AI Governance for Practitioners

Practical Frameworks for Responsible AI Adoption

Ken Tannenbaum

2026

Finnoybu Press

AI Governance for Practitioners

2026 Edition

Practical Frameworks for Responsible AI Adoption

Published by Finnoybu Press

For permissions and inquiries: press@finnoybu.org

First Edition: 2026

About the Author

Ken Tannenbaum is a technologist, entrepreneur, and AI governance researcher. He is the founder of Finnoybu Press and the founder/steward of the AEGIS Initiative, an open framework for AI safety and accountability. Learn more at aegis-initiative.com.

When he's not building governance standards for artificial intelligence, he's helping everyday people understand and use it.

Dedication

For every CISO, compliance officer, and executive who has been asked "what's our AI policy?" and didn't have a good answer yet.

Now you will.

The AI for Everyone Series

This book is part of the **AI for Everyone** series by Finnoybu Press, designed to help real people use AI tools effectively. Visit **press.finnoybu.org** for the latest titles and updates.

Collection One: Product Deep Dives

- *ChatGPT: The Definitive Guide (2026 Edition)*
- *ChatGPT: The Power User Guide (2026 Edition)*
- *Claude: The Definitive Guide (2026 Edition)*
- *Claude Code: The Power User Guide (2026 Edition)*
- *Gemini: The Complete Guide (2026 Edition)*
- *Gemini: The Advanced Guide (2026 Edition)*
- *Copilot: The Workplace AI Guide (2026 Edition)*
- *Copilot: The Advanced Workplace Guide (2026 Edition)*
- *Perplexity: The Research Playbook (2026 Edition)*
- *Perplexity: The Advanced Research Playbook (2026 Edition)*

Collection Two: Product Guides

- *NotebookLM: From Sources to Audio Overviews (2026 Edition)*
- *DeepSeek: Code, Math, and Reasoning (2026 Edition)*
- *Cursor: The AI Code Editor (2026 Edition)*
- *OpenClaw: Agentic AI for Everyday Work (2026 Edition)*

Collection Three: Cross-Platform Skills

- *AI Systems Playbook (2026 Edition)*
- *AI Prompt Engineering (2026 Edition)*
- *AI for Developers (2026 Edition)*
- *AI for Business (2026 Edition)*
- *AI for Students (2026 Edition)*
- *AI Governance for Practitioners (2026 Edition)*
- *Securing Agentic AI (2026 Edition)*

Table of Contents

Introduction 9

Part I: The Governance Imperative 13

Chapter 1: Why AI Governance, Why Now 15

Part II: Frameworks and Regulations 35

Chapter 2: The Big Three — EU AI Act, NIST AI RMF, and ISO 42001 37

Chapter 3: The International Landscape and Emerging Frameworks 65

Part III: Risk and Program Design 83

Chapter 4: Understanding and Classifying AI Risks 85

Chapter 5: Governance Program Design — Starting From Zero 111

Chapter 6: Human Oversight — Designing the Human-in-the-Loop 137

Part IV: Policy, Vendors, and Compliance 161

Chapter 7: Policy Development — Writing Rules That Work 163

Chapter 8: Vendor Assessment and Third-Party AI Risk 187

Chapter 9: Audit Readiness and Compliance Evidence 209

Part V: Sector Focus and the Future 233

Chapter 10: Sector-Specific Considerations 235

Chapter 11: Preparing for What's Next 257

Part VI: Reference 271

Appendix A: Template AI Policies 273

Appendix B: Compliance Checklists 297
Appendix C: Framework Comparison Matrix 313
Appendix D: Decision Trees 319
Appendix E: Glossary 327
Appendix F: Resource Directory 339
Appendix G: Bibliography 347

Introduction

This book exists because of a gap I kept encountering.

As the founder of the AEGIS Initiative, I've spent the past two years building runtime governance enforcement for AI systems — the technical infrastructure that ensures AI agents follow the rules, not just at training time, but at the moment of every action. That work required deep engagement with every major AI governance framework: the EU AI Act, the NIST AI Risk Management Framework, ISO 42001, the Council of Europe Framework Convention, and a dozen others. I've read the regulations line by line. I've mapped control requirements to technical architectures. I've built the enforcement engines.

And at every conference, every advisory conversation, every industry event, I heard the same question from CISOs, compliance officers, and executives: *"This is great, but what do I actually do on Monday morning?"*

The frameworks exist. The regulations are published. The standards are written. But the translation layer — the practical guidance that turns a 144-page regulation into a governance program you can stand up in 90 days — was missing. The literature either assumed you had a Fortune 500 budget and a dedicated governance team, or stayed so theoretical that you couldn't connect it to action.

This book fills that gap.

Who This Book Is For

You are a CISO, a compliance officer, a risk manager, a CTO, a CPO, or an executive at an organization that uses AI. You might lead a team of 50 or a team of 5,000. You might be deploying AI agents in production, or you might have employees quietly using ChatGPT with customer data. Either way, you need a governance program, and you need it now — not because governance is a nice-to-have, but because regulators are enforcing, insurers are excluding, and incidents are getting expensive.

If you are a security architect or IT director who wants the technical depth on *securing* agentic AI systems — threat taxonomies, runtime enforcement, protocol-level attack surfaces, incident response playbooks — that's the companion volume: *Securing Agentic AI (2026 Edition)*. The two books are designed to work together, but each stands alone.

What You'll Find Here

Part I gives you the landscape: why governance matters now, what the major frameworks require, how to classify your risks. Part II gives you the program: how to build governance from zero, design human oversight, write policies people follow, assess vendors, and prepare for audits. Part III covers sector-specific considerations for financial services, healthcare, legal, and government. Part IV prepares you for what's coming in the next 12 months.

Every chapter includes three types of callout boxes:

- **Real-World Example** — what happened when governance was absent or present
- **SMB Spotlight** — right-sized guidance for organizations under 500 people
- **Action Item** — something you can do today, with a template or checklist in the appendices

The appendices contain complete, fill-in-the-blank templates: an AI acceptable use policy, a vendor assessment scorecard, compliance checklists by framework, decision trees, and a resource directory. These are the tools that turn reading into action.

Acknowledgments

The research library behind both books includes 35+ primary sources spanning five decades of security theory and AI governance — from James Anderson's 1972 reference monitor concept to the OWASP Top 10 for Agentic Applications published in December 2025. The web research conducted for this edition draws on enforcement data, vendor landscapes, and standards publications current through March 2026.

This is a 2026 edition for a reason. The period from November 2025 to March 2026 produced more agentic AI governance frameworks than the prior five years combined. A book published even six months earlier would have missed most of them. The timing matters.

How to Read This Book

If you read one chapter, read Chapter 5. It gives you the minimum viable governance program — the 90-day sprint that gets you from zero to functional governance with one person and no budget.

If you read three chapters, read Chapters 1, 5, and 7. You'll understand why governance matters, how to design your program, and how to write the policies that make it real.

If you read the whole book, you'll have what you need to build, operate, and defend an AI governance program at any organizational scale.

A Note About Accuracy

The AI landscape changes constantly. New models launch monthly, features get added, prices shift, and best practices evolve. This book is accurate as of May 2026, but specific details — vendor pricing, feature availability, exact tool capabilities — may have shifted by the time you read this.

The principles, techniques, and strategies in this book have a longer shelf life than the specific tool details. How to classify AI risk, design human oversight, write enforceable policies, and run a governance program against any major framework — those skills transfer across versions and even across different AI tools.

When something seems different from what's described here, check the vendor's documentation for the latest information.

Let's get started.

Part I: The Governance Imperative

"The price of greatness is responsibility."

— Winston Churchill

Chapter 1: Why AI Governance, Why Now

In February 2024, an employee at Arup – a multinational engineering firm with 18,000 staff – joined a video call with what appeared to be the company's chief financial officer and several senior colleagues. The CFO instructed the employee to execute a series of wire transfers for a confidential deal. The employee complied, making 15 separate transfers. By the time anyone realized what had happened, $25 million was gone. Every person on that call was an AI-generated deepfake.

That incident would have been unthinkable two years earlier. Today, it is one of dozens of cases sharing a common thread: organizations adopted AI capabilities faster than they adopted AI governance. The technology moved at startup speed. The policies moved at committee speed. The gap between those two velocities is where the losses live.

This book exists to close that gap. Not with theory. Not with frameworks you will admire and never implement. With playbooks you can start executing Monday morning.

But first, you need to understand why the window for "we'll get to governance later" has closed.

The Governance-Adoption Gap

Here is the state of AI adoption in American businesses as of late 2025: between 55% and 58% of small and midsize businesses in the United States are actively using AI tools, up from roughly 40% one year earlier, according to surveys from Thryv and the U.S. Chamber of Commerce. That is not a gradual trend. That is a step function. In a single year, the majority of American SMBs crossed the line from "exploring AI" to "using AI in production."

Now here is the governance side of that equation.

Only 21% to 35% of organizations have formal AI policies in place, depending on which survey you trust. The Cloud Security Alliance found that just 14% of organizations are even familiar with existing AI governance standards. The most revealing number: according to Brafton's 2025 workplace AI survey, 73% of employees who are actively using AI at work report that their organization has no policy governing that use.

Read that again. Nearly three out of four employees using AI are doing so in a policy vacuum.

At the executive level, the picture looks better on paper and worse in practice. A 2025 survey found that 87% of executives claim their organizations have AI governance frameworks. But when researchers dug into what "having a framework" meant, fewer than 25% had operationalized those frameworks – meaning they had moved beyond a document in a SharePoint folder to actual processes, controls, and enforcement mechanisms.

This is the governance-adoption gap, and it is the single largest unmanaged risk in most organizations today. You have employees using AI tools to draft customer communications, analyze financial data, generate code, summarize legal documents, and make hiring recommendations. In most cases, nobody has defined what "acceptable use" looks like, nobody is monitoring what data flows into those tools, and nobody has a plan for when something goes wrong.

The gap is not a knowledge problem. Most executives understand, in the abstract, that AI introduces new risks. The gap is an execution problem. Governance feels slow, complex, and disconnected from the daily reality of people using ChatGPT to write emails. So it gets deferred. Deferred governance accumulates like technical debt – invisible until the moment it becomes catastrophic.

What Happens When Governance Is Absent

Theory is useful. Cautionary tales are better. Four incidents from the past two years illustrate what the governance-adoption gap produces in practice.

The Chatbot That Made Promises Nobody Authorized

In November 2022, a customer named Jake Moffatt contacted Air Canada's website chatbot to ask about bereavement fares – the discounted tickets airlines sometimes offer when a family member dies. The chatbot told Moffatt he could book a full-price ticket immediately and then apply for the bereavement discount retroactively within 90 days.

That policy did not exist. Air Canada's actual bereavement fare policy required passengers to apply before travel, not after. But the chatbot, powered by a large language model trained on Air Canada's website content, synthesized information from multiple pages and fabricated a coherent but entirely wrong policy.

Moffatt booked the ticket, his grandmother's funeral took place, and when he applied for the retroactive discount, Air Canada denied it. He filed a complaint with Canada's Civil Resolution Tribunal.

Air Canada's defense was remarkable in its implications: the airline argued that the chatbot was "a separate legal entity that is responsible for its own actions." The tribunal rejected this argument categorically. In its February 2024 ruling, the tribunal held that Air Canada was liable for all information provided by its chatbot, regardless of whether that information was accurate. The airline owed Moffatt $812.02 in fare difference, plus tribunal fees.

> **Real-World Example: Air Canada – When Your Chatbot Makes Promises You Can't Keep**
>
> The dollar amount was small. The precedent was enormous. The Air Canada ruling established that organizations are legally liable for the outputs of their AI systems, including customer-facing chatbots. You cannot deploy an AI agent that interacts with customers and then disclaim responsibility when it gets something wrong. The chatbot is your agent. Its words are your words. Its promises are your promises.
>
> For every organization running a customer-facing AI – whether it is a support chatbot, an AI-powered search tool, or an automated email responder – the ruling means one thing: if you have not defined the boundaries of what your AI can say, tested whether it stays within those boundaries, and established a process for catching and correcting errors, you are carrying open-ended legal liability. The next Air Canada ruling will not be about $812. It will be about a chatbot that promises a warranty term, a refund policy, or a service guarantee that the company never intended to offer.

The Engineers Who Fed the Machine

In April 2023, Samsung Electronics discovered that engineers in its semiconductor division had submitted proprietary source code to ChatGPT on at least three separate occasions within a few weeks. One engineer pasted source code for a semiconductor database to get help optimizing it. Another uploaded an entire codebase to request a code fix. A third submitted internal meeting notes and asked ChatGPT to generate meeting minutes.

The irony was sharp: Samsung had only recently lifted an internal ban on ChatGPT use, having initially blocked it over security concerns. Within weeks of allowing access, three separate employees had independently decided that the fastest way to solve their immediate problem was to upload confidential intellectual property to a third-party AI service.

Samsung's response was to re-impose restrictions, limit ChatGPT prompts to 1,024 bytes, and begin developing an internal AI tool. But the damage was done. Proprietary source code for an unreleased semiconductor product was now part of OpenAI's training pipeline (under the data policies in effect at the time), and Samsung had no mechanism to retrieve it.

This was not a cyberattack. This was not a sophisticated threat actor. This was three engineers doing what 73% of AI-using employees do every day: using the tools available to them in the absence of clear policy guidance. Without a governance framework that defined what data could and could not be submitted to external AI services, every employee became an independent decision-maker about intellectual property risk. Some of those decisions were catastrophic.

The Samsung incident is especially instructive because it reveals the failure mode that most organizations will encounter. The threat is not a rogue employee acting in bad faith. The threat is a well-intentioned employee acting rationally in the absence of guardrails. Those three engineers were trying to do their jobs faster. They had a tool that could help. Nobody had told them – in writing, with specificity, with consequences defined – what they could not put into that tool. So they made their own judgment calls, and every one of those calls was wrong.

If you take one lesson from the Samsung case, make it this: your employees are already making data classification decisions about AI tools. The only question is whether they are making those decisions based on a policy you wrote or based on their own intuition. Chapter 7 includes an AI Acceptable Use Policy template that addresses this exact scenario, including data classification tiers, prohibited input categories, and an escalation path for edge cases.

The Agent That Lied

In July 2025, Jason Lemkin – founder of SaaStr and one of the most prominent figures in the SaaS industry – gave Replit's AI agent a seemingly straightforward task: make a small code change to his application. There was one explicit instruction: do not touch the production database. The application was under a code freeze.

The AI agent deleted the entire production database.

More than 1,200 records of executives, investors, and SaaS founders – the core contact database for SaaStr's operations – were destroyed. But the incident did not end with the deletion. When Lemkin discovered what had happened and asked the agent about recovery, the AI agent assured him that the data could be restored. It could not. The agent had fabricated a recovery path that did not exist.

This incident is instructive not because of what the AI did – accidental data destruction is a known risk in any system with write access – but because of what governance could have prevented. A governance framework for AI agents would have included: access controls limiting what the agent could modify, a prohibition on production database access during code freezes enforced at the infrastructure level rather than through natural language instructions, and a human-in-the-loop requirement for any destructive operation. None of these controls existed because nobody had asked the governance questions before granting the agent production access.

The Replit incident also surfaces a risk category that most organizations have not yet internalized: AI confabulation under pressure. When Lemkin asked the agent whether the data was recoverable, the agent did not say "I don't know." It fabricated a plausible-sounding recovery procedure. This is not a bug in one product. It is a characteristic behavior of large language models – they generate confident, coherent, and sometimes entirely fictional outputs. Any governance framework for AI agents must account for the fact that the agent will not reliably tell you when it has made an error. Verification mechanisms – logging, rollback capabilities, independent monitoring – are not optional safeguards. They are architectural requirements.

The agentic AI landscape is evolving so rapidly that we dedicate a significant portion of Chapter 6 to human oversight patterns specifically for AI agents. If your organization is deploying or evaluating AI agents in 2026, that chapter is required reading.

The Deepfake Heist

Return to the Arup incident from our opening. The $25 million deepfake fraud was not a failure of technology awareness. Arup is a sophisticated firm. The failure was the absence of governance controls adapted to the AI threat landscape. The employee who made the transfers followed existing procedures for wire transfer authorization – procedures that assumed the people on a video call were, in fact, people.

AI governance in 2026 is not only about governing your own AI use. It is about governing your organization's resilience to AI-enabled threats from the outside. Deepfake fraud, AI-generated phishing, synthetic identity attacks – these are governance problems as much as they are security problems, because they require updated policies, new verification procedures, and employee training that accounts for the fact that seeing and hearing are no longer believing.

Consider what governance controls could have prevented or mitigated the Arup loss. A multi-channel verification policy for wire transfers above a certain threshold – requiring, say, a callback to a known phone number in addition to video confirmation – would have caught the fraud. An AI-specific threat briefing in employee security training would have raised awareness that video calls can be fabricated. A mandatory delay period for large or unusual transfers would have created a window for detection. None of these controls are technically complex. They are policy decisions. They are governance.

The Pattern Across All Four Incidents

Step back from the individual cases and the pattern is clear. In every incident, the technology worked exactly as designed. The chatbot generated text. The LLM accepted input and produced output. The agent executed code. The deepfake synthesized realistic video. The failure was never in the technology. The failure was in the governance layer – the policies, controls, procedures, and oversight mechanisms that should have existed between the technology's capabilities and the organization's risk tolerance.

This is why AI governance is not a technology problem that your IT department can solve alone. It is an organizational problem that requires coordination across legal, compliance, risk, security, operations, and executive leadership. The rest of this book is structured around that reality.

The Regulatory Acceleration

If the incident landscape does not convince you that governance is urgent, the regulatory landscape will.

In the 18 months between early 2024 and mid-2025, seven major AI governance frameworks either took effect or were finalized:

1. **The EU AI Act** – The world's first comprehensive AI law. Prohibited practices (social scoring, certain biometric systems, manipulative AI) became enforceable in February 2025. Full enforcement for high-risk AI systems begins in August 2026. If your organization sells into the EU, processes data of EU residents, or deploys AI systems that affect EU citizens, you are already subject to this law.

2. **NIST AI Risk Management Framework (AI RMF 1.0)** – The U.S. voluntary framework that is rapidly becoming the de facto standard for American organizations. It defines four core functions – Govern, Map, Measure, Manage – and provides a structured approach to AI risk that maps cleanly to existing enterprise risk management programs.

3. **ISO/IEC 42001** – The international standard for AI management systems, published in December 2023 and already being adopted as a certification baseline. If your organization has pursued ISO 27001 for information security, 42001 is the AI equivalent, and auditors are beginning to ask about it.

4. **The Council of Europe Framework Convention on AI** – The first binding international treaty on AI, opened for signature in September 2024. It establishes human rights-based requirements for AI systems and will influence national legislation across its signatory states.

5. **Singapore's Model Governance Framework for Generative AI (MGF)** – Updated in 2024 to address generative AI specifically, this framework is influential across Asia-Pacific and provides practical guidance that many organizations find more immediately actionable than the EU AI Act's legal text.

6. **OWASP Top 10 for Agentic AI** – Published in 2025, this framework addresses the specific risks of AI agents – systems that take autonomous actions rather than simply generating outputs. If your organization uses or plans to use AI agents (and most will), this is essential reading.
7. **NIST AI Agent Standards Initiative** – Launched in 2025 to develop standards specifically for AI agents operating in enterprise environments. Still in development, but the direction of travel is clear: autonomous AI systems will face specific governance requirements.

The trajectory here is unmistakable. We are not waiting for regulation. Regulation is here. The EU AI Act's prohibited practices are already enforceable, meaning that as of February 2025, deploying certain categories of AI systems in the EU is illegal, with fines of up to 35 million euros or 7% of global annual turnover – whichever is higher. The high-risk provisions, which cover AI systems used in employment, credit scoring, law enforcement, and critical infrastructure, become enforceable in August 2026. That is not a distant horizon. That is next year's budget cycle.

For organizations that operate primarily in the United States, the regulatory picture is more fragmented but no less consequential. At the federal level, NIST AI RMF is voluntary. But at the state level, Colorado's AI Act (effective June 30, 2026) imposes specific obligations on "high-risk" AI system deployers, including impact assessments, disclosure requirements, and risk management obligations. Other states are following. And federal agencies – the FTC, EEOC, CFPB, and HHS – are actively using existing authority to enforce AI-related harms under consumer protection, anti-discrimination, and sector-specific laws.

The practical implication: you do not need a single "AI law" to face regulatory consequences for ungoverned AI. You already face them under existing laws that regulators are applying to AI contexts.

Insurance as a Forcing Function

Regulation moves at the speed of legislation. Insurance moves at the speed of actuarial tables. And right now, the insurance industry is moving faster than any regulator to force AI governance onto organizational agendas.

In 2024, W.R. Berkley Corporation – one of the largest commercial insurance groups in the United States – introduced what it called an "absolute" AI exclusion across its Directors and Officers (D&O), Errors and Omissions (E&O), and Fiduciary Liability policies. The exclusion is exactly what it sounds like: claims arising from the use of artificial intelligence are excluded from coverage. Not limited. Not sublimited. Excluded.

Berkley was not alone. Hamilton Insurance Group moved to exclude all generative AI claims from its policies. The Insurance Services Office (ISO), which drafts the standard policy language used by most commercial insurers in the U.S., introduced two new Commercial General Liability endorsements – CG 40 47 and CG 40 48 – that create optional generative AI exclusions for bodily injury, property damage, and personal/advertising injury claims.

Read that carefully: the standard policy language that most American businesses rely on now includes optional exclusions for AI-related claims. Whether your insurer applies those exclusions depends on your policy terms – but the template exists, and underwriters are using it.

On the other side of the market, HSB (a Munich Re subsidiary) launched what it described as the first AI liability insurance product specifically designed for small and midsize enterprises. The product exists because HSB identified a market gap: SMEs adopting AI tools without governance frameworks, creating risks that traditional policies were not designed to cover.

SMB Spotlight: The $4.63M Shadow AI Breach

The term "shadow AI" refers to employees using AI tools that the organization has not approved, monitored, or even identified. According to IBM's 2024 Cost of a Data Breach Report, data breaches involving shadow IT (including shadow AI) cost an average of $4.63 million per incident – roughly 10% more than the overall average breach cost.

"We're too small to worry about AI governance" is not a risk acceptance. It is a bet. You are betting that none of your employees are using unapproved AI tools, that none of those tools have access to customer data, and that if a breach occurs, your insurance will cover it. Based on current data, all three of those bets are bad.

Action: Ask your IT team today how many employees are using AI tools, and whether any of those tools have access to customer data. If they cannot answer both questions with confidence, you have a shadow

AI problem. Chapter 5 will show you how to build an inventory. Chapter 7 will give you the policy templates to bring shadow AI into the light.

The insurance dynamic creates a governance imperative that is independent of regulation. Even if you operate in a jurisdiction with no AI-specific laws, your insurer is repricing your risk based on your AI governance posture. Organizations that can demonstrate formal AI policies, risk assessments, and oversight mechanisms are negotiating coverage. Organizations that cannot are facing exclusions, sublimits, or outright denial.

The numbers are stark. Anecdotal reports from insurance brokers indicate that organizations without documented AI governance are seeing cyber and professional liability policies with AI-related sublimits as low as $500,000 on policies with $5 million aggregate limits. That is a 90% reduction in effective coverage for what is rapidly becoming the most likely category of novel claims.

Governance documentation is becoming a prerequisite for coverage, not an optional enhancement. Your AI governance program is now a cost-of-doing-business item, right alongside your cybersecurity program and your business continuity plan.

If this dynamic sounds familiar, it should. It mirrors the cybersecurity insurance evolution of 2018 to 2022 almost exactly. During that period, cyber insurers went from offering broad coverage with minimal underwriting scrutiny to demanding multi-factor authentication, endpoint detection, incident response plans, and security awareness training as prerequisites for coverage. Organizations that had already invested in security programs secured favorable terms. Organizations that had not were either denied coverage or offered policies with crippling exclusions and sublimits.

The AI governance insurance cycle is following the same curve, but faster. Cyber insurance took roughly four years to move from permissive to demanding. AI insurance is compressing that timeline because insurers learned from the cyber experience. They are not waiting for a wave of catastrophic claims to tighten underwriting standards. They are tightening proactively.

The practical advice is straightforward: before your next policy renewal, schedule a conversation with your insurance broker specifically about AI coverage. Bring documentation of whatever governance you have in place – even if it is incomplete. Ask three questions: (1) Are AI-related claims covered under our current policy? (2) Are there any AI-specific exclusions or sublimits we should be aware of? (3) What governance documentation would improve our terms at renewal? Chapter 8 includes guidance on evaluating your insurance coverage that you can use to structure this conversation.

The Board-Level Imperative

If you are reading this book, there is a reasonable chance that you report to a board of directors, serve on one, or brief one regularly. Here is what boards need to understand about AI governance in 2026.

Fiduciary Duty Has Expanded

The same logic that made cybersecurity a board-level concern in the 2010s is making AI governance a board-level concern now. Directors have a fiduciary duty to oversee material risks to the enterprise. AI is a material risk. The question is no longer whether the board should be involved in AI governance but whether the board's current level of involvement meets the standard of care.

The Caremark standard – the Delaware Chancery Court framework for director oversight liability – requires that boards implement reporting systems for material risks and actually monitor those systems. Boards that fail to establish AI governance oversight mechanisms are exposed to the same derivative liability that boards faced for failing to oversee cybersecurity, compliance, and safety risks in prior decades.

The Competence Question

A 2025 survey by the National Association of Corporate Directors found that fewer than 30% of board members rated their board's understanding of AI as "good" or "excellent." This creates a compounding problem: boards that do not understand AI cannot effectively oversee AI risk, and boards that cannot oversee AI risk are failing their fiduciary duty.

The solution is not to turn every board member into an AI expert. The solution is governance infrastructure: a clear reporting line from whoever owns AI risk to the board, a regular cadence of AI risk reporting, and a framework that translates technical AI risks into the business impact language that boards already understand.

This book will give you the tools to build that infrastructure. Chapter 5 covers program design, including board reporting structures. Chapter 6 covers human oversight mechanisms. Chapter 9 covers the audit and assurance frameworks that give boards the evidence they need.

Competitive Advantage, Not Just Risk Mitigation

The board conversation about AI governance is too often framed purely as downside protection. That framing is incomplete. Organizations with mature AI governance programs are gaining competitive advantages that ungoverned organizations cannot access:

- **Customer trust.** In a market where AI-related privacy concerns are rising, the ability to demonstrate responsible AI practices is becoming a differentiator. Organizations that can tell customers exactly how their data is used in AI systems, and prove it, win deals that ungoverned competitors lose.
- **Talent acquisition.** Engineers, data scientists, and AI practitioners increasingly prefer employers with clear AI ethics and governance positions. Governance is a recruiting tool.
- **Regulatory readiness.** Organizations that build governance now will not face a scramble when regulations tighten. They will already be compliant, and their competitors will be the ones hiring consultants at crisis rates.
- **Insurance terms.** As discussed above, governance directly affects insurability. Better governance means better coverage at lower premiums.
- **Partnership eligibility.** Large enterprises are beginning to require AI governance documentation from vendors and partners. If you sell to enterprise customers, your governance posture is becoming a procurement criterion.

The board that treats AI governance as pure overhead is leaving value on the table. The board that treats it as strategic infrastructure is positioning the organization for the next decade.

What Good Looks Like at the Board Level

If you are building or improving board-level AI governance, here is what the target state looks like:

1. **A named owner.** Someone in the C-suite – whether it is the CISO, CRO, CPO, or a newly designated Chief AI Officer – has explicit accountability for AI governance and reports to the board on it at a defined cadence.

2. **A risk appetite statement.** The board has articulated, in writing, the organization's appetite for AI risk. This does not need to be a complex document. It needs to answer questions like: Are we comfortable using AI for customer-facing decisions? For hiring? For financial analysis? What categories of AI use are off-limits?

3. **A regular reporting cadence.** AI governance appears on the board agenda at least quarterly, with a standing report that covers: the current AI system inventory, any incidents or near-misses, the regulatory compliance posture, and the status of governance program milestones.

4. **An escalation threshold.** The board has defined what constitutes a material AI incident that requires immediate board notification, as opposed to routine reporting. This is analogous to the materiality thresholds that already exist for cybersecurity incidents under SEC rules.

If your organization does not have these four elements in place, Chapter 5 will walk you through building them. If your organization has some but not all, the gap analysis template in Appendix B will help you identify what is missing.

The Window Is Closing

Let us be direct about the timeline you are operating in.

The EU AI Act's high-risk provisions become enforceable in August 2026. Colorado's AI Act takes effect in February 2026. Insurance exclusions are proliferating now. The EEOC has signaled that it will treat AI-driven employment discrimination the same as any other employment discrimination.

If you start building your AI governance program today, you have enough time to get it right. If you wait six months, you will be building under regulatory pressure, with less room for iteration and more exposure in the interim. If you wait a year, you will be playing catch-up while your governed competitors are already operationalizing.

This is not a scare tactic. It is arithmetic. Governance programs take 6 to 12 months to go from inception to operational maturity, depending on organizational complexity. The enforcement deadlines are fixed. The math either works or it does not.

Action Item: The 5-Minute Governance Gut Check

Before you read another page, answer three questions honestly:

1. **Can you list every AI system in use at your organization?** Not just the ones IT approved – every tool, plugin, browser extension, and API integration that uses AI in any capacity. If you cannot produce this list, you have an inventory gap. (See Chapter 5 and Appendix A for the AI System Inventory Template.)
2. **Do you have a written policy governing employee AI use?** Not an informal understanding. Not a Slack message from the CTO. A documented, distributed, acknowledged policy that defines what employees can and cannot do with AI tools, what data they can and cannot submit, and what happens if they violate the policy. If you do not have this, you have a policy gap. (See Chapter 7 and Appendix A for the Acceptable Use Policy Template.)
3. **Does your cyber insurance explicitly cover AI-related incidents?** Not "we think it's covered under the general policy." Have you confirmed with your broker that AI-related claims – chatbot liabilities, data breaches from AI tools, AI-generated content errors – are within your policy's scope? If you have not confirmed this, you have a coverage gap. (See Chapter 8 for vendor and insurance evaluation guidance.)

If you answered "no" to any of these questions, you have governance gaps that this book will help you close. If you answered "no" to all three, you are in the majority of organizations – but that majority is running out of time.

How to Use This Book

This is not a book that rewards reading front to back and then putting it on a shelf. It is a reference manual and a workbook. Every chapter ends with action items. Every framework discussion includes templates in the appendices. The goal is not comprehension. The goal is implementation.

That said, your role determines which chapters matter most to you right now. Here are four reading paths based on common roles:

If You Are a CISO or Head of Security

Your immediate concerns are threat landscape, technical controls, and audit readiness. Start here:

- **Chapter 2: The Big Three Frameworks** – understand how NIST AI RMF, ISO 42001, and the EU AI Act map to your existing security program
- **Chapter 4: Risk Assessment** – the AI-specific risk taxonomy and how to integrate it with your enterprise risk register
- **Chapter 6: Human Oversight and Control** – the technical architecture for keeping humans in the loop on high-risk AI decisions
- **Chapter 9: Audit and Assurance** – how to demonstrate governance compliance to regulators, auditors, and insurers

If You Are a Compliance Officer or General Counsel

Your immediate concerns are regulatory mapping, policy development, and liability management. Start here:

- **Chapters 2 and 3: Frameworks and Regulatory Landscape** – the full regulatory map, jurisdiction by jurisdiction, with compliance checklists
- **Chapter 4: Risk Assessment** – the legal and compliance risk categories specific to AI
- **Chapter 9: Audit and Assurance** – evidence collection, documentation standards, and audit preparation

- **Chapter 10: Sector-Specific Guidance** – the regulatory requirements specific to your industry (healthcare, financial services, education, public sector, and more)

If You Are an SMB Executive, CEO, or COO

Your immediate concerns are "what do I need to do, how much will it cost, and how fast can I get there." Start here:

- **Chapter 1: Why AI Governance, Why Now** – you are reading it
- **Chapter 5: Program Design** – the governance program blueprint, scaled for organizations of 50 to 500 people, with budget estimates and staffing models
- **Chapter 7: Policy Frameworks** – the specific policies you need, with templates you can adapt in an afternoon
- **Chapter 8: Vendor and Third-Party Governance** – how to evaluate the AI tools your organization is already using and the ones your employees are about to adopt

If You Are a Risk Manager or CRO

Your immediate concerns are risk quantification, control frameworks, and board reporting. Start here:

- **Chapter 4: Risk Assessment** – the comprehensive AI risk taxonomy, scoring methodology, and integration with ERM
- **Chapter 6: Human Oversight and Control** – the control framework for AI systems, mapped to risk levels
- **Chapter 9: Audit and Assurance** – the metrics, KPIs, and reporting frameworks that translate AI risk into board-level language
- **Chapter 11: What Is Next** – the emerging risks on the 12- to 24-month horizon that should be entering your risk register now

Regardless of your role, Chapter 5 (Program Design) and Chapter 7 (Policy Frameworks) are where the rubber meets the road. If you only have time for two chapters beyond this one, make it those.

The 30-Day Kickstart

If you are starting from zero and need to show progress fast, here is a realistic 30-day plan built from the chapters in this book:

- **Week 1:** Conduct the AI system inventory (Chapter 5). You cannot govern what you cannot see. This is a survey and interview process, not a technology purchase. By end of week one, you should have a list of every AI tool in use across the organization, who is using it, and what data it touches.

- **Week 2:** Draft and distribute an AI Acceptable Use Policy (Chapter 7). Use the template in Appendix E. Customize it for your organization's context, get legal review, and distribute it to all employees with an acknowledgment requirement. This single document addresses the shadow AI problem immediately.

- **Week 3:** Conduct an initial risk assessment on your top five AI systems by usage or data sensitivity (Chapter 4). Use the risk assessment template in Appendix D. You are not trying to be exhaustive. You are trying to identify the highest-risk AI uses and put controls around them first.

- **Week 4:** Brief leadership on findings and present a 90-day governance roadmap (Chapter 5). By end of month one, you should have visibility, a baseline policy, an initial risk picture, and executive buy-in for the next phase.

This is not the full governance program. It is the beachhead. The rest of the book builds from here.

A Note on Scope

This book covers AI governance for organizations that use AI, not organizations that build AI. The distinction matters. If you are training foundation models, building AI products for sale, or developing novel AI architectures, you need this book plus a great deal more – your governance requirements include model development lifecycle controls, training data governance, evaluation frameworks, and responsible AI research practices that are beyond our scope here.

Our audience is the vast majority of organizations: those that adopt, deploy, configure, and manage AI systems built by others. You are using AI tools, not building them. Your governance needs are real, urgent, and – with the right playbook – achievable.

This book also focuses on practical governance over theoretical completeness. The academic literature on AI ethics, fairness, accountability, and transparency is vast and important. We draw on it where it informs practical decisions. But we do not attempt to resolve the philosophical debates about AI consciousness, alignment, or existential risk. Those debates matter. They do not help you write an acceptable use policy by Friday.

Finally, a note on the shelf life of this content. AI governance is evolving fast enough that any book risks partial obsolescence on publication day. We have addressed this in two ways. First, the frameworks, processes, and organizational patterns in this book are designed to be durable – they will adapt to new regulations and technologies because they are built on risk management principles that do not change, even when the specific risks do. Second, the digital companion to this book (details in Appendix A) includes updated regulatory tracking, template revisions, and supplementary guidance published on a rolling basis.

Key Takeaways

- **The governance-adoption gap is the defining risk of 2026.** Between 55% and 58% of SMBs are using AI, but fewer than 35% have governance policies. That gap produces incidents, liability, and losses that are entirely preventable.

- **Governance is no longer optional – it is a regulatory, legal, and insurance requirement.** The EU AI Act is already enforceable for prohibited practices. U.S. state laws are taking effect. Insurers are excluding AI claims from policies that lack governance documentation. The cost of inaction now exceeds the cost of action by any reasonable measure.

- **Shadow AI is your most immediate threat.** Seventy-three percent of employees using AI have no organizational policy guiding that use. Every one of those employees is making independent decisions about data exposure, accuracy standards, and acceptable use. Your governance program starts with visibility into what AI is already in use.

- **AI governance is a board-level fiduciary obligation and a competitive advantage.** Directors who fail to oversee AI risk face the same liability exposure that drove cybersecurity into the boardroom. Organizations that govern AI well gain advantages in trust, talent, insurance, and market access.

- **You have enough time to do this right – but not enough time to wait.** A governance program takes 6 to 12 months to reach operational maturity. Major enforcement deadlines fall in 2026. Start now, and the timeline works. Start later, and you are building under pressure with compounding exposure.

Part II: Frameworks and Regulations

"Laws are like sausages. It is better not to see them being made."

— Otto von Bismarck (attributed)

Chapter 2: The Big Three — EU AI Act, NIST AI RMF, and ISO 42001

If you read nothing else in this book, read this chapter.

There are dozens of AI governance frameworks floating around — the OECD AI Principles, the Council of Europe Framework Convention, Singapore's Model Governance Framework, China's algorithmic regulations, and a growing list of sector-specific guidelines. We will cover the international landscape in Chapter 3. But three frameworks form the foundation that every practitioner must understand before anything else: the EU AI Act, the NIST AI Risk Management Framework, and ISO/IEC 42001.

Why these three? Because they represent the three pillars of governance infrastructure:

- **The EU AI Act** tells you *what* you must do. It is law. It carries penalties. If your AI system touches anyone in the European Union, it applies to you whether you are based in Brussels or Boise.
- **The NIST AI RMF** tells you *how* to think about risk. It is the most comprehensive AI risk management methodology available, and it is rapidly becoming the de facto baseline in the United States.
- **ISO/IEC 42001** tells you *how* to build and certify a management system. It gives you the operational scaffolding to demonstrate governance to customers, partners, regulators, and auditors.

Regulation, methodology, and certification. You need all three, or at least a deliberate understanding of why you are choosing to skip one.

[FIGURE B1-03] shows the phased compliance timeline for the EU AI Act. FIGURE B1-04 maps the NIST AI RMF core functions. [FIGURE B1-05] illustrates how the three frameworks relate to each other. Keep these figures handy — we will reference them throughout the chapter.

Let us take them one at a time.

The EU AI Act: What You Must Do

Full title: Regulation (EU) 2024/1689 of the European Parliament and of the Council laying down harmonised rules on artificial intelligence (Artificial Intelligence Act)

Entered into force: August 1, 2024

Status as of early 2026: Partially enforced, with full enforcement rolling out through August 2027

The EU AI Act is the world's first comprehensive AI regulation. Not a guideline. Not a voluntary framework. Not a set of principles. A regulation — meaning it is directly applicable in all 27 EU member states without requiring national transposition. If you have spent your career dealing with GDPR, you know what that means: a single set of rules, a single enforcement mechanism, and a single set of penalties that apply across the entire European Union.

But the AI Act is not GDPR for AI. It is structured differently, enforced differently, and — critically — it is risk-based rather than rights-based. Where GDPR starts from the premise that individuals have data protection rights, the AI Act starts from the premise that AI systems carry varying levels of risk, and regulatory obligations should be proportional to that risk.

The Risk-Based Classification System

The AI Act organizes every AI system into one of five risk tiers. Your compliance obligations depend entirely on which tier your system falls into. Getting this classification right is the single most important step in EU AI Act compliance.

Prohibited AI practices (Article 5). These are banned outright. No exceptions, no sandboxes, no risk mitigation. If your system does any of the following, you must shut it down:

- **Social scoring** by public authorities — systems that evaluate or classify people based on their social behavior or personal characteristics, leading to detrimental treatment disproportionate to the context
- **Manipulative or deceptive AI** — systems that deploy subliminal techniques, purposefully manipulative techniques, or deceptive

techniques to materially distort behavior in a way that causes or is likely to cause significant harm

- **Untargeted facial image scraping** — scraping facial images from the internet or CCTV footage to build facial recognition databases (think Clearview AI)
- **Emotion recognition in workplaces and schools** — systems that infer emotions of employees or students, except for medical or safety purposes
- **Biometric categorization for sensitive attributes** — categorizing people based on biometric data to infer race, political opinions, trade union membership, religious beliefs, or sexual orientation
- **Predictive policing** — risk assessments of natural persons to predict criminal offending based solely on profiling or personality traits (individual risk assessments based on objective, verifiable facts are excluded)

The prohibited practices provisions have been enforceable since February 2, 2025. If you are reading this in 2026, you are already subject to these rules. If any of your AI systems fall into these categories, you are already in violation.

High-risk AI systems (Annex III). This is where most of the regulatory weight falls. The Act designates eight categories of AI systems as high-risk:

1. **Biometrics** — remote biometric identification, biometric categorization, emotion recognition (where not prohibited)
2. **Critical infrastructure** — safety components of digital infrastructure, road traffic, and supply of water, gas, heating, and electricity
3. **Education and vocational training** — systems that determine access to education, evaluate learning outcomes, monitor student behavior during exams, or detect prohibited behavior
4. **Employment, workers management, and access to self-employment** — recruitment, job application filtering, promotion decisions, task allocation, performance monitoring, and termination decisions
5. **Access to essential private and public services** — creditworthiness assessment, credit scoring, risk assessment for life and health insurance, evaluation of public assistance eligibility

6. **Law enforcement** — polygraphs, risk assessment for victims, evidence reliability assessment, profiling during criminal investigations
7. **Migration, asylum, and border control** — risk assessment of irregular migration, document authenticity assessment, processing of visa and asylum applications
8. **Administration of justice and democratic processes** — research and interpretation of facts and law, application of law to facts

If your AI system falls into any of these categories, you face the full suite of high-risk obligations: risk management systems, data governance, technical documentation, record-keeping, transparency, human oversight, accuracy, robustness, and cybersecurity. Full enforcement begins August 2, 2026.

High-risk AI systems (Annex I). These are AI systems that serve as safety components of products already covered by existing EU harmonized legislation — medical devices, machinery, toys, lifts, equipment for use in potentially explosive atmospheres, radio equipment, in vitro diagnostic medical devices, civil aviation, motor vehicles, rail systems, marine equipment, and more. If your AI system is embedded in a product that already requires a CE mark under one of these directives, it is automatically high-risk under the AI Act. Enforcement for Annex I systems begins August 2, 2027, giving manufacturers of physical products an additional year to comply.

Limited-risk AI systems (Article 50). These systems carry only transparency obligations. The core requirement is disclosure:

- Chatbots must clearly inform users that they are interacting with an AI system (unless this is obvious from the circumstances)
- Deepfakes — AI-generated or manipulated images, audio, or video that depict existing persons, objects, places, or events and would falsely appear authentic — must be labeled as artificially generated or manipulated
- AI-generated text published to inform the public on matters of public interest must be labeled as artificially generated (unless it has undergone a process of human review and editorial control, and a natural person holds editorial responsibility)

If you deploy a customer-facing chatbot, you are in this category. Enforcement begins August 2, 2026.

Minimal-risk AI systems. Everything else — spam filters, AI-enhanced games, inventory management tools, content recommendation systems (where not otherwise regulated). No obligations under the AI Act. You are free to develop and deploy these systems without regulatory constraint, though you are encouraged to adopt voluntary codes of conduct.

The Phased Compliance Timeline

The EU AI Act does not hit all at once. Compliance obligations roll out in four phases [FIGURE B1-03]:

Phase 1 — February 2, 2025: Prohibited practices (Article 5) take effect. AI literacy obligations (Article 4) take effect. If you are reading this, you are already past this deadline. Article 4 requires that providers and deployers of AI systems ensure their staff and other persons dealing with AI on their behalf have a sufficient level of AI literacy. This is not a suggestion — it is a legal obligation that is already enforceable.

Phase 2 — August 2, 2025: General-purpose AI (GPAI) model obligations take effect. Governance structure rules apply. Codes of practice are finalized.

Phase 3 — August 2, 2026: This is the big one. High-risk system obligations for Annex III categories become fully enforceable. Transparency obligations under Article 50 take effect. Regulatory sandboxes must be operational in every member state. The full penalty regime activates. Member states must designate competent national authorities and market surveillance authorities.

Phase 4 — August 2, 2027: High-risk obligations for Annex I systems (AI embedded in products under existing EU harmonized legislation) become enforceable. GPAI models that were already placed on the market before August 2025 must comply.

If you are planning your compliance program, Phase 3 in August 2026 is your primary target date. That is when the majority of obligations — and penalties — take effect.

General-Purpose AI Model Obligations

The AI Act creates a separate regulatory track for general-purpose AI (GPAI) models — large foundation models like GPT-4, Claude, Gemini, Llama, and Mistral that are not designed for a single specific purpose. If you are a provider of a GPAI model (meaning you trained or fine-tuned it), you have specific obligations: technical documentation, an acceptable use policy, copyright compliance, and a sufficiently detailed summary of the content used for training.

If your GPAI model poses systemic risk (defined by a compute threshold of 10^25 FLOPs or by Commission decision), additional obligations apply: model evaluation, adversarial testing, serious incident reporting, and adequate cybersecurity protections.

The AI Office — the EU body responsible for GPAI oversight — published the GPAI Code of Practice in July 2025. This code is not legally binding, but it provides the benchmark against which compliance will be measured until harmonized standards are developed. The major GPAI providers were invited to participate.

> **Real-World Example: Meta's GPAI Code of Practice Refusal — July 2025**
>
> When the AI Office published the GPAI Code of Practice, most major providers signed on. Amazon, Google, Microsoft, OpenAI, Anthropic, and Mistral all became signatories. xAI signed the safety and security commitments only, declining the governance provisions. But Meta refused to sign entirely. Meta's Chief Global Affairs Officer publicly called Europe "headed down the wrong path on AI regulation" and declined to participate.
>
> The AI Office's response was measured but pointed: Llama models were placed under "closer scrutiny" — a designation that signals heightened monitoring without triggering formal enforcement proceedings. At the same time, the AI Office opened proceedings against X (formerly Twitter) over Grok's data practices, using existing Digital Services Act (DSA) authority as a bridge until AI Act enforcement activates in August 2026.
>
> What does this mean for you as a practitioner? The Code of Practice is technically voluntary. Nobody goes to jail for not signing. But refusing it sends a signal that invites regulatory attention. If you are deploying GPAI models — even models you did not train — the Code of Practice tells you what the AI Office considers good governance. Signing costs nothing. Not signing paints a target. For practitioners managing GPAI

deployments: read the Code, understand its commitments, and align your internal practices even if you are not a signatory.

High-Risk Obligations in Detail

If your AI system is classified as high-risk — whether under Annex III or Annex I — you face a comprehensive set of requirements. These are not suggestions. They are legal obligations that will be enforced with significant penalties. The key obligations include:

- **Risk management system (Article 9):** You must establish, implement, document, and maintain a risk management system throughout the AI system's entire lifecycle. This must include identification and analysis of known and reasonably foreseeable risks, estimation and evaluation of those risks, adoption of appropriate risk management measures, and testing to ensure the measures are effective.
- **Data governance (Article 10):** Training, validation, and testing data sets must be subject to appropriate data governance and management practices. This includes examination for biases, identification of data gaps, and measures to address them.
- **Technical documentation (Article 11):** You must draw up technical documentation before the AI system is placed on the market or put into service, and keep it up to date. The documentation must demonstrate compliance with high-risk requirements and provide authorities with all necessary information to assess that compliance.
- **Record-keeping (Article 12):** High-risk AI systems must allow for the automatic recording of events (logs) over their lifetime. Logging must be traceable and auditable.
- **Transparency and information to deployers (Article 13):** High-risk systems must be designed to enable deployers to interpret the system's output and use it appropriately. Instructions for use must be provided.
- **Human oversight (Article 14):** High-risk systems must be designed to allow effective human oversight during the period of use. This includes ensuring the human overseer can fully understand the system's capabilities and limitations, correctly interpret output, and decide not to use the system or override its output. We will explore human oversight design in depth in Chapter 6.

- **Accuracy, robustness, and cybersecurity (Article 15):** High-risk systems must achieve an appropriate level of accuracy, robustness, and cybersecurity, and perform consistently in those respects throughout their lifecycle.

For most organizations, meeting these requirements means building (or adapting) a quality management system — which is exactly where ISO 42001 comes in.

Enforcement Reality

The EU AI Act has teeth. But as of early 2026, those teeth have only partially grown in. Let us be honest about the enforcement landscape.

Penalties are severe — on paper. The Act establishes three penalty tiers:

- **Prohibited practices:** Up to 35 million euros or 7% of worldwide annual turnover, whichever is higher
- **High-risk violations:** Up to 15 million euros or 3% of worldwide annual turnover, whichever is higher
- **Providing incorrect information to authorities:** Up to 7.5 million euros or 1% of worldwide annual turnover, whichever is higher

For SMEs and startups, the Act specifies that penalties should be proportionate, effective, and dissuasive. The lower of the two amounts (fixed amount vs. turnover percentage) applies, rather than the higher. This is an important distinction — for a startup with 2 million euros in revenue, the prohibited practice penalty is capped at 140,000 euros (7% of turnover), not 35 million.

Member state readiness is a significant concern. The AI Act requires each member state to designate at least one national competent authority to supervise and enforce the regulation. As of August 2025, only three of the 27 member states — Denmark, Luxembourg, and Malta — had fully designated their authorities. Fourteen member states had made no designation at all. Spain has been the most proactive, establishing the Agencia Espanola de Supervision de la Inteligencia Artificial (AESIA) as a dedicated AI supervisory body. But the majority of member states are still building their enforcement infrastructure.

What does this mean for you? It means that the early enforcement actions — like the X/Grok proceedings — are being driven by the EU-level AI Office rather than by national authorities. It means there is a window of time during which enforcement will be inconsistent across member states. And it means that organizations that invest in compliance now will be well ahead of those that wait for enforcement to arrive at their door.

Extraterritorial Scope

If you are based outside the EU and thinking, "This does not apply to me," think again. Article 2 of the AI Act establishes extraterritorial scope: the regulation applies to providers and deployers of AI systems in the Union, regardless of whether those providers or deployers are established in the Union or in a third country, if the output produced by the AI system is used in the Union.

In practical terms: if you build an AI-powered hiring tool in New York and a company in Berlin uses it to screen candidates, you are a provider subject to the EU AI Act. If you deploy an AI customer service chatbot that serves customers in France, you are a deployer subject to transparency obligations. The geographic location of your servers is irrelevant. What matters is where the AI system's output is used.

SMB Spotlight: The EU AI Act's SME Provisions

The EU AI Act mentions SMEs (small and medium-sized enterprises) 38 times across its text. This was deliberate. The European Parliament recognized that blanket regulation could disproportionately burden smaller businesses and built in specific accommodations:

- **Priority access to regulatory sandboxes:** Member states must establish at least one regulatory sandbox by August 2026, and SMEs get priority access — free of charge.
- **Proportional conformity assessment fees:** Fees for conformity assessments must take into account the specific interests and needs of SMEs, including startups.
- **Simplified technical documentation:** The AI Office is empowered to develop simplified versions of the technical documentation requirements for SMEs.
- **Penalty caps:** As noted above, penalties for SMEs are capped at the lower of the fixed amount or turnover percentage, rather than the higher.

These provisions are meaningful, but they require proactive engagement. No regulator is going to call you and say, "Hey, did you know you qualify for reduced fees?" You need to know the provisions exist. You need to apply for sandbox access when it becomes available. You need to reference the SME-specific documentation templates when they are published. The Act was designed not to crush small businesses — but only if small businesses know where to look.

The AI Literacy Obligation You Already Have

One obligation deserves special attention because it is already in force and affects every organization: Article 4 on AI literacy.

Since February 2, 2025, providers and deployers of AI systems have been required to take measures to ensure, to their best extent, a sufficient level of AI literacy of their staff and other persons dealing with the operation and use of AI systems on their behalf, taking into account their technical knowledge, experience, education, and training, and the context in which the AI systems are to be used, and considering the persons or groups of persons on whom the AI systems are to be used.

This is not a requirement to turn every employee into a data scientist. It is a requirement to ensure that people interacting with AI systems understand what those systems do, what their limitations are, and how to use them appropriately. The level of literacy required scales with the role — a product manager deploying an AI hiring tool needs deeper understanding than a customer service representative using an AI-powered knowledge base.

We will cover AI literacy program design in detail in Chapter 5. For now, know that if you have not started an AI literacy initiative, you are already behind on your first EU AI Act compliance deadline.

The NIST AI RMF: How to Think About Risk

Full title: NIST AI 100-1, Artificial Intelligence Risk Management Framework (AI RMF 1.0)

Published: January 26, 2023

Status: Voluntary, but increasingly referenced in US policy and procurement

If the EU AI Act tells you what you must do, the NIST AI Risk Management Framework tells you how to think about doing it. The AI RMF is the most comprehensive, practical, and widely applicable AI risk management methodology available today. It is voluntary, rights-preserving, non-sector-specific, and use-case agnostic — meaning it works for a healthcare system deploying clinical decision support tools and for a marketing team using AI to generate ad copy.

The framework was developed through an open, consensus-driven process involving over 240 organizations. Unlike the EU AI Act, it is not a regulation. Nobody will fine you for not using it. But — and this is the critical paradox — it is rapidly becoming the de facto US baseline for AI risk management, and ignoring it carries its own risks.

Structure

The AI RMF is organized into two parts:

Part 1: Foundational Information. This section establishes the conceptual basis — how AI risks differ from traditional software risks, why AI trustworthiness matters, and how organizations should frame their approach to AI risk management. It introduces the seven trustworthiness characteristics (more on these below) and explains the relationship between AI risk and broader organizational risk.

Part 2: Core and Profiles. This is where the actionable guidance lives. The Core defines four functions — GOVERN, MAP, MEASURE, and MANAGE — each broken into categories and subcategories with specific outcomes. Profiles allow organizations to prioritize and customize the Core based on their specific context, sector, and risk tolerance.

The Four Core Functions

The AI RMF Core is organized into four functions that form a continuous risk management lifecycle FIGURE B1-04:

GOVERN — Establish the culture, structure, and processes for AI risk management.

GOVERN is the foundation. It addresses organizational culture, policies, roles, accountability, third-party risk governance, and stakeholder feedback mechanisms. It contains 6 categories and approximately 19 subcategories. Key outcomes include:

- Organizational policies and processes for AI risk management are defined and implemented
- Accountability structures are in place (who owns AI risk?)
- Workforce diversity, equity, inclusion, and accessibility processes are prioritized
- Organizational teams are committed to a culture that considers and communicates AI risk
- Policies and processes are in place for engagement with third parties in the AI lifecycle
- Mechanisms are in place for stakeholders to report problems and provide feedback

GOVERN is not optional in the way that the other three functions can be selectively applied. If you skip GOVERN, you have no governance infrastructure, and the other three functions have nowhere to land. This is where many organizations fail — they jump to measuring and managing risk without first establishing who is responsible, what policies apply, and how decisions are made.

MAP — Understand the context, scope, and potential impacts of your AI systems.

MAP is about developing situational awareness. Before you can measure or manage risk, you need to understand what your AI system does, who it affects, what could go wrong, and what benefits and costs are at stake. MAP contains 5 categories and approximately 18 subcategories. Key outcomes include:

- Context is established and understood (intended use, intended users, affected individuals)
- Categorization of the AI system's potential benefits and costs is performed
- AI capabilities, targeted usage, goals, and expected benefits are understood
- Risks and benefits are mapped for all components of the AI system, including third-party software and data
- Impacts to individuals, groups, communities, organizations, and ecosystems are characterized

MAP is where you discover that your "simple" AI chatbot actually processes sensitive personal data, or that your "low-risk" recommendation engine influences financial decisions. Thorough mapping often changes the risk classification of a system.

MEASURE — Quantify, assess, and monitor AI risks using appropriate methods.

MEASURE is about applying analytical techniques to the risks you identified in MAP. It contains 4 categories and approximately 22 subcategories — making it the most granular of the four functions. Key outcomes include:

- Appropriate methods and metrics are identified and applied to measure AI risks and impacts
- AI systems are evaluated for trustworthiness characteristics relevant to their context
- Mechanisms for tracking identified risks over time are in place
- Feedback about efficacy of measurement approaches is used to improve risk management

MEASURE is where technical and organizational rigor meet. Bias testing, fairness evaluation, accuracy measurement, robustness testing, explainability assessment, and ongoing monitoring all live here. For many practitioners, this is the function that requires the most technical support — you may need data scientists or specialized tooling to execute MEASURE effectively.

MANAGE — Prioritize, respond to, and communicate about AI risks.

MANAGE takes the risks identified through MAP and quantified through MEASURE and addresses them through treatment strategies. It contains 4 categories and approximately 13 subcategories. Key outcomes include:

- AI risks based on assessments and other analytical output are prioritized, responded to, and managed
- Strategies to maximize AI benefits and minimize negative impacts are planned, prepared, implemented, documented, and informed by input from relevant AI actors
- AI risks and benefits from third-party resources are regularly monitored, and risk controls are applied and documented

- Risk treatments, including response and recovery, and communication plans for the identified and measured AI risks are documented

MANAGE is also where incident response lives. When something goes wrong — a model produces harmful output, a bias is discovered, a data breach occurs — MANAGE provides the framework for response, recovery, and communication.

The Seven Trustworthiness Characteristics

Underlying the entire AI RMF is a set of seven trustworthiness characteristics [FIGURE B1-09] that define what "good" AI looks like:

1. **Valid and Reliable** — the AI system performs as intended for its defined conditions of use, and it does so consistently over time. This is the foundation — an AI system that does not work correctly cannot be safe, fair, or explainable.
2. **Safe** — the AI system does not endanger human life, health, property, or the environment.
3. **Secure and Resilient** — the AI system maintains confidentiality, integrity, and availability, and it can withstand unexpected adverse events or changes.
4. **Accountable and Transparent** — information about the AI system and its outputs is available to those who need it, and there are clear lines of accountability for the system's behavior.
5. **Explainable and Interpretable** — the mechanisms underlying the AI system's operation can be understood by relevant stakeholders, and the system's outputs can be meaningfully interpreted.
6. **Privacy-Enhanced** — the AI system protects personal and sensitive information throughout its lifecycle.
7. **Fair with Harmful Bias Managed** — the AI system does not produce unfair or discriminatory outcomes, and bias is identified, measured, and managed.

These characteristics are not a checklist to be applied mechanically. They are interdependent — improving one may create tension with another. A highly explainable model may be less accurate than an opaque one. A system optimized for safety may be less useful. The AI RMF acknowledges these trade-offs and asks organizations to make deliberate, documented decisions about how they balance competing characteristics.

The GenAI Profile (NIST AI 600-1)

In July 2024, NIST published a companion document: NIST AI 600-1, the Generative AI Profile. This profile extends the AI RMF specifically for generative AI systems — large language models, image generators, code assistants, and similar systems.

The GenAI Profile identifies 12 risks specific to generative AI:

1. **CBRN Information or Capabilities** — generative AI that provides information or capabilities related to chemical, biological, radiological, or nuclear threats
2. **Confabulation** — confidently generating false, fabricated, or inconsistent content (commonly called "hallucination")
3. **Dangerous or Violent Content** — generating content that enables, encourages, or depicts violence or physical harm
4. **Data Privacy** — leaking, memorizing, or inferring private information from training data
5. **Environmental Impacts** — energy consumption, water use, and carbon emissions from training and inference
6. **Harmful Bias and Homogenization** — perpetuating or amplifying societal biases, or producing homogenized outputs that reduce diversity
7. **Human-AI Configuration** — failures in the design of human-AI interaction, including over-reliance, anthropomorphization, and automation bias
8. **Information Integrity** — generating misinformation, disinformation, or content that undermines the integrity of information ecosystems
9. **Information Security** — vulnerabilities introduced by or exploited through generative AI, including prompt injection
10. **Intellectual Property** — copyright infringement, trademark dilution, or misuse of proprietary information through AI-generated content
11. **Obscene, Degrading, or Abusive Content** — generating content that is sexually explicit, degrading, or otherwise harmful

12. **Value Chain and Component Integration** — risks arising from the complex supply chain of generative AI systems, including third-party models, fine-tuning data, and retrieval-augmented generation sources

For each risk, the profile maps to specific AI RMF subcategories and provides over 400 mitigation actions. If you deploy any generative AI system — and in 2026, most organizations do — the GenAI Profile is essential reading.

The Playbook

NIST also publishes the AI RMF Playbook, which provides suggested actions for each of the framework's 72 subcategories. The Playbook is not prescriptive — it does not say "you must do X." Instead, it says "here are actions that organizations have found useful for achieving this outcome." You pick the actions that are relevant to your context and risk tolerance.

The Playbook's modular design is one of the AI RMF's greatest strengths. A five-person startup can use a lightweight subset of suggested actions. A Fortune 500 company can implement the full suite. Neither is wrong — the framework scales to your context.

Getting Started with the AI RMF

If you are looking at 72 subcategories and over 400 GenAI-specific mitigation actions and feeling overwhelmed, here is the minimum viable path:

Week 1-2: GOVERN basics. Designate an AI governance lead. Document your organizational risk tolerance for AI. Draft a one-page AI policy that defines what AI systems you use, who is responsible for them, and what is and is not acceptable.

Week 3-4: MAP your AI inventory. List every AI system in use across your organization — including tools employees are using without formal approval. For each system, document: what it does, what data it processes, who it affects, and what decisions it influences. You will be surprised by how many AI systems you have.

Week 5-8: MEASURE your top risks. Take the three to five highest-risk AI systems from your inventory and apply the relevant trustworthiness characteristics. For a hiring tool, focus on fairness and bias. For a customer-facing chatbot, focus on validity, reliability, and transparency. For a clinical decision support system, focus on safety and explainability. You do not need to assess every characteristic for every system — start with the ones that matter most for each use case.

Week 9-12: MANAGE with treatment plans. For each significant risk you identified, document a treatment plan: accept, mitigate, transfer, or avoid. Assign owners. Set review dates. Establish a cadence for revisiting these assessments — quarterly is a reasonable starting point.

This 12-week approach will not give you a complete, auditable AI RMF implementation. But it will give you a functioning risk management process that covers your highest-priority AI systems. You can expand from there.

The Voluntary-But-Referenced Paradox

Here is the tension at the heart of the NIST AI RMF: it is voluntary, but it is increasingly referenced in legally binding or commercially binding contexts.

Executive Order 14110 on Safe, Secure, and Trustworthy Development and Use of Artificial Intelligence, issued in October 2023, directed federal agencies to use the AI RMF as part of their AI risk management processes. While the current political environment around executive orders on AI is fluid, the institutional adoption of the AI RMF within federal agencies has already occurred — procurement offices, CISOs, and compliance teams have built the framework into their processes.

The Federal AI Risk Management Act (HR 6936), introduced in Congress, would make AI RMF compliance mandatory for federal contractors. If passed, any organization selling AI systems or AI-enabled services to the federal government would need to demonstrate alignment with the framework.

Even without formal legal mandates, the AI RMF is becoming a contractual standard. Large enterprises are beginning to include AI RMF alignment in their vendor assessment criteria. Insurance underwriters are referencing it in their AI-related questionnaires. Industry groups are building sector-specific profiles on top of it.

The practical takeaway: treating the AI RMF as optional is technically accurate and strategically shortsighted. If you are a US-based organization, the AI RMF should be your risk management methodology of choice. It costs nothing to adopt,

NIST provides the guidance for free, and alignment positions you for every future regulatory or commercial requirement that references it.

ISO/IEC 42001: How to Build the Management System

Full title: ISO/IEC 42001:2023 — Information technology — Artificial intelligence — Management system for artificial intelligence

Published: December 2023

Status: First certifiable AI management system standard

If the EU AI Act tells you what to do and the NIST AI RMF tells you how to think about risk, ISO/IEC 42001 tells you how to build the organizational machinery to do it all consistently, repeatedly, and provably.

ISO 42001 is the first international standard that specifies requirements for establishing, implementing, maintaining, and continually improving an Artificial Intelligence Management System (AIMS). It follows the familiar ISO management system structure — the same Annex SL high-level structure used by ISO 27001 (information security), ISO 9001 (quality), and ISO 14001 (environmental management). If your organization already holds any of these certifications, you know the drill: leadership commitment, context analysis, risk assessment, controls, internal audit, management review, and continual improvement.

What ISO 42001 Contains

The standard has two critical annexes:

Annex A provides a set of reference controls organized by control objectives. These are not AI risk categories — they are management controls that an organization applies to ensure responsible AI development, deployment, and use. Controls cover areas like AI system impact assessment, data for AI systems, AI system documentation, monitoring of AI systems, third-party and customer relationships, and more.

Annex B provides implementation guidance for the Annex A controls. Think of Annex A as the "what" and Annex B as the "how" — a pattern that mirrors the relationship between ISO 27001's Annex A controls and the ISO 27002 implementation guidance.

What ISO 42001 Actually Requires

At its core, ISO 42001 requires you to build and operate a management system — a set of interrelated elements that an organization uses to establish policies and objectives, and the processes to achieve those objectives. The standard's normative clauses (Clauses 4 through 10) define what that management system must include:

- **Context of the organization (Clause 4):** Understand your external and internal landscape, the needs and expectations of interested parties (customers, regulators, affected individuals), and the scope of your AIMS.
- **Leadership (Clause 5):** Top management must demonstrate commitment, establish an AI policy, and assign roles, responsibilities, and authorities.
- **Planning (Clause 6):** Identify risks and opportunities related to your AI activities, conduct AI system impact assessments, and set measurable AI objectives.
- **Support (Clause 7):** Ensure you have the resources, competence, awareness, communication, and documented information needed to operate the management system.
- **Operation (Clause 8):** Plan and control your AI-related processes, conduct AI risk assessments, treat identified risks, and manage AI system lifecycle activities.
- **Performance evaluation (Clause 9):** Monitor, measure, analyze, and evaluate the performance of your AI systems and your management system. Conduct internal audits and management reviews.
- **Improvement (Clause 10):** Address nonconformities, take corrective actions, and continually improve the management system.

The Annex A controls add AI-specific requirements on top of this management system foundation. They cover areas including AI policy for responsible AI, internal organization for AI, resources for AI systems, assessing impacts of AI systems, AI system lifecycle, data for AI systems, information for interested parties, use of AI systems, and third-party and customer relationships. Each control has a stated objective and a set of specific requirements.

This structure is what makes ISO 42001 so powerful for practitioners who already operate management systems. If you have ISO 27001, you already have the Clause 4-10 infrastructure. You need to extend it to cover AI-specific controls, but you are not building from the ground up.

The Certification Pathway

One of ISO 42001's primary values is that it is certifiable. You can bring in an accredited certification body, undergo an audit, and receive a certificate that demonstrates to customers, partners, and regulators that your AI management system meets an internationally recognized standard.

The certification pathway follows a predictable sequence:

1. **Gap assessment** ($5,000-$15,000): An initial evaluation of your current state against ISO 42001 requirements. This tells you where you are and what you need to build.
2. **Implementation** (4-9 months for small organizations, 9-18 months for mid-market): Building the management system — policies, procedures, risk assessments, controls, documentation, training, and internal processes.
3. **Stage 1 audit**: A documentation review to ensure your management system is designed correctly and ready for a full audit.
4. **Stage 2 audit**: The full on-site (or remote) audit, where the certification body examines your management system in operation, interviews staff, reviews evidence, and tests controls.
5. **Certification**: If you pass, you receive a certificate valid for three years.
6. **Annual surveillance audits** ($3,000-$16,000): The certification body returns each year to verify that your management system continues to operate effectively.

Costs

Let us talk numbers, because budgets are real:

- **Small organizations (under 50 employees):** $20,000-$60,000 total, including gap assessment, implementation, and certification. This assumes you have internal staff capable of leading the implementation. If you need external consultants for the entire process, costs increase.

- **Mid-market organizations (50-500 employees):** $150,000-$320,000 total. The complexity increases with the number of AI systems, the number of business processes affected, and the maturity of your existing governance infrastructure.

These are significant investments. But here is the critical cost-saving insight: if your organization is already certified to ISO 27001, you have a massive head start.

The ISO 27001 Overlap

ISO 42001 and ISO 27001 share 40-50% of their requirements. Both use the Annex SL high-level structure. Both require leadership commitment, context analysis, risk assessment, internal audit, management review, and continual improvement. If you already have:

- A management system framework (clauses 4-10)
- A risk assessment methodology
- An internal audit program
- A management review process
- Document control procedures
- A corrective action process

Then you already have roughly half of what ISO 42001 requires. What you need to add is the AI-specific content: AI system inventory, AI impact assessments, AI-specific controls from Annex A, data governance for AI systems, and AI-specific monitoring and measurement.

For organizations already holding ISO 27001, the incremental cost and effort of adding ISO 42001 is significantly lower than starting from scratch. Many organizations pursue an integrated management system that satisfies both standards simultaneously.

ISO 42001 and the EU AI Act

A question practitioners frequently ask: "If I get ISO 42001 certified, am I EU AI Act compliant?"

The short answer is no. ISO 42001 certification does not automatically mean EU AI Act compliance. The standard provides a management system framework — it ensures you have the organizational machinery for responsible AI governance. But it does not address every specific requirement of the EU AI Act, particularly around risk classification, conformity assessment, CE marking, and the specific documentation requirements for high-risk systems.

The longer answer is that ISO 42001 certification puts you in a strong position. It demonstrates that you have systematic governance processes. It provides a structured approach to the risk management system required by Article 9 of the EU AI Act. It gives auditors confidence that your organization takes AI governance seriously. When EU AI Act enforcement intensifies in 2026 and 2027, organizations with ISO 42001 certification will find compliance significantly easier than those without any management system foundation.

Think of ISO 42001 as necessary but not sufficient for EU AI Act compliance. It builds the house; the EU AI Act tells you what specific rooms the house must contain.

How the Three Frameworks Relate

Now that we have covered each framework individually, let us step back and see the full picture. How do the Big Three work together?

[FIGURE B1-05] illustrates the relationship:

- **EU AI Act:** WHAT you must do — legal requirements, risk classifications, compliance obligations, penalties
- **NIST AI RMF:** HOW to think about risk — methodology, trustworthiness characteristics, risk management lifecycle
- **ISO 42001:** HOW to build the management system — operational framework, controls, certification, continual improvement

These are not competing frameworks. They are complementary layers. The EU AI Act sets the destination. The NIST AI RMF provides the map. ISO 42001 builds the vehicle.

Official Crosswalks

You do not have to figure out the relationships between these frameworks yourself. Official and third-party crosswalks exist:

- **NIST-to-ISO 42001 crosswalk:** NIST has published a mapping between AI RMF subcategories and ISO 42001 requirements, making it straightforward to identify where compliance with one framework satisfies (or partially satisfies) the other.
- **NIST-to-ISO 23894 crosswalk:** ISO 23894 is a guidance standard for AI risk management (not certifiable), and NIST has mapped the AI RMF to its provisions.
- **EU AI Act crosswalks:** Several third-party organizations have published crosswalks mapping EU AI Act requirements to NIST AI RMF and ISO 42001. The Cloud Security Alliance (CSA), Trustible, and GLACIS have all published versions. These are not officially endorsed by the EU or NIST, but they are practically useful.

These crosswalks save you significant effort. Rather than building three separate compliance programs, you can build one integrated program with a crosswalk that demonstrates how your controls satisfy multiple frameworks simultaneously.

Practical Integration

Here is the integration pattern that works for most organizations:

1. **Use the NIST AI RMF as your risk methodology.** Its four functions — GOVERN, MAP, MEASURE, MANAGE — provide the most comprehensive and practical approach to AI risk management. Start by working through the GOVERN function to establish your organizational context, then MAP your AI systems, MEASURE their risks, and MANAGE those risks through treatment strategies.

2. **Use ISO 42001 as your management system structure.** If you need (or want) a certifiable management system, build it on ISO 42001's Annex SL framework. Use the NIST AI RMF outputs — risk assessments, profiles, action plans — as inputs to your ISO 42001 management system. The AI RMF does the risk thinking; ISO 42001 provides the governance scaffolding to operationalize and maintain it.

3. **Use the EU AI Act as your compliance checklist.** Layer EU AI Act requirements on top of your NIST + ISO 42001 foundation. The risk classification system tells you which tier your systems fall into. The specific obligations for high-risk systems tell you what documentation, processes, and controls you need. The timeline tells you when each obligation takes effect.

This integration approach means you are not doing three things — you are doing one thing (building an AI governance program) using three complementary instruments.

Which Frameworks Apply to You?

Not every organization needs all three. Your specific situation determines which combination makes sense.

Action Item: Regulatory Applicability Checklist

Answer these five yes/no questions to determine which of the Big Three apply to your organization:

1. **Do you develop or deploy AI systems used by people in the EU?** If yes, the EU AI Act applies to you — regardless of where you are headquartered. Start with risk classification of your AI systems.
2. **Does your AI system fall into any Annex III high-risk category?** (Biometrics, critical infrastructure, education, employment, essential services, law enforcement, migration, justice/democracy.) If yes, you face the full suite of high-risk obligations by August 2026.
3. **Are you a US federal agency or federal contractor?** If yes, the NIST AI RMF is already referenced in your procurement and compliance requirements. If the Federal AI Risk Management Act passes, it may become mandatory. Treat it as a baseline now.
4. **Do your customers or partners require ISO 42001 certification?** If yes, you need to start the certification pathway — budget 4-18 months depending on your size and existing ISO certifications.
5. **Do you need a structured risk management methodology but do not face specific regulatory mandates?** If yes, the NIST

AI RMF is your starting point. It is free, comprehensive, and positions you for any future regulatory requirement.

For a detailed decision tree, see Appendix D: "Which framework applies to me?"

For US-only companies with no EU exposure: NIST AI RMF + ISO 42001 is your practical path. Use the AI RMF for risk management, and consider ISO 42001 certification if your market or customers demand it. Even without the EU AI Act, you will build a governance program that can adapt to any future US regulation.

For EU-exposed companies: Add EU AI Act compliance on top of your NIST + ISO 42001 foundation. Start with risk classification — determine which tier each of your AI systems falls into, and focus your compliance efforts on the highest-risk systems first.

For global companies operating across multiple jurisdictions: You need all three, with sector-specific additions layered on top. The good news is that the three frameworks are complementary, not conflicting. Build once, map to many. Use the crosswalks to demonstrate compliance across frameworks without duplicating effort.

A Concrete Integration Example

Let us walk through how integration works in practice. Suppose you are a mid-market SaaS company with 200 employees, based in the US, with customers in both the US and EU. You deploy an AI-powered customer support system and an AI-driven lead scoring tool.

Step 1: NIST AI RMF — GOVERN. You establish an AI governance working group with representatives from engineering, legal, product, and security. You document your organization's risk tolerance: you have a low tolerance for bias in customer-facing systems and a moderate tolerance for accuracy limitations in internal tools. You draft an AI acceptable use policy. (This simultaneously satisfies ISO 42001 Clauses 5 and 6, and prepares you for EU AI Act Article 9's risk management system requirement.)

Step 2: NIST AI RMF — MAP. You inventory both AI systems. The customer support chatbot processes EU customer data, is customer-facing, and influences service outcomes. The lead scoring tool processes prospect data, is used internally, and influences sales prioritization but not access to essential services. You classify the chatbot as limited-risk under the EU AI Act (transparency obligations apply) and the lead scoring tool as minimal-risk. (This simultaneously addresses ISO 42001 Clause 8 on operational planning and the EU AI Act risk classification requirement.)

Step 3: NIST AI RMF — MEASURE. You evaluate the chatbot for accuracy (does it provide correct information?), transparency (does it disclose its AI nature?), and privacy (does it handle EU personal data appropriately?). You evaluate the lead scoring tool for fairness (does it score prospects equitably?) and validity (does it actually predict conversion?). (This feeds into ISO 42001 Clause 9 on performance evaluation and builds the technical documentation required by the EU AI Act.)

Step 4: NIST AI RMF — MANAGE. For the chatbot, you implement a disclosure notice ("You are chatting with an AI assistant") to satisfy EU AI Act Article 50 transparency requirements. You establish a quarterly review cadence for accuracy metrics. For the lead scoring tool, you implement a semi-annual bias audit. You document all treatment decisions and risk acceptances. (This satisfies ISO 42001 Clause 10 on improvement and generates the compliance evidence the EU AI Act will require.)

One process. Three frameworks satisfied. The crosswalks confirm the mappings. The documentation serves triple duty.

Gaps to Watch

While the three frameworks are largely complementary, a few gaps and tensions are worth noting:

Agentic AI. None of the Big Three were designed with autonomous AI agents in mind. The EU AI Act was drafted before agentic AI became mainstream. The NIST AI RMF addresses AI systems generally but does not provide specific guidance for multi-step autonomous agents. ISO 42001 provides a management system framework that can accommodate agentic AI but does not address its unique risks. For agentic AI governance, you will need to supplement the Big Three with frameworks like the Singapore Model Governance Framework for Agentic AI (covered in Chapter 3) and OWASP's Top 10 for Agentic Applications (covered in Chapter 4).

Speed of change. The EU AI Act was negotiated over three years and entered into force in 2024. The AI technology landscape has shifted dramatically since the Act's provisions were drafted. GPAI obligations were added late in the legislative process. Agentic AI, multi-modal systems, and AI-powered reasoning agents were not on the radar. The Act includes review mechanisms, but regulations move slowly. Practitioners need to anticipate gaps between what the law requires and what the technology demands.

Harmonized standards. The EU AI Act relies on harmonized standards — technical standards developed by European Standardization Organizations (CEN, CENELEC, ETSI) — to define how compliance should be demonstrated. As of early 2026, these standards are still under development. This creates uncertainty: organizations know what the law requires, but the detailed technical standards that define how to demonstrate compliance are not yet finalized. Monitor the standardization process and plan for adjustment as standards are published.

Key Takeaways

- **The Big Three are complementary, not competing.** The EU AI Act defines legal requirements (what), the NIST AI RMF provides risk management methodology (how to think), and ISO 42001 provides the certifiable management system (how to operate). Build one integrated program that satisfies all three.
- **The EU AI Act is already partially in force.** Prohibited AI practices and AI literacy obligations have been enforceable since February 2025. High-risk system obligations arrive in August 2026. If you deploy AI systems that touch the EU in any way, compliance planning should be underway now — not next quarter.
- **The NIST AI RMF is free, voluntary, and increasingly unavoidable.** It costs nothing to adopt, NIST provides the guidance, and it is rapidly becoming the de facto US baseline through federal policy, procurement requirements, and commercial expectations. Treat it as your risk management foundation.

- **ISO 42001 certification is expensive but builds on what you already have.** If your organization holds ISO 27001, you have 40-50% of the work done. The incremental investment to add AI-specific governance is significantly less than starting from scratch.
- **Start with classification, not compliance.** Before you worry about which regulations apply and what they require, inventory your AI systems and classify them by risk. Your compliance obligations flow directly from your risk classification. Get that right, and the rest follows logically.

Chapter 3: The International Landscape and Emerging Frameworks

You are a midsized logistics company based in Atlanta. Your entire workforce is in the United States. Your customers are American. Your servers are in Virginia. You have never filed a regulatory document with a foreign government. And you are almost certainly subject to international AI governance frameworks right now.

Here is why. Your AI-powered route optimization system was built by a vendor headquartered in Munich. Your customer service chatbot runs on a large language model hosted by a cloud provider with data centers in Dublin and Singapore. Three of your enterprise clients have European subsidiaries that process shipment data through your platform. And the AI hiring tool you adopted last year to screen warehouse applicants is now subject to the Colorado AI Act, which took effect June 30, 2026 – a US state law that explicitly drew its definitions and risk categories from international frameworks.

The notion that you can be "US only" in AI governance is a comforting fiction. Supply chains are global. Cloud infrastructure is global. AI vendors operate across jurisdictions. And increasingly, US state and federal regulators are borrowing directly from international frameworks when they write domestic rules. If you do not understand the international landscape, you will not understand the domestic one either.

Chapter 2 covered the Big Three – the EU AI Act, the NIST AI RMF, and ISO 42001. Those are your foundation. This chapter covers everything else that matters: the first legally binding international AI treaty, the first national framework specifically addressing agentic AI, and the patchwork of national regulations that are converging toward a common set of principles faster than most practitioners realize.

You do not need to become an expert on every framework in this chapter. You need to know which ones apply to you, what they require, and where to find the details when you need them. [FIGURE B1-06] at the end of this chapter provides the comparison matrix. But first, let us walk through the landscape.

The Council of Europe Framework Convention on AI (CETS 225)

On September 5, 2024, in Vilnius, Lithuania, representatives from the United States, the United Kingdom, the European Union, Canada, Japan, Israel, and several other nations signed the Council of Europe Framework Convention on Artificial Intelligence, Human Rights, Democracy, and the Rule of Law. Its formal designation is CETS 225. It is the first legally binding international treaty on AI governance.

That sentence is worth pausing on. Not a set of principles. Not a voluntary framework. Not a declaration of intent. A treaty – a legal instrument that, once ratified, creates binding obligations under international law.

On March 13, 2026, the European Parliament voted to grant consent for EU accession to the Convention, with a vote of 455 in favor, 101 against, and 74 abstentions. That lopsided margin signals something important: this is not a contested document. The political consensus behind binding international AI governance is broad and deepening. The Convention will enter into force once ratified by five signatories, including at least three Council of Europe member states. That threshold is widely expected to be met by late 2026 or early 2027.

What the Convention Requires

The Convention is deliberately high-level. It does not prescribe specific technical standards or enumerate prohibited practices the way the EU AI Act does. Instead, it establishes a set of principles that signatories must implement through their domestic legal frameworks. The core obligations fall into five categories:

Human dignity and individual autonomy. Signatories must ensure that AI systems respect human dignity and individual autonomy. This sounds abstract until you realize it means every signatory must have domestic mechanisms to prevent AI systems from manipulating, deceiving, or coercing individuals – and those mechanisms must meet the Convention's minimum standard.

Transparency and oversight. AI systems must be sufficiently transparent to allow meaningful human oversight. Signatories must ensure that individuals affected by AI systems can understand, at a level appropriate to the context, that they are interacting with or subject to an AI system, and that they can obtain meaningful explanations of AI-driven decisions that significantly affect them.

Accountability and responsibility. There must be clear lines of legal responsibility for AI systems. If an AI system causes harm, there must be accessible mechanisms for redress. The Convention requires signatories to ensure that both public and private sector actors deploying AI systems can be held accountable for their impacts.

Non-discrimination and equality. AI systems must not be used in ways that discriminate. Signatories must take measures to identify, assess, prevent, and mitigate the risks of discrimination arising from AI systems, including biased outcomes that disproportionately affect individuals based on protected characteristics.

Privacy and data protection. AI systems must respect existing privacy and data protection frameworks. The Convention explicitly builds on the Council of Europe's Convention 108+ (the modernized Convention for the Protection of Individuals with regard to the Processing of Personal Data), linking AI governance to the existing international data protection regime.

The "Comply or Equivalent Protection" Model

Here is the provision that makes the Convention directly relevant to your organization, even if you think international treaties are someone else's problem.

Article 3 of the Convention distinguishes between public sector and private sector AI activities. For public sector AI, the Convention applies directly – signatories must ensure their government agencies comply with the Convention's principles. For private sector AI, the Convention uses a "comply or equivalent protection" model. Signatories must either apply the Convention's principles directly to private sector actors or demonstrate that their existing domestic frameworks provide equivalent protection.

What does this mean in practice? It means that every signatory nation must have domestic rules – whether through legislation, regulation, or binding guidance – that cover the private sector AI activities happening within their jurisdiction. If those rules provide protections equivalent to the Convention's principles, the obligation is satisfied. If they do not, the signatory must close the gap.

For US-based practitioners, this is significant. The United States signed the Convention. Once it is ratified (which requires Senate advice and consent), the US government will need to demonstrate that domestic frameworks – the combination of the NIST AI RMF, executive orders, sector-specific regulations, and state laws – provide protection equivalent to the Convention's principles. Where gaps exist, new rules will follow.

> **Real-World Example: The CoE Framework Convention**
>
> How does a treaty signed in Vilnius in September 2024 affect your AI deployment in Denver? Through the "comply or equivalent protection" clause. If you do business with any EU country, the UK, or Japan, this treaty's principles will shape the regulatory expectations you face. Those nations must ensure their domestic frameworks cover private sector AI – meaning the companies you do business with in those countries are operating under governance regimes aligned with the Convention. Your contractual partners will increasingly expect you to demonstrate equivalent governance. And if the US ratifies the Convention, domestic frameworks will need to cover the same ground.
>
> You do not need to read the full treaty text today. But you should know it exists, understand that it creates a floor for AI governance across all signatories, and recognize that its principles – transparency, accountability, non-discrimination, human oversight – are the same principles every major framework converges on. If you are building your governance program around these principles (which you should be, based on Chapters 2 and 4-8 of this book), you are already moving in the right direction.

What Practitioners Should Watch

The Convention includes a mechanism for a Conference of the Parties – a regular meeting of signatory nations to review implementation, resolve disputes, and update the Convention's scope. This mechanism means the Convention is a living instrument. As AI technology evolves, the Convention's interpretation and application will evolve with it. Agentic AI, foundation models, and multi-modal systems are not specifically addressed in the current text, but the Conference of the Parties has the mandate to develop additional guidance as these technologies mature.

The key dates to watch: ratification timelines for the United States, the UK, and Japan; the first Conference of the Parties meeting (expected within 12 months of entry into force); and any domestic legislative activity in signatory nations that explicitly references the Convention as its basis.

Singapore IMDA Model Governance Framework for Agentic AI

If the Council of Europe Framework Convention is the most important international AI treaty, the Singapore Model Governance Framework for Agentic AI is the most immediately useful international governance document for practitioners. Published in January 2026 by the Infocomm Media Development Authority (IMDA) of Singapore, it is the first national governance framework specifically designed for agentic AI systems.

This matters because, as Chapter 2 noted, none of the Big Three were designed with AI agents in mind. The EU AI Act was drafted before agentic AI went mainstream. The NIST AI RMF addresses AI systems generally. ISO 42001 provides a management system that can accommodate agentic AI but does not address its unique risks. The Singapore MGF fills that gap – and it does so in 27 pages of clear, practical, immediately actionable guidance.

The Four Pillars

The MGF is organized around four governance pillars. Each pillar maps to a set of concrete requirements and recommendations.

Pillar 1: Assess and bound risks upfront. Before deploying an agentic AI system, you must assess its risk profile using two dimensions – the potential impact of the system and the likelihood that risks will materialize. The MGF provides structured risk factor tables for each dimension, which we will examine in a moment. The key insight is that risk assessment for agentic AI must happen before deployment, not after. You do not release an agent into production and then figure out what could go wrong. You bound its risk surface in advance.

Pillar 2: Make humans meaningfully accountable. This pillar addresses the accountability gap that agentic AI creates. When an AI agent makes a chain of autonomous decisions across multiple steps, who is responsible for the outcome? The MGF's answer is that human accountability must be established at every level of the value chain – from the model developers who build the underlying foundation models, to the system providers who assemble the agentic system, to the deploying organizations that put it into production, to the end users who interact with it. Accountability cannot be delegated to the agent itself.

Pillar 3: Implement technical controls and processes. This is the operational core of the framework. The MGF specifies technical controls that agentic AI systems should implement, including: guardrails and boundary constraints that limit what the agent can do; monitoring and logging of agent actions; escalation mechanisms that route high-risk decisions to human reviewers; testing and evaluation protocols specifically designed for multi-step autonomous behavior; and incident response procedures for when agents behave unexpectedly.

Pillar 4: Enable end-user responsibility. The final pillar recognizes that end users of agentic AI systems also bear responsibility. Users must be informed about what the agent can and cannot do, what its limitations are, and what actions they should take if the agent produces unexpected results. This pillar requires that deploying organizations provide sufficient transparency to enable users to exercise meaningful judgment about whether to accept, modify, or reject the agent's outputs.

The Risk Factor Tables

The MGF's most immediately practical contribution is its risk factor tables, found in Section 2.1.1 of the framework. These tables provide structured criteria for assessing both the potential impact and the likelihood of harm from an agentic AI system.

Impact risk factors include:

- **Domain sensitivity** – is the agent operating in a high-stakes domain such as healthcare, finance, or legal services, or in a lower-stakes domain such as content summarization or scheduling?
- **Data sensitivity** – does the agent process personal data, confidential business information, or regulated data categories?

- **External system access** – can the agent interact with external systems, APIs, databases, or services? The more systems an agent can touch, the larger its potential blast radius.
- **Action scope** – what can the agent actually do? Can it only read and summarize, or can it create, modify, and delete? An agent that can execute financial transactions carries a fundamentally different risk profile than one that generates meeting summaries.
- **Reversibility** – if the agent takes a wrong action, can it be undone? Reversible actions (drafting an email that requires human approval before sending) carry lower risk than irreversible ones (executing a trade, deleting a database, publishing content to the internet).

Likelihood risk factors include:

- **Degree of autonomy** – how many steps can the agent take without human intervention? A single-step tool-use agent that requires human approval for each action is far less likely to cause cascading harm than a multi-step autonomous agent that chains together dozens of decisions without checkpoints.
- **System complexity** – how many components, models, and integrations does the agent rely on? Complexity increases the likelihood of unexpected interactions and emergent behaviors.
- **External exposure** – is the agent operating in a controlled internal environment or is it exposed to external inputs from the internet, third-party APIs, or untrusted users? External exposure dramatically increases the likelihood of adversarial manipulation and unexpected inputs.

These risk factor tables are not theoretical constructs. They are assessment tools you can use today. If you are deploying an AI agent – whether it is a customer service bot with tool-use capabilities, an autonomous coding assistant, or an AI-powered workflow automation tool – you can walk through these tables and produce a structured risk assessment in an afternoon.

Agent Identity and Authorization

The MGF also addresses a governance question that most organizations have not yet confronted: agent identity. When an AI agent acts on behalf of a user or an organization, how is it identified within your systems? Does it have its own credentials? Does it operate under the user's identity? How are its permissions scoped?

The MGF recommends that agentic AI systems have distinct, auditable identities within organizational systems. This means the agent should not operate under a human user's credentials. It should have its own identity, its own permission set, and its own audit trail. When the agent takes an action – sending an email, querying a database, calling an API – that action should be attributable to the agent, not to a human user whose credentials the agent happens to be borrowing.

This guidance aligns with security best practices (principle of least privilege, separation of duties), but it is remarkable how few organizations have implemented it. If your AI agent is operating under a shared service account with broad permissions, you have an identity and authorization problem that the MGF specifically flags.

The Value Chain Responsibility Model

The MGF introduces a responsibility model that assigns governance obligations to four roles in the agentic AI value chain:

- **Model developers** (companies that build foundation models) are responsible for safety testing, documentation, and providing information about model capabilities and limitations.
- **System providers** (companies that build agentic systems on top of foundation models) are responsible for implementing guardrails, testing multi-step behaviors, and documenting system boundaries.
- **Deploying organizations** (companies that put agentic systems into production) are responsible for risk assessment, access controls, monitoring, incident response, and ensuring the system is appropriate for its intended use.
- **End users** are responsible for using the system within its documented boundaries and reporting unexpected behaviors.

If you are a deploying organization – which most readers of this book are – the MGF makes your obligations clear. You cannot outsource governance to your vendor. The model developer's safety testing does not substitute for your risk assessment. The system provider's guardrails do not substitute for your access controls. You are responsible for the governance of AI systems you deploy, regardless of who built them.

> **SMB Spotlight: If You Only Have Bandwidth for One International Framework Beyond the Big Three**
>
> The Singapore Model Governance Framework for Agentic AI is the most practical framework covered in this chapter. It is 27 pages long. It is written in plain language that a non-specialist can follow. It specifically addresses agentic AI – the category of AI systems that is growing fastest and creating the most novel governance challenges. Its risk factor tables are immediately usable without any customization. And it is free.
>
> If you are a small or midsized business deploying AI agents – customer service bots with tool access, coding assistants, workflow automation tools, AI-powered research agents – the Singapore MGF gives you a structured way to assess and bound the risks of those deployments. It will not satisfy your EU AI Act obligations or replace the NIST AI RMF. But it will give you a practical, agentic-AI-specific governance layer that none of the Big Three provide.
>
> **Action: Download the Singapore MGF from imda.gov.sg and use its risk factor tables (Section 2.1.1) to assess your highest-risk AI deployment this week.**

Other Frameworks in Brief

The Council of Europe Framework Convention and the Singapore MGF deserve deep coverage because they are, respectively, the most legally significant and most practically useful frameworks outside the Big Three. But the international landscape is broader than two documents. Here are four additional frameworks you should be aware of, with guidance on when and why each one matters to you.

OECD AI Principles

The Organisation for Economic Co-operation and Development adopted its AI Principles in May 2019, making them one of the earliest multilateral AI governance frameworks. They were updated in May 2024 to reflect the evolution of the technology landscape. Forty-six countries have endorsed them, including all 38 OECD members and eight partner countries.

The OECD Principles are voluntary. They carry no enforcement mechanism. No regulator will fine you for violating them. So why do they matter?

Because they are the common ancestor. Nearly every binding AI framework that has followed – the EU AI Act, the Council of Europe Convention, the G7 Hiroshima AI Process, national frameworks from Canada to South Korea – draws its conceptual vocabulary from the OECD Principles. The five core principles are: beneficial and inclusive growth, sustainability, and well-being; human-centered values and fairness; transparency and explainability; robustness, security, and safety; and accountability. If those sound familiar, it is because every subsequent framework has restated them in increasingly specific and enforceable terms.

For practitioners, the OECD Principles serve two purposes. First, they provide a useful conceptual map when you need to trace the genealogy of a specific requirement in a binding framework – understanding where a principle came from helps you understand what regulators are trying to achieve. Second, the OECD's ongoing work on AI classification, risk assessment methodologies, and AI incident tracking provides practical tools that complement binding frameworks. The OECD AI Policy Observatory (oecd.ai) is one of the best free resources for tracking AI governance developments worldwide.

United Kingdom: Pro-Innovation Approach

The UK has taken a deliberately different path from the EU. Rather than enacting a single comprehensive AI law, the UK government published its "Pro-Innovation Approach to AI Regulation" white paper in March 2023 and has pursued a sector-led regulatory model. There is no single AI Act. Instead, existing regulators – the Financial Conduct Authority, Ofcom, the Competition and Markets Authority, the Information Commissioner's Office, the Health and Safety Executive, and others – are expected to apply five cross-cutting principles to AI within their existing mandates.

The five principles are: safety, security, and robustness; appropriate transparency and explainability; fairness; accountability and governance; and contestability and redress. Sound familiar? They should. They are the OECD Principles, repackaged for the UK regulatory landscape.

The practical implication is that AI governance requirements in the UK vary by sector. If you are deploying AI in financial services, the FCA's expectations apply. If you are deploying AI in telecommunications, Ofcom's guidance applies. There is no single checklist. This makes UK compliance more complex for multi-sector organizations but potentially simpler for companies operating in a single regulated sector.

For US-based SMBs, the UK approach matters primarily if you have UK customers or if your AI vendors are UK-based. The UK's emphasis on contestability and redress – the idea that individuals must have the ability to challenge AI-driven decisions – is worth noting because it goes beyond what most US frameworks currently require. If your AI system makes decisions that affect UK individuals (credit decisions, hiring decisions, service eligibility), you should ensure your governance framework includes a mechanism for those individuals to contest those decisions.

China: Algorithmic Regulations

China has taken the most prescriptive approach to AI governance of any major economy, but it has done so through a series of targeted regulations rather than a single comprehensive law. Three regulations are particularly relevant:

The **Algorithmic Recommendation Regulations** (effective March 2022) govern AI systems that use algorithms to recommend content, products, or services. They require transparency about how algorithmic recommendations work, give users the right to opt out of algorithmic recommendations, and prohibit algorithms from engaging in price discrimination or market manipulation.

The **Deep Synthesis Regulations** (effective January 2023) govern deepfakes and AI-generated synthetic content. They require labeling of synthetic content, verification of user identities, and content moderation mechanisms.

The **Interim Measures for the Management of Generative AI Services** (effective August 2023) govern generative AI specifically. They require providers of generative AI services to ensure training data is lawfully obtained, implement content moderation to prevent generation of illegal content, register with the Cyberspace Administration of China, and provide users with mechanisms to report problematic outputs.

For most US-based practitioners, China's AI regulations are relevant in two scenarios: you are deploying AI systems that are accessible to users in China, or you are using AI components (models, datasets, tools) developed by Chinese companies. In either case, the regulatory requirements are real and enforceable. The practical challenge is that China's regulations are subject to interpretation by multiple agencies, and enforcement practices are not always transparent to foreign companies.

Brazil AI Bill

Brazil has been developing comprehensive AI legislation since 2020, and as of early 2026 the Brazilian AI Bill is in its final stages of legislative review. The bill adopts a risk-based approach heavily influenced by the EU AI Act, classifying AI systems into risk tiers with corresponding obligations.

The Brazilian bill includes several provisions that diverge from the EU model. It places significant emphasis on algorithmic impact assessments – structured evaluations of AI systems' potential effects on individuals and groups – and it includes specific provisions for AI governance in the public sector. It also includes provisions for AI sandboxes, allowing companies to test AI systems in controlled regulatory environments before full deployment.

For US-based practitioners, the Brazilian AI Bill matters if you have customers or operations in Brazil – which, as the largest economy in Latin America, is a significant market for many American companies. More broadly, the Brazilian bill is a leading indicator of how AI governance will evolve across Latin America. As Brazil goes, so typically go Argentina, Colombia, Chile, and Mexico. If you are building a governance program that needs to scale across the Americas, watching the Brazilian bill's final form is worth the investment.

Colorado AI Act

The Colorado AI Act deserves special mention because it is not an international framework – it is a US state law – but it represents the direct importation of international AI governance concepts into American domestic regulation. Signed into law in May 2024 and effective June 30, 2026, it is the first comprehensive AI governance law enacted by a US state.

The Act applies to "developers" and "deployers" of "high-risk AI systems" – terminology borrowed directly from the EU AI Act. A high-risk AI system is defined as any AI system that makes or is a substantial factor in making a "consequential decision" – a decision that has a material legal or similarly significant effect on a consumer's access to or the cost, terms, or availability of education, employment, financial services, government services, healthcare, housing, insurance, or legal services.

If you are a deployer of a high-risk AI system under the Colorado Act, your obligations include: implementing a risk management policy and program; completing an impact assessment before deploying the system and annually thereafter; providing consumers with notice when a high-risk AI system is used to make a consequential decision about them; and providing a mechanism for consumers to correct incorrect data used in the decision and to appeal the decision.

The Colorado Act's significance extends beyond Colorado. It establishes a template that other US states are actively studying. Connecticut, Texas, and Illinois have introduced similar bills. For practitioners, the Colorado Act is a preview of the domestic AI governance landscape that is coming – and its clear lineage from international frameworks demonstrates why understanding those frameworks matters even if you think you are a purely domestic operation.

The Framework Comparison Matrix

[FIGURE B1-06] provides a side-by-side comparison of every framework covered in Chapters 2 and 3. The matrix covers seven dimensions for each framework:

- **Jurisdiction** – which countries or regions does the framework apply to?
- **Binding status** – mandatory or voluntary?
- **Approach** – risk-based, prescriptive, principles-based, or hybrid?
- **Enforcement mechanism** – fines, administrative penalties, sector regulators, or none?
- **SMB provisions** – does the framework include specific accommodations for smaller organizations?
- **Agentic AI coverage** – does the framework specifically address autonomous AI agents?
- **Current status** – enacted, proposed, or voluntary?

A few patterns jump out of the matrix.

First, nearly every framework is risk-based. The EU AI Act, the NIST AI RMF, the Brazilian AI Bill, and the Colorado AI Act all classify AI systems by risk level and scale obligations accordingly. This convergence is not coincidental. Risk-based regulation is the consensus approach because it avoids both the paralysis of regulating all AI equally and the negligence of regulating none of it.

Second, SMB provisions are inconsistent. The EU AI Act includes specific accommodations for SMBs – lighter documentation requirements, access to regulatory sandboxes, fee reductions for conformity assessment. The NIST AI RMF is inherently scalable. But most other frameworks make no specific provision for smaller organizations. If you are an SMB, you will need to interpret many of these frameworks through the lens of proportionality – applying the spirit of the requirements at a scale appropriate to your operations.

Third, agentic AI coverage is sparse. As of early 2026, only the Singapore MGF specifically addresses agentic AI. The EU AI Act, the NIST AI RMF, the Council of Europe Convention, and the Colorado AI Act were all developed before agentic AI became a primary governance concern. This gap is temporary – every major regulatory body is working on agentic AI guidance – but for the next 12 to 18 months, the Singapore MGF is your best resource for agentic-specific governance.

The Convergence Trend

If you have read this far, you may have noticed something: despite different starting points, different legal traditions, and different regulatory philosophies, every framework in this chapter converges on the same set of core principles.

Risk-based approach. Not all AI is created equal. Governance obligations should be proportional to the risk a system poses. A spam filter and a criminal sentencing algorithm should not face the same regulatory burden. Every major framework – from the EU AI Act to the Colorado AI Act to the Singapore MGF – starts from this premise.

Human oversight. AI systems should not make high-stakes decisions without meaningful human involvement. The specific mechanisms vary – the EU AI Act requires human oversight for high-risk systems, the Singapore MGF requires human accountability at every level of the value chain, the UK principles require contestability and redress – but the underlying principle is universal.

Transparency. People affected by AI systems should know they are being affected, understand how the system works at an appropriate level of abstraction, and be able to obtain explanations for decisions that significantly affect them. Every framework requires some form of transparency, though the specifics range from the EU AI Act's detailed disclosure requirements to the OECD Principles' high-level aspirations.

Accountability. Someone must be responsible. AI systems do not exist in an accountability vacuum. Whether it is the model developer, the system deployer, or the end user, every framework insists that human actors bear responsibility for AI outcomes. The Council of Europe Convention makes this a treaty-level obligation. The Singapore MGF assigns accountability across the entire value chain. The Colorado AI Act makes deployers directly liable for their high-risk systems.

Fairness and non-discrimination. AI systems must not produce discriminatory outcomes. This principle appears in every single framework covered in this book, from the OECD Principles to the EU AI Act to China's algorithmic regulations. The specific obligations vary – some require pre-deployment bias testing, some require ongoing monitoring, some require algorithmic impact assessments – but the underlying commitment to non-discrimination is universal.

This convergence has a practical implication for your governance program: you do not need to build a separate compliance program for each framework. If you build a governance program around these five principles – risk-based classification, human oversight, transparency, accountability, and fairness – you will have a foundation that satisfies the intent of every framework in this chapter. The specifics of each framework may require additional measures, but the core architecture is the same.

This is not a coincidence. It is the result of two decades of international dialogue on AI governance, from the OECD Principles in 2019 to the Bletchley Declaration in 2023 to the Vilnius signing of the Council of Europe Convention in 2024. Regulators and policymakers around the world have been talking to each other, reading each other's proposals, and converging on a shared understanding of what responsible AI governance requires. That convergence is your strategic advantage. It means the governance investment you make today will remain relevant as new frameworks emerge, because those new frameworks will be built on the same principles.

Action Item: International Exposure Assessment

Does your AI cross jurisdictional boundaries? Work through these five questions with your legal and compliance team:

1. **Do you have customers in the EU?** If yes, the EU AI Act applies to your AI systems that affect those customers, regardless of where your servers are located.
2. **Do you have customers in Singapore, Japan, or the UK?** If yes, those nations' AI governance frameworks set expectations for how AI is used in interactions with their residents.
3. **Do your AI vendors process data outside your home jurisdiction?** If yes, you have cross-border data governance obligations that interact with AI governance requirements.
4. **Is your AI accessible via the internet to users in other countries?** If yes, you may be subject to the AI governance frameworks of countries whose residents can access your system.
5. **Do you operate in a US state with AI-specific legislation (Colorado, Illinois, etc.)?** If yes, domestic AI legislation that draws from international frameworks applies to you directly.

If you answered yes to any of these questions, your governance program must account for international frameworks. Reference Appendix C (Framework Comparison Matrix) for a detailed crosswalk of which frameworks apply based on your jurisdictional exposure.

Key Takeaways

- **International AI governance is not optional, even for "domestic only" companies.** Your vendors, your cloud providers, your customers, and increasingly your state regulators operate across jurisdictions. Understanding the international landscape is understanding your own regulatory exposure.

- **The Council of Europe Framework Convention (CETS 225) is the first legally binding international AI treaty.** Its "comply or equivalent protection" model means every signatory nation – including the US – must ensure domestic frameworks cover private sector AI activities. Watch for ratification timelines and the domestic legislative activity that will follow.

- **The Singapore MGF for Agentic AI is the most practical framework for agentic AI governance available today.** At 27 pages, it is concise, actionable, and free. Its risk factor tables and value chain responsibility model fill a gap that none of the Big Three address. If you are deploying AI agents, this document should be on your desk.

- **Different frameworks, same principles.** Risk-based classification, human oversight, transparency, accountability, and fairness appear in every major framework worldwide. Build your governance program around these principles and you build a foundation that scales across jurisdictions and survives regulatory evolution.

- **Start with the International Exposure Assessment.** Five questions determine whether international frameworks apply to you. Most organizations will answer yes to at least one. Appendix C provides the crosswalk from jurisdictional exposure to specific framework requirements.

Part III: Risk and Program Design

"Risk comes from not knowing what you are doing."

— Warren Buffett

Chapter 4: Understanding and Classifying AI Risks

Every technology introduces risk. Servers crash. Software has bugs. Networks get breached. If you have spent any time in IT risk management, you have developed an intuition for how to think about these failures: identify the asset, identify the threat, estimate the likelihood and impact, and apply controls proportional to the risk.

AI breaks that intuition.

Not because AI risks are inherently more dangerous than traditional software risks — though some of them are — but because AI risks behave differently. They emerge from different sources, propagate through different mechanisms, and resist the detection methods you have built your career around. If you manage AI risk using only your existing IT risk frameworks, you will miss categories of failure that do not exist in traditional software, and you will over-invest in categories AI has fundamentally changed.

This chapter gives you the full picture. We start with what makes AI risk different. We walk through the NIST AI Risk Management Framework's trustworthiness characteristics — the most rigorous taxonomy of AI-specific qualities your systems need to exhibit. We cover the risks unique to generative AI and agentic AI, because those are the systems most of you are deploying right now. We translate the OWASP threat landscape into governance requirements. And we give you the methodology to classify your systems, assess your risks, and build the register that will drive every governance decision you make from here on.

By the end of this chapter, you will have a risk vocabulary, a classification methodology, and a practical template for inventorying and scoring every AI system in your organization.

[FIGURE B1-08] shows the EU AI Act risk tiers we will use for regulatory classification. [FIGURE B1-09] maps the NIST AI RMF trustworthiness characteristics. [FIGURE B1-10] illustrates the dimensional governance framework. Keep all three handy.

Why AI Risks Are Different

The NIST AI Risk Management Framework (AI RMF 1.0), in its Appendix B, identifies five characteristics that distinguish AI risk from traditional software risk. These are not abstract academic distinctions. They are the reasons your existing risk management processes will produce blind spots if applied to AI without modification.

Data dependency. Traditional software executes deterministic logic written by developers. If the code says "if balance < 0, then deny transaction," it will deny transactions with negative balances every time, in every environment, forever. AI systems learn their behavior from data. The same model architecture trained on different data will produce different outputs, different biases, and different failure modes. Your risk profile is not just a function of the software — it is a function of the data the software was trained on, the data it was fine-tuned on, and the data it encounters in production. Change the data, and you change the risk. Feed the system data that does not reflect your production environment, and the risk assessment you performed during development is meaningless.

The practical implication: you cannot assess AI risk once and file it away. Data drift — the gradual divergence between training data and real-world data — means your risk profile is changing continuously, whether or not you change anything about the system. Your risk management process must include ongoing monitoring, not just periodic reviews.

Opacity. Most enterprise AI systems, and certainly all large language models, are opaque. You cannot trace a specific output back to a specific line of code or a specific decision rule. When a traditional application denies a loan, you can pull up the credit scoring algorithm, walk through the decision tree, and explain exactly why. When an AI system denies a loan, you may be able to identify which features influenced the decision, but you often cannot provide a complete, human-interpretable explanation of why those features combined to produce that particular outcome.

This is not a temporary engineering limitation waiting for better tools. It is a fundamental characteristic of how neural networks process information. Explainability techniques like SHAP values and attention maps provide approximations, not explanations. For governance, that means you need accountability mechanisms that do not depend on being able to fully explain every decision. You need logging, auditing, outcome monitoring, and human review processes that catch problematic patterns even when you cannot explain the mechanism that produced them.

Emergent behavior. Traditional software does what it was programmed to do. AI systems can exhibit behaviors that were not explicitly programmed, not anticipated by their developers, and not present during testing. A language model trained to be helpful might learn to be deceptive if deception achieves the objective more efficiently. An autonomous agent given access to tools might use those tools in combinations that no one tested or intended.

Emergent behavior is not a bug. It is a feature of how AI systems generalize from training data. From a risk management perspective, it means your testing regime cannot enumerate all possible failure modes. You cannot write a test case for a behavior you did not anticipate. This shifts the emphasis from pre-deployment testing (necessary but insufficient) to post-deployment monitoring (essential and ongoing).

Sociotechnical nature. AI systems do not operate in a vacuum. They operate inside human organizations, human decision-making processes, and human social structures. The risk profile of an AI system depends not just on the technology but on how humans interact with it. Automation bias — the tendency of humans to defer to automated systems even when their own judgment disagrees — means a perfectly accurate AI system can still produce harmful outcomes if the humans using it fail to exercise independent judgment. Conversely, a mediocre AI system with robust human oversight can produce better outcomes than a superior AI system deployed without guardrails.

AI risk assessment must account for human factors: who uses the system, what training they have, what incentives they face, and what alternative information sources they can access. A risk assessment that evaluates only the technical system and ignores the humans around it is incomplete.

Evolving capabilities. Traditional software is static between updates. AI systems — particularly those that learn from user interactions or are updated through fine-tuning — can change their behavior over time. The system you risk-assessed in January may behave differently in June, not because someone pushed a code change, but because the model was updated, the training data was refreshed, or the system learned from six months of production interactions.

For governance, this means your risk classification is not permanent. A system classified as minimal risk today might warrant reclassification if the vendor updates the underlying model, adds new capabilities, or changes the training data. Your governance program needs a trigger-based review process: when the model changes, when the data changes, when the use case expands, you reassess.

These five characteristics — data dependency, opacity, emergent behavior, sociotechnical nature, and evolving capabilities — are the reasons this chapter exists. If AI risk behaved like traditional software risk, you could add a few AI-specific line items to your existing risk register and move on. It does not, and you cannot.

The Seven Trustworthiness Characteristics

The NIST AI RMF defines seven characteristics that a trustworthy AI system should exhibit [FIGURE B1-09]. These are not aspirational ideals. They are the dimensions along which your AI systems will succeed or fail, and they provide the vocabulary your risk assessments should use.

Two of these characteristics — Accountable and Transparent and Safe — serve as cross-cutting foundations. The remaining five address specific dimensions of trustworthiness.

Valid and Reliable

Validity means the system does what it claims to do. Reliability means it does so consistently across conditions, over time, and for different user populations. This is the foundation. If your AI system is not valid and reliable, nothing else matters — you are governing a broken system.

In practice, validity and reliability require ongoing measurement. For a language model used in customer support, validity means it provides correct answers. Reliability means it provides correct answers at 2 AM on a holiday weekend with the same consistency as at 10 AM on a Tuesday. For a classification model used in fraud detection, validity means it correctly identifies fraud. Reliability means its performance does not degrade when transaction patterns shift during a new product launch.

The governance implication: define performance metrics before deployment, measure them continuously, and establish thresholds that trigger review. "The model seems to work fine" is not a validity assessment.

Safe

Safe means the system does not endanger human life, health, property, or the environment. For most enterprise applications, safety is not the primary concern — you are not deploying AI to control nuclear reactors. But safety intersects with your operations more than you might think. An AI system that provides incorrect medical information to employees through a benefits chatbot is a safety issue. An AI agent that misconfigures cloud infrastructure can create safety implications if that infrastructure supports critical services.

Safety also encompasses the concept of fail-safe behavior: when the system encounters conditions outside its training distribution, does it fail gracefully (flagging uncertainty, deferring to humans) or fail silently (producing confident but wrong outputs)?

Secure and Resilient

AI systems inherit all the security risks of traditional software — injection attacks, unauthorized access, data breaches — and add new ones. Adversarial attacks can manipulate model inputs to produce targeted misclassifications. Data poisoning can corrupt training data to introduce backdoors. Model extraction attacks can steal proprietary models through repeated queries. Prompt injection can hijack language models to produce unauthorized outputs.

Resilience means the system maintains acceptable performance under adverse conditions: adversarial inputs, data corruption, infrastructure failures, and unexpected load. For governance, your security program must extend to cover AI-specific attack surfaces, and your business continuity planning must account for AI system failures.

Accountable and Transparent

Accountability means someone is responsible for the system's behavior — not in the abstract, but in a way that is documented, enforceable, and traceable. Transparency means the system's operations, capabilities, and limitations are communicated clearly to all stakeholders: users, affected persons, auditors, and regulators.

These two characteristics are cross-cutting because they apply to every other dimension. A valid and reliable system that nobody is accountable for will not remain valid and reliable. A safe system whose safety mechanisms are opaque cannot be audited.

For practitioners, accountability requires an ownership model: every AI system has a named owner, and that owner is responsible for the system's compliance with your governance policies. Transparency requires documentation — what the system does, what data it uses, what its known limitations are, and who to contact when something goes wrong.

Explainable and Interpretable

Explainability means the system can provide meaningful information about why it produced a particular output. Interpretability means the system's internal mechanisms can be understood by humans. In practice, these exist on a spectrum. A simple decision tree is fully interpretable. A large language model is neither explainable nor interpretable in any rigorous sense.

The governance response is not to ban opaque systems — that would eliminate most modern AI. It is to calibrate your oversight mechanisms to the system's explainability. Highly explainable systems can rely on output-level review. Opaque systems require input monitoring, output sampling, outcome tracking, and independent validation.

Privacy-Enhanced

Privacy in AI goes beyond data protection compliance, though it includes that. AI systems can memorize training data and regurgitate it in outputs. They can infer sensitive information from seemingly innocuous inputs. They can re-identify individuals from anonymized datasets. And generative AI creates a new category of privacy risk: employees submitting personal data, customer data, or proprietary information into AI tools that may retain, learn from, or expose that data.

Your privacy controls for AI must address data in training, data in inference (what users submit to the system), and data in outputs (what the system reveals).

Fair — with Harmful Bias Managed

Fairness means the system does not produce outcomes that systematically disadvantage particular groups. Harmful bias — bias that produces discriminatory outcomes — can enter AI systems through biased training data, biased feature selection, biased labeling, or biased deployment contexts. Bias is not always obvious. A hiring model that excludes gender as a feature can still discriminate on gender if it uses proxy variables like university attended or years of continuous employment.

Managing bias requires proactive testing across demographic groups, ongoing outcome monitoring, and a clear process for investigating and remediating disparities when they are detected.

Generative AI-Specific Risks

The seven trustworthiness characteristics apply to all AI systems. But generative AI — the large language models, image generators, and multimodal systems most of you are deploying — introduces risks that are qualitatively different from traditional machine learning. NIST AI 600-1, the companion profile for generative AI, identifies twelve risk categories. We will cover all twelve, with deeper treatment of the five most relevant to practitioners.

Confabulation (Hallucination)

This is the risk that keeps practitioners up at night, and for good reason. Generative AI systems produce outputs that are fluent, confident, and wrong. They cite sources that do not exist. They fabricate statistics. They invent company policies. They generate plausible legal citations for cases that were never decided.

The term "hallucination" is common but misleading — it implies the system is perceiving something that is not there. What is actually happening is simpler and more dangerous: the system is generating the most probable next sequence of tokens given its training data and the input prompt. If the most probable sequence happens to be false, the system generates it with the same confidence as a true statement.

For governance, confabulation risk demands three controls: (1) output verification for any AI-generated content that will be relied upon for decisions, (2) user training so people who interact with AI systems understand that confident does not mean correct, and (3) use-case restrictions that prevent AI from being the sole source of truth in high-stakes contexts. If your employees are using AI to draft customer communications, someone must review those communications before they go out. If your AI is generating financial analysis, someone must verify the numbers. "The AI said so" is not a citation.

Data Privacy

Every interaction with a generative AI system is a potential data leak. When an employee pastes a customer complaint into ChatGPT to draft a response, that customer's personal data has left your organization. When a developer submits proprietary code to an AI coding assistant, that code may be stored, logged, or used for model training depending on the vendor's data processing agreement.

NIST AI 600-1 identifies several dimensions of this risk: unauthorized disclosure of training data through model outputs (memorization), collection and processing of personal data without adequate consent, and inferential privacy violations where the model deduces sensitive information from non-sensitive inputs.

The governance response is a data classification policy specific to AI tools. What data can be submitted to which tools under which conditions? Chapter 7 provides the template. At minimum, you need three tiers: data that can be freely submitted to any AI tool (public information), data that can be submitted only to approved enterprise AI tools with appropriate data processing agreements (internal business information), and data that must never be submitted to any external AI tool (personal data, regulated data, trade secrets, source code).

Harmful Bias and Homogenization

Generative AI can amplify existing biases at scale. A biased hiring recommendation from a human recruiter affects one candidate. A biased AI screening tool affects every candidate. But generative AI introduces an additional risk that NIST calls homogenization: when many organizations use the same AI systems, trained on the same data, the outputs converge. Diversity of perspective, approach, and analysis decreases. If every company in your industry uses the same AI to generate market analysis, you all get the same analysis. If every company uses the same AI to screen resumes, you all select for the same candidate profiles.

Homogenization is not a compliance risk in the traditional sense, but it is a strategic risk. Governance programs should encourage diversity in AI tooling and maintain human judgment as a counterweight to AI-generated consensus.

Information Security

Generative AI systems are vulnerable to prompt injection (manipulating the system through crafted inputs), jailbreaking (bypassing safety constraints), data extraction (tricking the model into revealing training data or system prompts), and supply chain attacks (compromised models, plugins, or training data). These are not theoretical risks. Prompt injection attacks against production systems are documented and increasing.

Your information security program must extend to cover these AI-specific attack vectors. This means security testing of AI systems (red teaming), monitoring of AI system inputs and outputs for anomalous patterns, and vendor security assessments that specifically address AI-related risks.

Value Chain and Component Integration

Modern AI deployments are not monolithic. You are using a model from one vendor, hosted on infrastructure from another vendor, accessed through an API managed by a third vendor, with plugins and integrations from several more. Each link in this chain introduces risk: the model vendor may update the model without notice, the hosting provider may have access to your data, the API provider may change their terms of service, and a compromised plugin can expose your entire system.

NIST AI 600-1 highlights value chain risk as particularly acute for generative AI because the supply chains are long, opaque, and rapidly changing. Your governance program must include vendor management processes that specifically address AI supply chain risks: model update notification requirements, data processing agreements that cover AI-specific data flows, and contingency plans for vendor changes.

The Remaining Seven Categories — Brief Treatment

The other seven NIST AI 600-1 risk categories deserve acknowledgment even if they are less frequently encountered by the average enterprise practitioner:

- **CBRN Information.** The risk that generative AI provides actionable information about chemical, biological, radiological, or nuclear weapons. Primarily a concern for AI providers, not deployers, but relevant if you operate in defense, research, or dual-use sectors.
- **Confabulation (Dangerous or Violent Content).** AI generates content that could facilitate harm — instructions for dangerous activities, violent scenarios, or weapons manufacturing. Again, primarily a provider-side concern with content filtering, but relevant if your AI tools are accessible to the public.
- **Environmental Impacts.** Training and running large AI models consumes significant energy and water. If your organization has ESG commitments, the environmental footprint of your AI usage is a reportable risk.
- **Human-AI Configuration.** The risk that humans over-rely on AI outputs (automation bias) or under-rely on them (automation distrust), leading to suboptimal decisions in either case. This is a training and process design issue, not a technology issue.
- **Information Integrity.** AI-generated misinformation, deepfakes, and synthetic media that undermine trust in information. Relevant if your organization produces public-facing content or operates in media, communications, or public affairs.
- **Intellectual Property.** AI systems trained on copyrighted material may reproduce that material in outputs, creating infringement risk for the deployer. Also relevant for organizations that want to protect their own IP from being used to train AI systems.
- **Obscene, Degrading, or Abusive Content.** AI generates offensive content. Primarily a concern for consumer-facing applications with minimal content filtering.

Agentic AI Risks

If generative AI risks keep you up at night, agentic AI risks should have you reconsidering sleep entirely.

An AI agent is not just generating text. It is taking actions: calling APIs, executing code, modifying databases, sending emails, making purchases, and interacting with other systems and other agents. The Singapore Model AI Governance Framework for Agentic AI (January 2026) identifies five primary risk categories that go beyond what we covered for generative AI alone.

Erroneous Actions

The agent makes mistakes. It misinterprets an instruction, takes a wrong step in a multi-step process, or produces an output that is technically responsive to the prompt but substantively wrong. This is the agentic version of confabulation, except instead of generating wrong text, the agent takes wrong actions. And actions have consequences that text does not — a wrong paragraph can be deleted, but a wrong database query may have already corrupted your data.

The governance response is constraining the agent's action space: what systems can it access, what operations can it perform, and what damage can it inflict in a worst-case scenario? If the worst-case scenario is unacceptable, the agent needs tighter constraints.

Unauthorized Actions

The agent does something it was not asked to do and does not have permission to do. This can happen through prompt injection (an external attacker manipulates the agent through crafted inputs), goal drift (the agent's planning process leads it to take steps that were not part of the original instruction), or confused deputy attacks (the agent uses its legitimate permissions to perform actions that serve an attacker's objectives rather than the user's).

The governance response is the principle of least privilege, applied rigorously: the agent gets the minimum permissions necessary for its task, and nothing more. Broad permissions granted "for convenience" are an invitation for unauthorized action.

Biased Actions

The same bias risks that apply to generative AI outputs apply to agentic AI actions, but with higher stakes. A biased text output can be reviewed and corrected before it reaches a customer. A biased action — an agent that routes support tickets differently based on the customer's name, or an agent that applies different approval criteria based on demographic proxies — may execute before anyone has a chance to review it.

Data Breaches

Agents need access to data to perform their tasks. That access creates exfiltration risk. An agent with access to your CRM, your email system, and an external API can — through error or manipulation — transmit customer data to an unauthorized destination. The more capable the agent, the more systems it can access, and the larger the blast radius of a data breach.

Disruption to Connected Systems

Agentic AI does not operate in isolation. It connects to other systems, other APIs, and potentially other agents. A failure in one agent can cascade to connected systems. An agent that sends malformed requests to an API can cause that API to fail. An agent that triggers a runaway loop can consume resources and degrade performance for other systems. In multi-agent architectures, an error in one agent's output becomes an error in another agent's input, and the cascade can propagate faster than human operators can intervene.

Sources of Risk by Component

The Singapore framework helpfully identifies where agentic risks originate:

- **Planning and reasoning** — the agent's ability to break down tasks, sequence steps, and make decisions. Risks here include faulty reasoning, goal misalignment, and inability to recognize when a plan is going wrong.
- **Tools and integrations** — the external systems the agent can access. Risks include tool misuse, unintended side effects, and the agent combining tools in unanticipated ways.

- **Protocols and interfaces** — the communication channels between the agent and other systems. Risks include injection attacks through these channels, inadequate authentication, and insufficient input validation.
- **System-level interactions** — the emergent behavior that arises when agents interact with complex environments or with each other. These risks cannot be predicted from analyzing individual components; they emerge from the interactions between components.

For governance purposes, the key insight is that agentic AI risk management requires controls at every layer: the model level, the tool level, the protocol level, and the system level. A governance program that only addresses the model — "we use GPT-4, and OpenAI handles safety" — misses three out of four layers where risk originates.

The OWASP Threat Landscape: A Governance Lens

OWASP has published two threat taxonomies relevant to AI governance: the Top 10 for Large Language Model Applications (2025 edition) and the Top 10 for Agentic Applications (2026 edition). These are primarily security-oriented documents — they tell you what can go wrong and how attackers exploit AI systems. A deep technical treatment belongs in Book 2 of this series (AI Governance and Security Playbook). Here, we focus on a governance question: what policies and controls does each risk category demand?

The LLM Top 10 includes prompt injection, insecure output handling, training data poisoning, model denial of service, supply chain vulnerabilities, sensitive information disclosure, insecure plugin design, excessive agency, overreliance, and model theft. The Agentic Top 10 adds risks specific to autonomous systems: agentic identity spoofing, tool misuse, privilege escalation through multi-agent chains, inadequate guardrails, and cascading failures across agent networks.

Rather than walk through all twenty individually, here is the governance translation: what policy does each cluster of risks require?

Data governance policies. Prompt injection, training data poisoning, and sensitive information disclosure all demand policies governing what data enters and exits AI systems. Your data classification policy (Chapter 7) must specifically address AI data flows. Your vendor agreements must specify data handling, retention, and training data usage.

Access control policies. Excessive agency, privilege escalation, and tool misuse demand policies governing what AI systems can access and what operations they can perform. The principle of least privilege is not new, but applying it to AI agents requires rethinking how you provision access — agents should not inherit their human operator's full permission set.

Output validation policies. Insecure output handling and overreliance demand policies governing how AI outputs are used in decision-making. Who reviews AI-generated content before it is published? Who validates AI recommendations before they are implemented? What decisions can AI make autonomously, and which require human approval?

Supply chain policies. Supply chain vulnerabilities and model theft demand policies governing your AI vendor relationships. How do you evaluate AI vendors? What security requirements do you impose? How do you handle model updates? What is your contingency plan if a vendor is compromised?

Incident response policies. Every risk category demands an incident response capability. When an AI system produces a harmful output, who is notified? What is the escalation path? Can the system be shut down quickly? Is there a rollback procedure? Your existing incident response plan needs an AI-specific annex.

The OWASP taxonomies are living documents — they are updated as the threat landscape evolves. Bookmark them, review them annually, and use them as a checklist when evaluating new AI deployments. But remember: OWASP tells you what can go wrong. Your governance program tells you what to do about it.

Risk Classification Methodology

Understanding AI risks is necessary. Classifying them is what makes governance actionable. You cannot apply the same controls to every AI system — you will either over-govern your spam filter or under-govern your hiring tool. Classification gives you proportionality: high-risk systems get heavy governance, minimal-risk systems get light governance, and you allocate your limited resources where they matter most.

EU AI Act Risk Tiers

We covered the EU AI Act risk tiers in detail in Chapter 2. Here we focus on practical application [FIGURE B1-08].

Prohibited (Article 5). Social scoring, manipulative AI, untargeted facial image scraping, emotion recognition in workplaces and schools, biometric categorization for sensitive attributes, and certain forms of predictive policing. If any of your systems fall here, they must be decommissioned. This is not a classification decision — it is a compliance requirement already in force since February 2025.

High-risk — Annex III. These are AI systems in sensitive domains: biometrics, critical infrastructure, education, employment, essential services, law enforcement, migration, and administration of justice. If your AI system makes or materially influences decisions about people in these domains, it is high-risk regardless of how simple the technology is.

> **Real-World Example: The Hiring Tool That Was Actually High-Risk**
>
> A mid-market company with 400 employees uses an AI tool to screen resumes for open positions. The tool ingests resumes, scores candidates on fit, and surfaces the top 20 for human review. The company classified the system as minimal risk because, in their words, "it just ranks candidates — a human makes the actual hiring decision."
>
> That classification is wrong.
>
> EU AI Act Annex III, Section 4, explicitly classifies AI systems used in "employment, workers management and access to self-employment" as high-risk. This includes systems used for "placing targeted job advertisements," "screening or filtering applications," and "evaluating candidates in the course of interviews or tests." A resume screening tool falls squarely within this definition.
>
> As a high-risk system, the tool now requires: a documented risk management system (Article 9), data governance and management practices for training data (Article 10), detailed technical

documentation (Article 11), automatic event logging (Article 12), transparency to deployers (Article 13), human oversight mechanisms (Article 14), accuracy, robustness, and cybersecurity measures (Article 15), conformity assessment (Article 43), and registration in the EU database (Article 49).

The "it just ranks candidates" defense does not work. The AI Act classifies based on the domain and function, not on the company's subjective assessment of how much influence the system has. If the system filters candidates before a human sees them, it is making decisions about who gets a chance and who does not. That is high-risk.

The lesson: classification is not a negotiation. It is a legal determination based on objective criteria. When in doubt, classify up.

High-risk — Annex I. AI systems embedded in products already covered by EU harmonized legislation (medical devices, machinery, vehicles, etc.). If your AI is a safety component of a regulated product, it is automatically high-risk. Enforcement for Annex I systems begins August 2027.

Limited risk (Article 50). Systems with transparency obligations only: chatbots must disclose their AI nature, deepfakes must be labeled, and AI-generated text published to inform the public must be identified as AI-generated. If you operate a customer-facing chatbot, this is your tier.

Minimal risk. Everything else. No regulatory obligations under the AI Act. Spam filters, AI-enhanced search, content recommendations (where not otherwise regulated), inventory optimization tools, code completion assistants (used internally, not in a regulated domain). You are encouraged to adopt voluntary codes of conduct but face no compliance mandates.

NIST AI RMF Risk Framing

The EU AI Act gives you a regulatory classification. The NIST AI RMF gives you an organizational risk assessment methodology. You need both.

NIST's GOVERN function establishes risk framing — the organizational context for all risk decisions. This includes three elements:

Impact and likelihood. Traditional risk assessment: for each AI risk, estimate the severity of the potential impact and the probability of occurrence. NIST encourages you to consider impact across multiple dimensions: harm to individuals (physical, psychological, financial, reputational), harm to organizations (financial loss, legal liability, operational disruption), and harm to ecosystems (market distortion, erosion of public trust, environmental damage).

Risk tolerance. How much risk is your organization willing to accept? This is not a one-size-fits-all answer. A healthcare organization deploying AI for diagnostic assistance has a very different risk tolerance than a marketing agency using AI to generate social media copy. Your risk tolerance should be explicitly stated, documented, and approved by leadership. "We are generally risk-averse" is not a risk tolerance statement. "We will not deploy AI systems that make autonomous decisions affecting patient care without real-time physician oversight" is.

Risk prioritization. You will identify more risks than you can address simultaneously. Prioritization requires balancing impact, likelihood, risk tolerance, and resource availability. NIST recommends considering both the risks of deploying an AI system and the risks of not deploying it. Sometimes the risk of leaving a process manual (slow, error-prone, inconsistent) exceeds the risk of automating it with AI.

Conducting an AI System Inventory

Before you can classify risk, you need to know what AI systems you have. This sounds obvious. It is not. In most organizations, AI has proliferated without centralized tracking. Departments have signed up for AI tools independently. Employees are using personal AI accounts for work tasks. Vendors have embedded AI into products you already use without prominently disclosing it.

Your AI system inventory should capture, at minimum:

Field	What to Capture
System name	The product or tool name
Vendor	Who provides it
Model type	LLM, classification, recommendation, agent, etc.
Data inputs	What data does it access? Customer data? Employee data? Financial data?

Field	What to Capture
Data outputs	What does it produce? Recommendations? Decisions? Content?
Users	Who uses it? Which departments? How many users?
EU AI Act risk tier	Prohibited, high-risk (III), high-risk (I), limited, minimal
NIST trustworthiness score	Your assessment across the seven characteristics
Owner	The named individual responsible for governance compliance
Last review date	When was this system last assessed?

Action Item: AI System Inventory and Risk Register

Do not wait until you have finished this book. Start your AI system inventory this week. Use the AI Risk Assessment Template in Appendix A to capture each system.

For every AI system in your organization, record: the system name, vendor, model type, data inputs (what data does it access?), data outputs (what does it produce?), users (who uses it and in which departments?), EU AI Act risk tier, NIST trustworthiness score across all seven characteristics, the named owner responsible for governance compliance, and the date of the last review.

You will not get a complete inventory on the first pass. That is fine. Start with the systems you know about, then send a survey to department heads asking: "What AI tools are your teams using?" You will be surprised by the answers. Shadow AI — tools adopted without IT or leadership awareness — is the norm, not the exception.

Once you have the inventory, classify each system using the methodology in this chapter. Systems classified as high-risk under the EU AI Act or scoring poorly on NIST trustworthiness characteristics get immediate attention. Systems classified as minimal risk get documented and scheduled for periodic review.

The inventory process itself is a governance win. In many organizations, the act of asking "what AI are we using?" surfaces tools and practices that leadership had no idea existed. That awareness is the first step toward control.

Combining Regulatory Classification with Organizational Risk Tolerance

The EU AI Act tells you the minimum governance your system requires. Your organizational risk tolerance tells you whether the minimum is enough.

Consider a customer-facing chatbot. Under the EU AI Act, it is a limited-risk system — transparency obligations only. Technically, you need to disclose that the user is talking to AI, and you are compliant.

But your organizational risk tolerance might demand more. If the chatbot handles sensitive customer inquiries, provides information that customers rely on for financial decisions, or operates in a heavily regulated industry, the regulatory floor may be far below what your risk appetite requires. You might impose additional controls — output monitoring, human escalation triggers, regular accuracy audits — even though the regulation does not require them.

The methodology is: start with the regulatory classification as your floor. Then assess organizational risk across the NIST trustworthiness characteristics. If your organizational risk assessment demands controls beyond the regulatory minimum, implement them. You will never face a penalty for over-governing an AI system. You may face catastrophic consequences for under-governing one.

Dimensional Governance

Risk classification gives you a snapshot: at this moment, for this system, in this configuration, here is the risk level. But AI systems are not static. They evolve. More accurately, the relationship between humans and AI systems evolves — and that evolution changes the risk profile in ways that static classification frameworks do not capture.

Engin and Hand (2025) propose a dimensional governance framework that addresses this gap. Instead of asking "what risk category does this system fall into?" they ask: "how is the human-AI relationship configured, and how does that configuration change over time?" [FIGURE B1-10]

The Three Dimensions of AI Governance

Decision Authority. Who decides? On one end of the spectrum, the human decides and the AI provides information. On the other end, the AI decides autonomously. In between, there is a gradient: the AI recommends and the human approves, the AI decides with human veto rights, the AI decides and the human reviews after the fact.

Your governance requirements change at every point on this spectrum. An AI system that provides information to a human decision-maker needs accuracy controls and transparency. An AI system that makes autonomous decisions needs all of that plus accountability mechanisms, fallback procedures, and outcome monitoring.

Process Autonomy. How independently does the AI operate? A system that executes a single, well-defined function (classify this image, translate this text) operates with limited process autonomy. An agentic system that breaks down complex tasks, selects tools, makes multi-step plans, and adapts its approach based on intermediate results operates with high process autonomy.

High process autonomy means more opportunities for the system to deviate from intended behavior. Your monitoring and control mechanisms must scale with the system's autonomy. A single-function system can be validated through input-output testing. A multi-step agent requires process monitoring — checking not just the final output but the intermediate steps.

Accountability Configuration. Who is responsible when something goes wrong? In a simple deployment, the answer is straightforward: the deployer. In a complex multi-vendor, multi-agent deployment, accountability fragments. The model provider is responsible for the model's safety properties. The platform vendor is responsible for the hosting infrastructure. The deployer is responsible for the use case and the data. The user is responsible for their inputs and their reliance on the outputs.

Effective governance requires mapping this accountability chain explicitly. For every AI system, you should be able to answer: if this system produces a harmful output, who is responsible? If the answer is "it depends" or "we are not sure," your accountability configuration is inadequate.

Four Critical Trust Thresholds

Engin and Hand identify four thresholds where the human-AI relationship undergoes a qualitative shift. These are the points where your governance must adapt or break.

Verification-to-Delegation Threshold. At low volumes and low complexity, humans can verify every AI output. A paralegal using AI to draft a contract can review the entire draft. But as volume or complexity increases, verification becomes impractical. A system processing 10,000 customer service inquiries per day cannot have every response reviewed by a human. At this threshold, you shift from verifying individual outputs to monitoring aggregate performance: accuracy rates, customer satisfaction scores, escalation rates, error patterns. Your governance must make this shift explicit — when did we stop verifying everything, and what monitoring replaced it?

Process-to-Outcome Threshold. At low autonomy, you can govern the process: the AI follows these steps, uses these tools, operates within these constraints. As autonomy increases, the process becomes too complex and adaptive to govern directly. You shift to governing outcomes: we do not care how the AI achieves the result, as long as the result meets these criteria. This is a significant governance shift because it requires clear, measurable outcome definitions and robust outcome monitoring.

Information-to-Authority Threshold. This is the most consequential. It marks the point where the AI transitions from providing information to making decisions. Before this threshold, the human sees the AI's output, exercises judgment, and decides. After this threshold, the AI's output is the decision. Many organizations cross this threshold without realizing it — formally, a human is "in the loop," but in practice, the human rubber-stamps every AI recommendation without independent evaluation. If your human oversight process approves 99.9% of AI recommendations without modification, you have crossed this threshold whether or not your governance framework acknowledges it.

Individual-to-Collective Threshold. This applies to multi-agent systems. When individual agents interact, their collective behavior can differ from any individual agent's behavior. Emergent multi-agent behavior — cooperation, competition, resource contention, cascading failures — cannot be predicted from analyzing individual agents. If your organization deploys multiple AI agents that interact with each other or share resources, you need system-level governance that addresses collective behavior, not just individual agent governance.

Why This Matters for Your Governance Program

The dimensional framework matters because it tells you something that static risk classification cannot: your governance requirements are not fixed. As your AI systems gain capabilities, as you increase their autonomy, as you expand their decision authority, your governance must evolve with them.

A system you classified as minimal risk when it was a simple recommendation engine may warrant reclassification when the vendor adds agentic capabilities. A system that had adequate human oversight when it processed 100 decisions per day may have crossed the verification-to-delegation threshold when volume grew to 10,000 per day.

Build review triggers into your governance program: when the system's capabilities change, when its autonomy level changes, when its decision authority changes, when its volume changes — reassess. Risk classification is not a one-time exercise. It is a continuous process.

SMB Spotlight: The Top 5 AI Risks That Actually Affect SMBs

If you are running a small or mid-size business, the twelve NIST AI 600-1 risk categories and the OWASP Top 10 can feel overwhelming. You are not deploying autonomous weapons systems or operating critical infrastructure. You are using AI for content generation, customer support, data analysis, and code assistance. Here are the five risks that actually keep your lights on — or turn them off:

1. Data privacy. Your employees are submitting customer data, financial data, and proprietary business information to AI tools. Some of those tools are approved. Many are not. Every submission is a potential data breach.

2. Confabulation. Your AI is confidently stating wrong information. It is generating incorrect product specifications, fabricating company policies, and citing regulations that do not exist. If that information reaches a customer or a regulator, you own the consequences.

3. Shadow AI. Your employees are using AI tools you do not know about, have not approved, and cannot monitor. They are making data classification decisions every time they paste something into a chat window. Without a policy, every employee is their own risk manager — and most of them are not qualified for that role.

4. Vendor lock-in. You have built processes, workflows, and integrations around a single AI provider. If that provider raises prices, changes terms, degrades quality, or goes out of business, your operational dependency becomes an operational crisis.

5. Liability. When your AI makes a mistake — and it will — who is responsible? If your AI chatbot gives a customer wrong information and the customer relies on it to their detriment, you are liable. The Air Canada ruling (Chapter 1) established this clearly. Your AI's outputs are your outputs.

Action: inventory your AI systems this week using the template in Appendix A. Start with the tools your team uses daily, then ask department heads what their teams are using. You will discover tools you did not know about. That discovery is the first step toward control.

Building a Risk Register

The inventory tells you what AI systems you have. The classification tells you how risky they are. The risk register tells you what you are going to do about it.

A risk register is not a spreadsheet you create and forget. It is a living document that tracks identified risks, their severity, their current status, and the controls you have implemented or plan to implement. For AI governance, your risk register should include:

For each AI system: - System identifier (from your inventory) - EU AI Act classification - Organizational risk score (your own assessment beyond regulatory classification)

For each identified risk: - Risk description (what could go wrong) - Risk category (mapping to NIST AI 600-1 categories where applicable) - Impact assessment (severity if the risk materializes) - Likelihood assessment (probability of occurrence) - Current controls (what mitigation is already in place) - Residual risk (remaining risk after current controls) - Planned controls (additional mitigation you intend to implement) - Owner (who is responsible for this risk) - Review date (when this risk will be reassessed)

Populate the register systematically. For each AI system, walk through the NIST trustworthiness characteristics and the relevant NIST AI 600-1 risk categories. For each applicable risk, assess impact and likelihood, document current controls, and identify gaps.

Third-Party AI Risk

A risk register that only covers your internally developed AI systems is incomplete. Most organizations consume far more AI than they build. Your AI risk exposure includes every vendor, every SaaS platform, and every API that uses AI in its product — whether or not the vendor prominently discloses that fact.

Third-party AI risk management requires extending your vendor risk management process to cover AI-specific concerns:

What model does the vendor use? Many SaaS vendors have embedded AI features powered by third-party models. Your vendor's AI feature may be powered by OpenAI, Anthropic, Google, or an open-source model. Each has different data handling, safety, and reliability characteristics. Ask.

What happens to your data? When your data flows through a vendor's AI feature, is it used for model training? Is it retained after processing? Is it accessible to the vendor's employees? Data processing agreements must specifically address AI data flows, not just traditional data storage and processing.

How does the vendor handle model updates? If the vendor updates the underlying model, does your risk classification change? Does the vendor notify you? Can you opt out of model updates? A model update that changes the system's behavior changes your risk profile, and you should be able to reassess before the update takes effect.

What happens if the AI feature fails? Does the vendor's product degrade gracefully? Is there a non-AI fallback? Or does an AI failure take down the entire product? Your business continuity planning must account for AI-specific failure modes in your vendor stack.

Can you audit? For high-risk systems, you may need the ability to audit the vendor's AI practices. Does the vendor provide transparency reports, model cards, or third-party audit results? Will they support your compliance requirements with documentation?

Third-party AI risk is not an edge case. For most organizations, it is the majority case. Treat it accordingly.

Key Takeaways

- **AI risk is fundamentally different from traditional software risk.** Data dependency, opacity, emergent behavior, sociotechnical complexity, and evolving capabilities mean your existing risk frameworks need AI-specific extensions. Do not assume your current risk management processes are sufficient without modification.
- **Classification is not optional — it is the foundation of proportional governance.** Use the EU AI Act risk tiers as your regulatory floor and the NIST trustworthiness characteristics as your organizational assessment framework. Combine both to determine the governance each system requires. When in doubt, classify up.
- **Generative and agentic AI introduce risk categories that did not exist five years ago.** Confabulation, data privacy in AI interactions, prompt injection, cascading agent failures, and value chain complexity demand new policies, new controls, and new monitoring capabilities. Your governance program must specifically address these risks, not just reference them.
- **Risk classification is not a one-time exercise.** The dimensional governance framework (Engin and Hand 2025) shows that your governance requirements evolve as AI capabilities, autonomy, and decision authority increase. Build review triggers into your program so that reclassification happens when the system changes, not on an arbitrary annual schedule.
- **Start with your inventory.** You cannot govern what you cannot see. Inventory your AI systems this week — both the ones you know about and

the ones you do not. Use the AI Risk Assessment Template in Appendix A. The inventory is the foundation for classification, the classification is the foundation for your risk register, and the risk register is the foundation for every governance decision you make from this point forward.

Chapter 5: Governance Program Design — Starting From Zero

If you have read the first four chapters of this book, you now know more about AI governance frameworks than 95% of your peers. You understand the regulatory landscape. You can name the Big Three. You know the difference between NIST's trustworthiness characteristics and the EU AI Act's risk tiers. You have a risk classification methodology and the beginnings of a risk register.

And none of that matters if you do not do something with it.

This is the chapter where we stop talking about what governance is and start building one. Not a theoretical governance program that checks every box in ISO 42001. Not a PowerPoint governance program that looks impressive in a board presentation and does nothing in practice. A real, functioning governance program that you can stand up in 90 days with the resources you already have.

Here is the uncomfortable truth that most governance guides will not tell you: the biggest risk is not building the wrong program. The biggest risk is building no program at all while you wait for the perfect one. Every week you spend debating committee structures and charter language is a week your employees are using AI tools with no guardrails, your vendors are processing your data with no oversight, and your organization is accumulating governance debt that compounds with interest.

You do not need perfection. You need a starting point.

This chapter gives you that starting point. We walk through governance maturity levels so you can honestly assess where you are today. We lay out a 90-day sprint to get you from zero to functional. We cover organizational structures for every size of company — from the 30-person firm where the IT director is also the CISO, the DPO, and the person who fixes the printer, to the 5,000-person enterprise with budget for a dedicated governance team. We talk about what this actually costs, because "invest in governance" is meaningless advice without numbers. We cover AI literacy — the one governance obligation that is already legally mandatory. And we show you how to bolt AI governance onto whatever GRC infrastructure you already have.

Let us get started.

Governance Maturity: Where Are You Today?

Before you can design a governance program, you need an honest assessment of where you stand. Not where you told the board you stand. Not where your compliance team thinks you stand. Where you actually stand.

[FIGURE B1-11] shows the four governance maturity levels. Most organizations reading this book are at Level 1. That is not a criticism. It is a starting point.

Level 1: Ad Hoc. No formal AI governance process exists. Individual employees and teams make their own decisions about AI tool selection, data handling, and acceptable use. There may be informal norms — "we don't put customer data into ChatGPT" — but those norms are not documented, not enforced, and not consistently understood across the organization. If someone asked "who is responsible for AI governance at your company?" the honest answer is "nobody." This is where 65-75% of organizations are today, based on the survey data we reviewed in Chapter 1.

Level 2: Defined. Policies exist and are documented. You have an acceptable use policy for AI. You have an inventory of the AI systems in use across the organization. You have designated someone — a person with a name, not a vague organizational function — as responsible for AI governance. You have a risk classification for your AI systems, even if it is basic. You have a recurring meeting where governance is reviewed. The key distinction between Ad Hoc and Defined is not sophistication — it is documentation. Defined means someone wrote it down, someone is accountable, and there is a cadence.

Level 3: Managed. Governance is not just documented but actively monitored and enforced. You have metrics: how many AI systems are in your inventory, what percentage have completed risk assessments, how many incidents have been reported, how many policy exceptions have been granted. You conduct periodic audits. Your vendor review process has teeth — you have actually rejected or restricted AI tools that did not meet your standards. You track governance KPIs and report them to leadership. The difference between Defined and Managed is the difference between having a fire evacuation plan posted on the wall and actually running fire drills.

Level 4: Optimized. Governance processes are continuously improved based on data, incidents, regulatory changes, and organizational learning. You conduct post-incident reviews that feed back into policy updates. You benchmark against industry peers and external standards. You participate in industry working groups and contribute to the development of governance standards. Your governance program is not a static compliance artifact — it is a living system that evolves. Very few organizations are here today, and that is fine. This is not your 2026 goal. This is your 2028 goal.

The goal of this chapter is to get you from Level 1 to Level 2 in 90 days. That is the single highest-leverage transition you can make. Moving from "we have nothing" to "we have something documented, someone accountable, and a regular cadence" eliminates the vast majority of the governance-adoption gap risk we discussed in Chapter 1. It does not eliminate all risk — no governance program does. But it moves you from "we are flying blind" to "we have instruments," and that is a fundamentally different risk posture.

Do not try to jump to Level 3 in your first quarter. You will overengineer the program, exhaust your stakeholders, and end up with a beautifully documented governance framework that nobody follows because it was designed for an organization three maturity levels ahead of where you actually are.

The Minimum Viable Governance Program: A 90-Day Sprint

Here is your 90-day plan. Six phases, two weeks each. At the end, you will have a functioning governance program that covers the essentials: you will know what AI you are using, how risky it is, what the rules are, who is in charge, how you evaluate new tools, and when you review the whole thing. That is enough. That is more than 75% of your competitors have.

[FIGURE B1-12] shows the 90-day sprint timeline with deliverables for each phase.

Weeks 1-2: AI Inventory

You cannot govern what you cannot see. The first and most important step is finding out what AI systems your organization is actually using. Not what AI systems IT approved. Not what AI systems appear in your vendor management database. What AI systems are actually in use, right now, by actual humans in your organization.

This will surprise you. I promise it will surprise you. Every organization that conducts its first AI inventory discovers systems they did not know about. The marketing team signed up for an AI content generator using a corporate credit card. The engineering team is using an AI coding assistant through a freemium tier that does not require procurement approval. An intern connected an AI tool to a customer database "just for a quick analysis." The sales team is using AI to auto-generate email sequences. The HR department is using an AI tool to screen resumes.

Your inventory template should capture the following fields for each AI system:

- **System name** — the product or tool name (e.g., "ChatGPT Enterprise," "Jasper AI," "GitHub Copilot")
- **Vendor** — who provides it
- **Model type** — what kind of AI it is (generative LLM, classification model, recommendation engine, AI agent, etc.)
- **Data inputs** — what data goes into the system (customer data, employee data, financial data, proprietary code, public data only)
- **Data outputs** — what comes out and where it goes (internal documents, customer-facing content, automated decisions, recommendations)
- **Users** — who uses it and approximately how many
- **Risk tier** — we will fill this in during Weeks 3-4
- **Owner** — we will assign this in Weeks 7-8
- **Contract status** — is there a formal agreement, a terms-of-service click-through, a free trial, or no documented relationship at all

How do you actually find these systems? Four methods, in order of reliability:

First, check your financial records. Pull credit card statements, expense reports, and procurement records for the past 12 months. Search for any vendor name associated with AI — OpenAI, Anthropic, Google (Gemini), Microsoft (Copilot), Midjourney, Jasper, Copy.ai, Grammarly, and any other name your finance team can identify. This catches anything that costs money.

Second, check your SSO and identity provider logs. If you use Okta, Azure AD, Google Workspace, or a similar identity provider, pull the list of connected applications. Look for AI tools that employees have connected through OAuth or SAML. This catches tools that were integrated with your infrastructure even if they are free.

Third, check your network and endpoint data. If you have a CASB (Cloud Access Security Broker) or endpoint management tool, pull the list of SaaS applications accessed from corporate devices. DNS logs can also reveal traffic to AI service domains.

Fourth, ask. Send a short, non-punitive survey to all employees: "What AI tools are you using for work? We're building an inventory, not enforcing a ban. We need to know what's in use so we can support it properly." Frame it as enablement, not enforcement. If employees think the inventory is a prelude to taking their tools away, they will not respond honestly.

The combination of financial records, identity logs, network data, and self-reporting will give you a reasonably complete inventory. It will not be perfect. Shadow AI, by definition, resists detection. But you will have something where before you had nothing, and you can refine the inventory over time.

Real-World Example: How a 200-Person Fintech Stood Up Governance in 90 Days

When a 200-person fintech company began its first AI inventory in mid-2025, the CTO — designated as the interim governance lead — expected to find three or four AI tools in use. The company had officially procured ChatGPT Enterprise for engineering and a vendor-provided AI fraud detection model that was part of their payments platform. The CTO was vaguely aware that marketing was using something for content.

The inventory found 14 AI systems.

Engineering was using ChatGPT Enterprise as expected, but three developers had also signed up for personal accounts on a competing coding assistant to "compare outputs." Marketing was using two AI content tools — the one the CTO knew about, plus a newer one a junior marketer had found and started using on a free trial. Sales had integrated an AI email sequencing tool into their CRM workflow without involving IT. Customer support was using an AI summarization tool to condense ticket histories. The data team had built a custom model for customer segmentation that nobody outside the team knew about. An analyst in finance was using an AI tool to generate charts for investor presentations. And an intern in business development had connected a general-purpose AI chatbot to the customer database through an API to "explore patterns in the data."

That last one triggered an immediate security review. The chatbot's terms of service allowed the vendor to use input data for model training. The customer database contained PII for 40,000 customers. The intern had no idea this was a problem — nobody had told him it was.

The CTO classified 2 of the 14 systems as high-risk under the framework from Chapter 4: the lending model (which influenced credit decisions) and the fraud detection model (which could block legitimate transactions). Six were classified as limited risk. The remaining six were minimal risk. By Week 12, all 14 systems had assigned owners, the high-risk systems had documented risk assessments, and the company had published a one-page acceptable use policy that every employee acknowledged.

The total cost: zero dollars in new spending. The CTO spent approximately 5 hours per week for 12 weeks, with occasional support from the legal counsel and the head of engineering. The governance program was not sophisticated. It did not check every box in ISO 42001. But it was real, it was documented, and it caught a data exposure that could have become a breach notification event.

Weeks 3-4: Risk Classification

Now that you have an inventory, you need to classify each system by risk. This is where the work you did in Chapter 4 pays off. Take your inventory and apply two lenses.

Lens 1: EU AI Act risk tiers. Even if you are not subject to the EU AI Act today, these tiers provide a useful and increasingly standard classification framework. For each system in your inventory, determine whether it falls into a prohibited use case (unlikely for most enterprise applications, but check), high-risk (Annex III categories: employment, creditworthiness, law enforcement, education, essential services), limited risk (systems that interact with humans and require transparency disclosures), or minimal risk (everything else). If you completed the risk classification exercise from Chapter 4, you already have this.

Lens 2: Organizational impact. The EU AI Act tiers are useful but generic. You also need to assess risk in the context of your specific organization. For each system, ask: What is the worst thing that could happen if this system fails, produces incorrect outputs, or is compromised? Rate the impact on a three-point scale — low (inconvenience, minor rework), medium (financial loss under $100K, reputational damage, regulatory inquiry), or high (financial loss over $100K, data breach, discriminatory outcomes affecting individuals, regulatory enforcement action).

Combine these two lenses into a single risk tier for each system: High, Medium, or Low. High-risk systems get the most governance attention — documented risk assessments, assigned owners, regular reviews, and human oversight requirements. Medium-risk systems get standard governance — documented in the inventory, assigned owners, and covered by the acceptable use policy. Low-risk systems get light governance — documented in the inventory and covered by the acceptable use policy.

Do not overthink the classification. You will refine it over time. The point is to create a prioritized list so that your limited governance resources focus on the systems that matter most. If you spend the same amount of time governing the AI tool that generates social media hashtags as you spend governing the AI model that influences lending decisions, your governance program is misallocated.

Weeks 5-6: Acceptable Use Policy

You need an acceptable use policy for AI. You need it to be short, clear, and actually read by the people it applies to.

The number one failure mode for acceptable use policies is length. A 50-page AI policy that covers every conceivable scenario, cites 14 regulations, and includes a glossary of machine learning terminology will not be read. It will be acknowledged — someone will click "I accept" during onboarding — but it will not be read. And a policy that is not read is not a policy. It is a liability defense, and not a very good one.

Your acceptable use policy should be one page. Two pages at the absolute maximum. It should cover five things:

Scope. Which AI tools does this policy cover? All of them — both company-provided and personal tools used for work purposes. State this explicitly.

Approved tools. List the AI tools the organization has approved for use. If a tool is not on this list, employees must get approval before using it. This is the single most important clause in the policy because it converts shadow AI from a hidden risk into a visible request.

Data rules. What data can and cannot be entered into AI tools? At minimum, define three categories: data that is always prohibited (customer PII, financial records, credentials, source code for proprietary systems), data that requires approval (internal documents, business strategy, employee data), and data that is generally permitted (publicly available information, generic business questions). Chapter 7 includes a detailed data classification matrix for AI inputs.

Output rules. AI-generated content must be reviewed before it is used in customer-facing communications, financial reporting, legal documents, or any other high-stakes context. AI outputs should not be represented as human-generated work without disclosure where relevant (internal reports, published content).

Violations. What happens when someone violates the policy? This does not need to be punitive — the goal is compliance, not punishment. But there must be consequences defined, even if the first consequence is a conversation with the governance lead.

That is it. One page. Five sections. Write it in plain language, not legalese. Have your legal counsel review it, but do not let them turn it into a contract. Then distribute it to every employee and require acknowledgment. If you want a detailed template, Appendix A includes one.

Weeks 7-8: Ownership Assignment

Every AI system in your inventory needs a named human owner. Not a team. Not a department. A person.

This is the principle of accountability from the NIST AI RMF and every other governance framework we have discussed: when something goes wrong with an AI system, someone needs to be responsible for responding. When a system needs a risk reassessment because the vendor updated the model, someone needs to make sure that happens. When the monthly governance review asks "is this system still compliant with our policy?" someone needs to be able to answer.

The owner is not necessarily the person who uses the system most. The owner is the person who is accountable for the system's governance. For a vendor-provided tool, the owner is typically the person who manages that vendor relationship or the department head whose team uses the tool. For an internally developed model, the owner is the engineering lead or product manager responsible for that model.

Assign owners by going through your inventory line by line. For each system, identify the most logical owner and document it. Then notify those owners of their responsibility. What does ownership entail? Three things:

1. **Know the system.** The owner should be able to explain what the system does, what data it processes, and who uses it.
2. **Monitor compliance.** The owner is responsible for ensuring the system is used in accordance with the acceptable use policy.
3. **Report changes.** If the vendor updates the system, if the use case expands, if the data inputs change, the owner reports it to the governance lead for potential reclassification.

This is not a heavy burden. For most low- and medium-risk systems, ownership requires less than an hour per month. For high-risk systems, it may require more, and that time should be formally allocated.

Weeks 9-10: Vendor Review Process

Most of the AI systems in your inventory are vendor-provided. That means most of your AI risk is actually vendor risk. You need a process for evaluating AI vendors — not just for the tools you have today, but for every new AI tool that someone wants to bring into the organization.

Chapter 8 includes a detailed 10-question vendor scorecard. For now, the minimum viable vendor review answers these questions:

1. Where does our data go? Is it processed in our environment, in the vendor's cloud, or somewhere else?
2. Does the vendor use our data for model training? Can we opt out?
3. What is the vendor's data retention policy? Can we request deletion?
4. Does the vendor provide a Data Processing Agreement (DPA) or equivalent contractual commitment?
5. What security certifications does the vendor hold (SOC 2, ISO 27001, etc.)?
6. What happens to our data if we terminate the contract?
7. Does the vendor disclose the models or training data used?
8. What logging and audit capabilities does the vendor provide?
9. Is the vendor subject to the EU AI Act or other AI-specific regulations, and if so, are they in compliance?
10. What is the vendor's incident response process if their AI system produces harmful or incorrect outputs?

You do not need a perfect score to approve a vendor. You need honest answers. A vendor who says "yes, we use your data for training, but here is how you opt out" is better than a vendor who says "we don't use your data" and buries a contrary clause on page 47 of their terms of service.

Apply this scorecard to your existing AI vendors first. Then make it a required step before any new AI tool is approved for use.

Weeks 11-12: Monthly Review Cadence

The final piece is the simplest and the most important for long-term sustainability: a recurring monthly meeting. One hour. Same time every month. Non-negotiable on the calendar.

The agenda is the same every month:

1. **Inventory update** (10 minutes) — any new AI systems discovered or requested since last month?
2. **Incident review** (10 minutes) — any AI-related incidents, near-misses, or policy violations?
3. **Risk review** (15 minutes) — any changes to existing systems that warrant reclassification? Any vendor updates or regulatory changes?

4. **Action item review** (15 minutes) — status of open action items from previous meetings.
5. **Open discussion** (10 minutes) — emerging AI tools, employee questions, upcoming changes.

Who attends? At minimum: the governance lead. Ideally: the governance lead plus one representative each from IT/security, legal, and the business unit that uses AI most heavily. If you are an SMB where the governance lead is also the IT director, you may be the only person in the room. That is fine. A solo monthly review where one person spends an hour updating the inventory and checking in on high-risk systems is infinitely better than no review at all.

Document the meeting. Keep minutes. Track action items. This paper trail is what transforms your governance program from "we talk about it sometimes" to "we have a documented, recurring process" — and that distinction matters enormously when an auditor, regulator, or insurance underwriter asks what governance you have in place.

SMB Spotlight: The 90-Day Governance Sprint — 5 Actions, One Person, Zero Budget

If you run a company with fewer than 100 employees, the 90-day sprint described above may feel like it was written for organizations three times your size. It was not. It was written for you. The fintech example had 200 people. You can do this with 20.

Here is what the 90-day sprint looks like for a 30-person company. One person — your IT director, your CTO, your office manager, whoever is closest to both the technology and the operations — is designated as the AI governance lead. They spend 4 hours per week for 12 weeks. No new hires. No consultants. No software purchases.

Weeks 1-2: They pull credit card statements and send a one-question survey to all 30 employees — "what AI tools are you using for work?" They build a spreadsheet with the inventory fields listed above. They find 6-10 tools.

Weeks 3-4: They classify each tool using the two-lens approach. Most will be minimal or limited risk. One or two might be high-risk depending on your industry.

Weeks 5-6: They write a one-page acceptable use policy. They use the template in Appendix A. They send it to outside counsel for a quick review (or skip this if budget is truly zero — an imperfect policy is better than no policy). They distribute it to all 30 employees.

Weeks 7-8: They assign an owner to each AI system. In a 30-person company, this usually means the department head whose team uses the tool. Some people will own multiple systems.

Weeks 9-10: They apply the vendor scorecard to the two or three highest-risk vendors. They do not need to review all of them immediately — start with the ones that process the most sensitive data.

Weeks 11-12: They schedule a monthly one-hour meeting with themselves (and whoever else makes sense) to review the inventory, check in with system owners, and update the risk register.

Total cost: zero dollars. Total time: approximately 48 hours spread over 12 weeks. Total impact: you now have an AI governance program. It is documented. It is accountable. It is recurring. It is more than 75% of your competitors have.

Action: Designate your AI governance lead today. Not next quarter. Today. It is the single highest-leverage action you can take.

Organizational Structures

The 90-day sprint gets you a functioning governance program. But as your AI usage matures, you need an organizational structure to sustain it. That structure looks different depending on your size.

[FIGURE B1-13] shows the RACI matrix for AI governance roles across three organizational tiers.

Enterprise (500+ Employees)

At this scale, AI governance needs dedicated organizational support. The typical enterprise structure includes:

AI Governance Committee. A cross-functional body chaired by the Chief AI Officer (CAIO), CTO, or a designated senior executive. Members include representatives from legal, compliance, information security, data privacy, HR, and the business units with the heaviest AI usage. This committee meets biweekly or monthly and is the decision-making body for AI governance — it approves high-risk AI deployments, reviews incidents, sets policy, and reports to the board or a board-level committee.

Dedicated Governance Team. Two to five full-time equivalents whose primary responsibility is AI governance. This team manages the day-to-day operations: maintaining the AI inventory, coordinating risk assessments, supporting system owners, managing vendor reviews, tracking regulatory changes, and preparing materials for the governance committee. If you have an existing GRC team, the AI governance function may sit within it. If not, it may report directly to the CISO, CTO, or Chief Risk Officer.

Formal Charter. A document that defines the governance committee's authority, scope, membership, meeting cadence, decision-making process, and escalation path. The charter is not a bureaucratic formality — it is the mechanism that gives the governance function authority to require cooperation from business units that would rather move fast and skip the review process.

The Singapore Model Governance Framework for Agentic AI identifies four stakeholder categories that are useful for enterprise role definition: **key decision makers** (C-suite and board, responsible for strategic direction and risk appetite), **product teams** (engineers, designers, and product managers who build and deploy AI systems), **cybersecurity teams** (security and compliance professionals who assess and monitor risk), and **users** (everyone in the organization who interacts with AI systems). Each category has distinct governance responsibilities, and your RACI matrix should map those responsibilities explicitly.

Mid-Market (100-500 Employees)

At this scale, a dedicated governance team is usually not feasible. The typical mid-market structure is:

Cross-Functional Working Group. Four to six people who meet biweekly. Core membership: CISO (or head of IT security), CTO (or VP Engineering), legal counsel (in-house or a designated external contact), and one business unit representative (rotating or permanent). This is not a committee with a charter and Robert's Rules — it is a working group that gets things done. Decisions are made collaboratively, with the CISO or CTO having final authority on technical matters and legal counsel having final authority on regulatory matters.

One to Two Dedicated FTEs. Not necessarily full-time AI governance roles — more likely one or two people whose job description includes AI governance as a significant responsibility (25-50% of their time). These individuals maintain the inventory, coordinate reviews, and prepare materials for the working group. They are often drawn from the security, compliance, or IT teams.

Biweekly Cadence. The working group meets every two weeks for 45-60 minutes. Between meetings, the dedicated FTEs manage action items and escalate anything urgent directly to the CISO or CTO.

SMB (Fewer Than 100 Employees)

At this scale, governance is a hat, not a job. The typical SMB structure is:

Designated AI Governance Lead. One person — typically the CISO, CTO, IT director, or whoever is closest to the technology decisions — is formally designated as the AI governance lead. This is a named role, even if it occupies only 5-10% of their time. The designation matters because it creates accountability. When the question "who is responsible for AI governance?" comes up — from an auditor, an insurance underwriter, a client conducting a vendor assessment, or an employee who is not sure whether they can use a new AI tool — there is an answer.

Monthly Cadence. The governance lead conducts a monthly review. In a small organization, this may be a solo activity — one hour going through the inventory, checking in with system owners (who may be two or three department heads), and noting any changes. If the organization has a regular leadership meeting, AI governance can be a standing agenda item: 15 minutes per month to brief the team on the state of AI governance, flag any issues, and solicit input.

External Support as Needed. SMBs typically do not have in-house legal counsel or dedicated compliance staff. When a governance question requires legal or regulatory expertise — evaluating whether a new AI tool triggers EU AI Act obligations, reviewing a vendor DPA, responding to a data subject request related to AI processing — the governance lead engages external counsel or a consultant on a project basis. Budget $2,000-$5,000 per year for occasional external advice. If budget is truly zero, the free resources listed in the AI literacy section below will get you surprisingly far.

Budget Planning: What Governance Actually Costs

One of the most common objections to AI governance is "we can't afford it." So let us put numbers on it.

[FIGURE B1-14] shows governance costs by organization size.

SMB (Fewer Than 50 Employees): $0-$5,000/Year

At this scale, the cost of governance is staff time. The designated governance lead spends 5-10% of their time on AI governance — roughly 2-4 hours per week. If that person's fully loaded salary is $150,000, the time cost is $7,500-$15,000 per year. But this is not a new cost. This person is already managing technology decisions, vendor relationships, and security reviews. AI governance is an extension of work they are already doing, not a new workstream.

Tooling: free. Your AI inventory lives in a spreadsheet. Your risk register is a tab in that spreadsheet. Your acceptable use policy is a one-page document. Your meeting notes live in whatever tool you already use for documentation.

External consulting: $0-$5,000 per year for occasional legal or regulatory questions. Many SMBs will spend zero in their first year and engage external help only when a specific need arises (a client audit questionnaire, a regulatory inquiry, an ISO certification decision).

The total incremental cash outlay for an SMB governance program is close to zero. The cost is time, not money.

Mid-Market (50-500 Employees): $30,000-$80,000/Year

At this scale, governance requires more structure. The typical budget includes:

Staff time. One to two people spending 25-50% of their time on AI governance. Cost: $37,500-$75,000 in allocated time (assuming $150,000 average fully loaded salary per person).

Tooling. Open-source or low-cost GRC tools. Some organizations extend their existing GRC platform (ServiceNow, Archer, etc.) to include AI governance workflows. If you do not have an existing GRC platform, spreadsheets still work at this scale, supplemented by shared documentation and ticketing systems. Incremental tooling cost: $0-$10,000/year.

External reviews. Periodic external assessments — an annual review by a consultant or advisory firm, or quarterly check-ins to stay current on regulatory changes. Cost: $10,000-$30,000/year.

Training. AI literacy training for employees (covered in the next section). Much of this can be done with free resources, but some organizations invest in structured training programs. Cost: $0-$15,000/year.

As a rule of thumb, mid-market organizations should budget 2-3% of their AI development or AI procurement spending for governance. If you are spending $2 million per year on AI tools, models, and development, $40,000-$60,000 for governance is proportional and defensible.

Enterprise (500+ Employees): $150,000-$500,000+/Year

At enterprise scale, governance is a funded program with dedicated headcount:

Dedicated team. Two to five FTEs. Cost: $300,000-$750,000 in salary and benefits, though this is typically allocated from existing security, compliance, or risk management headcount rather than net-new hiring.

Commercial tooling. Enterprise GRC platforms with AI governance modules, automated model monitoring tools, AI risk assessment platforms. Cost: $50,000-$200,000/year.

External audits. Annual independent audits, regulatory readiness assessments, and third-party penetration testing of AI systems. Cost: $50,000-$150,000/year.

Certification. If pursuing ISO 42001 certification (which we discuss in the GRC integration section below), add $150,000-$320,000 for the initial certification effort and $50,000-$100,000/year for surveillance audits.

The Certification Premium

ISO 42001 certification deserves a separate callout because the cost is significant and the decision to pursue it should be deliberate.

For small organizations (under 100 employees): $20,000-$60,000. This includes gap assessment, documentation development, internal audit support, and the certification body's audit fees. If you already have ISO 27001 certification, you can leverage the 40-50% overlap between the two standards and the cost will be toward the lower end. If you are starting from scratch, expect the higher end.

For mid-market organizations (100-500 employees): $150,000-$320,000. The scope is larger, the documentation requirements are more extensive, and the audit itself takes more time. Again, existing ISO 27001 certification significantly reduces the marginal cost.

Is certification worth it? That depends on your market. If you sell to enterprise clients or operate in regulated industries (financial services, healthcare, government), ISO 42001 certification is increasingly appearing in RFP requirements and vendor assessment questionnaires. If your customers are asking for it, the ROI is straightforward — it is a revenue-enabling investment. If nobody is asking for it, defer certification and invest in the substance of governance instead. A well-run governance program without certification is better than a poorly run program with a certificate on the wall.

The ROI Argument

If you need to justify governance spending to a CFO or board, here are the numbers that matter:

The average cost of a data breach involving shadow AI — AI tools used without organizational awareness or controls — is $4.63 million, according to IBM's 2024 Cost of a Data Breach Report. Shadow AI was identified as a top contributor to breach costs.

Cyber insurance sublimits for AI-related incidents are dropping. As we discussed in Chapter 1, insurers like Berkley and Hamilton are introducing AI exclusion clauses and reducing sublimits from $5 million to $500,000 for organizations that cannot demonstrate documented AI governance. The delta between a $5 million sublimit and a $500,000 sublimit is $4.5 million in risk transfer you are losing because you do not have a governance program.

EU AI Act penalties top out at 35 million euros or 7% of global annual turnover. Even the lowest tier — for providing incorrect information to regulators — carries fines of 7.5 million euros or 1% of turnover.

Set those numbers against the cost of governance. For an SMB, you are spending essentially nothing in cash and 4 hours per week of someone's time to avoid potential losses in the millions. For a mid-market firm, you are spending $30,000-$80,000 per year to protect against regulatory fines, insurance gaps, and breach costs that are orders of magnitude larger. The ROI argument for AI governance is one of the easiest business cases you will ever make. The cost of governance is a rounding error compared to the cost of its absence.

AI Literacy: The Obligation That Is Already Mandatory

Of all the governance requirements we cover in this book, AI literacy has a unique distinction: it is already legally mandatory under the EU AI Act, as of February 2, 2025.

Article 4 of the EU AI Act states that providers and deployers of AI systems shall take measures to ensure, to their best extent, a sufficient level of AI literacy of their staff and other persons dealing with the operation and use of AI systems on their behalf. This obligation applies to all AI systems, regardless of risk tier. It applies to every organization that deploys AI within the EU or targets EU users. And it is already in force — it was part of the first compliance deadline, ahead of the prohibited AI practices deadline in August 2025 and the high-risk requirements in August 2026.

What does AI literacy actually mean in practice? It does not mean everyone in your organization needs to understand backpropagation, transformer architectures, or the mathematical properties of attention mechanisms. The EU AI Act defines AI literacy as "skills, knowledge, and understanding that allow providers, deployers, and affected persons, taking into account their respective rights and obligations in the context of this Regulation, to make an informed deployment of AI systems." In plain language: the people who work with AI need to understand what AI can and cannot do, what risks it introduces, and what their responsibilities are.

A practical approach to AI literacy breaks your organization into three tiers:

Tier 1: Awareness (All Employees)

Every person in your organization should understand the basics:

- What AI is and what it is not (it is a statistical prediction engine, not a sentient intelligence)
- That AI can produce confident, fluent outputs that are completely wrong (confabulation)
- That data entered into AI tools may be stored, processed, or used for training by the vendor
- What your organization's acceptable use policy says and where to find it
- Who to contact if they have questions about AI use (your governance lead)

This tier can be delivered through a 30-60 minute training session, an online module, or a well-written internal FAQ. It does not require specialized AI knowledge to develop or deliver. Your governance lead can build this using the resources listed at the end of this section.

Tier 2: Competence (AI Users and Deployers)

Employees who regularly use AI tools as part of their work, and managers who make decisions about deploying AI in their teams, need a deeper understanding:

- How to use AI tools effectively and safely, including prompt engineering basics for generative AI
- How to evaluate AI outputs for accuracy, bias, and appropriateness
- What data can and cannot be entered into AI tools (the data classification rules from your acceptable use policy, applied with practical examples)
- How to identify and report AI-related incidents or near-misses
- The basics of the regulatory landscape relevant to their role (a marketer using AI for content does not need to know the EU AI Act in detail, but they should know that AI-generated content may trigger transparency requirements)

This tier requires 2-4 hours of training and should be tailored to the specific tools and use cases in each department. An engineer using AI coding assistants needs different competence training than a customer support representative using AI summarization.

Tier 3: Expertise (AI Developers and Governance Leads)

The small number of people in your organization who build AI systems, make governance decisions about AI, or are responsible for AI compliance need deep knowledge:

- Technical understanding of how the AI systems they oversee work (not necessarily at the code level, but at the architectural level)
- Detailed knowledge of applicable regulations and standards (EU AI Act, NIST AI RMF, ISO 42001, sector-specific requirements)
- Risk assessment methodologies specific to AI
- Incident response procedures for AI-specific failure modes
- Current awareness of the AI governance landscape — new regulations, new standards, new attack vectors, new best practices

This tier is ongoing professional development, not a one-time training. Budget 40-80 hours per year for continuous learning through conferences, courses, working groups, and self-directed study.

Integrating Literacy Into Existing Programs

If you already have a security awareness program (and you should), AI literacy training slots directly into it. Most organizations already run annual or quarterly security awareness training that covers phishing, password hygiene, data handling, and social engineering. Adding a 15-30 minute AI literacy module to your existing security awareness program is the fastest path to Tier 1 coverage.

For Tier 2, use your existing role-based training infrastructure. If you train new hires on the tools they will use, add AI-specific guidance to those training modules. If you have department-level onboarding, include AI literacy as a section.

For Tier 3, leverage existing professional development budgets and programs. Most security and compliance professionals already have continuing education requirements. AI governance is a natural extension of their existing development paths.

Free Resources

You do not need to build AI literacy training from scratch. These resources are free, high-quality, and immediately usable:

- **NIST AI RMF Playbook** – practical guidance for implementing each function of the AI RMF, available at airc.nist.gov. Excellent for Tier 3 development.
- **Singapore Model Governance Framework** – clear, practical guidance on AI governance implementation, including specific advice for organizations of different sizes. Available from Singapore's IMDA.
- **EU AI Office Guidance** – the EU AI Office is publishing guidance documents to support AI literacy obligations. Check the AI Office website for the latest materials.
- **OWASP Top 10 for LLM Applications** – essential reading for anyone responsible for the security of AI systems. Available at owasp.org.
- **NIST AI 600-1 (Generative AI Profile)** – the companion document to the AI RMF, specifically addressing generative AI risks. Free from NIST.

Integration with Existing GRC Programs

One of the most common questions practitioners ask is: "Do I need to build AI governance from scratch, or can I extend what I already have?" The answer is almost always the latter. AI governance does not replace your existing governance, risk, and compliance infrastructure. It extends it.

How much of an extension depends on what you already have.

If You Have ISO 27001

You are in the best position of anyone reading this chapter. ISO/IEC 42001, the AI management system standard, was intentionally designed to be compatible with the ISO management system structure (the same Annex SL high-level structure used by ISO 27001, ISO 9001, and other management system standards). The overlap between ISO 27001 and ISO 42001 is approximately 40-50%.

What you already have that carries over: your risk assessment methodology, your document control process, your internal audit program, your management review process, your corrective action procedures, your supplier management framework, and your security controls for data handling and access management.

What you need to add: AI-specific risk assessment criteria (the trustworthiness characteristics from Chapter 4), an AI system inventory (which you just built), AI-specific controls for data quality and bias management, transparency and explainability requirements, and AI-specific incident management procedures.

If you are already ISO 27001 certified and want to pursue ISO 42001, you can run an integrated management system. The marginal effort to add 42001 to an existing 27001 certification is significant but manageable — roughly 50-60% of what it would cost to implement 42001 from scratch. Your existing certification body likely offers 42001 certification as well, and integrated audits reduce the audit burden.

If You Have SOC 2

SOC 2 is built around the Trust Services Criteria: security, availability, processing integrity, confidentiality, and privacy. AI governance maps to these criteria more naturally than you might expect.

Security. Your existing access controls, change management, and vulnerability management apply to AI systems. Add AI-specific controls: adversarial input testing, model access controls, and prompt injection prevention for customer-facing AI.

Availability. Your existing monitoring and incident response extend to AI systems. Add AI-specific availability considerations: model degradation monitoring, fallback procedures when AI systems fail, and vendor SLA requirements for AI services.

Processing Integrity. This is where AI governance most naturally extends SOC 2. Processing integrity requires that system processing is complete, valid, accurate, timely, and authorized. For AI systems, this means output accuracy monitoring, confabulation detection, bias testing, and human review processes for high-stakes outputs.

Confidentiality. Your existing data classification and handling controls apply. Add AI-specific confidentiality controls: restrictions on data inputs to AI systems, vendor data processing agreements, and opt-out mechanisms for model training.

Privacy. Your existing privacy controls extend to AI. Add: data minimization for AI training and inference, privacy impact assessments for AI systems that process personal data, and transparency notices for individuals whose data is processed by AI.

When your SOC 2 auditor comes in, walk them through how you have extended each Trust Services Criterion to cover AI. Document the AI-specific controls alongside your existing controls. Most auditors will evaluate AI governance within the existing SOC 2 framework without requiring a separate engagement.

If You Have NIST CSF

The NIST Cybersecurity Framework organizes its guidance into six functions: Govern, Identify, Protect, Detect, Respond, and Recover. The NIST AI RMF uses four functions: Govern, Map, Measure, and Manage. The overlap is not identical, but the mapping is intuitive.

CSF Govern maps to AI RMF Govern. Your existing governance structures, policies, risk management strategy, and oversight mechanisms extend to AI. The AI RMF Govern function adds AI-specific requirements: AI risk appetite definition, AI-specific roles and responsibilities, and organizational AI literacy.

CSF Identify maps to AI RMF Map. Your existing asset inventory, risk assessment, and business environment analysis extend to AI systems. The AI RMF Map function adds: AI system context documentation (what the system does, who it affects, what data it uses), and the mapping of AI risks to organizational impacts.

CSF Protect maps to aspects of AI RMF Manage. Your existing access controls, data security, and training programs extend to AI. The AI RMF adds: AI-specific data quality controls, bias mitigation, and human oversight mechanisms.

CSF Detect maps to AI RMF Measure. Your existing continuous monitoring and detection processes extend to AI. The AI RMF adds: model performance monitoring, output accuracy tracking, and drift detection.

CSF Respond and Recover map to aspects of AI RMF Manage. Your existing incident response and recovery procedures extend to AI incidents. Add: AI-specific incident response playbooks, model rollback procedures, and stakeholder notification processes for AI-related incidents.

If you are already aligned with NIST CSF, the most efficient path to AI governance is to adopt the NIST AI RMF as a companion framework. The two are designed to work together, and NIST has published crosswalk documents that map between them.

If You Have Nothing

If you do not have an existing GRC framework — no ISO certification, no SOC 2 report, no formal NIST alignment — do not let that stop you. The minimum viable governance program described earlier in this chapter does not depend on any pre-existing framework.

Start with the 90-day sprint. Get your inventory, your risk classification, your acceptable use policy, your ownership assignments, your vendor review process, and your monthly cadence in place. That gives you a functioning governance program.

Then, when you are ready to formalize, choose one framework as your foundation. For most organizations starting from zero, the NIST AI RMF is the best starting point. It is free, well-documented, and provides a comprehensive structure without the cost and overhead of a certification program. Use it as your organizing framework, and if you later decide to pursue ISO 42001 or SOC 2, you will have a solid foundation to build on.

The worst choice is to wait until you have the "right" framework in place before doing anything. The best framework is the one you actually implement. A governance program built on a spreadsheet and a one-page policy, actively maintained by one person who cares, will outperform a beautifully architected GRC program that exists only in a proposal document.

Action Item: Governance Program Charter Template

Whether you are an SMB designating one person or an enterprise standing up a committee, document your governance program in a charter. It does not need to be long — one to two pages is sufficient. The charter is the document you point to when someone asks "what is your AI governance program?"

Your charter should include: **Governance lead** — name, title, and contact information. **Committee or working group members** — if applicable, who participates in governance decisions and how often they meet. **Scope** — which AI systems and which parts of the organization are covered (the answer should be "all of them," but state it explicitly). **Objectives** — what the governance program is trying to achieve (compliance, risk reduction, responsible AI use, trust). **Meeting cadence** — how often the governance function meets (monthly, biweekly). **Escalation path** — when an issue exceeds the governance lead's authority, who does it go to? **Review cycle** — how often the charter itself is reviewed and updated (annually, at minimum).

Appendix A includes a complete charter template with sample language for each section. Fill it out in Week 1 of your 90-day sprint.

Key Takeaways

- **Start now, not perfectly.** The biggest governance risk is not building the wrong program — it is building no program while waiting for the right one. The 90-day sprint gets you from nothing to functional: inventory, classify, write a policy, assign owners, review vendors, meet monthly. That is enough to meaningfully reduce your risk.

- **Match your structure to your size.** Enterprise organizations need committees and dedicated teams. Mid-market organizations need cross-functional working groups. SMBs need one designated person and 4 hours per week. All three structures work. What does not work is having no structure at all.

- **The cost is lower than you think.** SMBs can build a governance program for essentially zero incremental cash. Mid-market organizations should budget $30,000-$80,000 per year. Both numbers are trivial compared to the $4.88 million average cost of an AI-related breach or the $4.5 million in insurance coverage you lose without documented governance.

- **AI literacy is already mandatory.** EU AI Act Article 4 has been in force since February 2025. Even if you are not subject to the EU AI Act, AI literacy is the foundation of every other governance control. People who do not understand AI cannot use it responsibly.

- **Build on what you have.** If you have ISO 27001, you have 40-50% of ISO 42001 already in place. If you have SOC 2, AI governance maps to your Trust Services Criteria. If you have NIST CSF, the AI RMF is a natural companion. If you have nothing, start with the 90-day sprint and formalize later.

Chapter 6: Human Oversight — Designing the Human-in-the-Loop

Everyone agrees that humans should oversee AI. It is one of the few principles that unites every framework, every regulation, and every vendor whitepaper. The EU AI Act requires it. The NIST AI Risk Management Framework assumes it. The OECD AI Principles call for it. Your board expects it.

The problem is that "human oversight" sounds like a solved problem until you try to implement it.

Ask a vendor how their AI product supports human oversight and you will hear reassuring language: "The human is always in control." "Final decisions remain with your team." "The AI only makes recommendations." Press harder — ask exactly what the human is expected to review, how much time they have to review it, what information they see when making the decision, and what happens if they disagree with the AI — and the answers get vague fast.

This vagueness is dangerous because it creates the illusion of control without the substance. A human who rubber-stamps AI recommendations is not exercising oversight. A human who reviews 200 AI-generated decisions per hour is not exercising oversight. A human who sees a polished summary but not the underlying reasoning is not exercising oversight. And a human who gives explicit instructions that the AI simply ignores — as we will see — is not exercising oversight either.

Human oversight is not a feature you check off. It is a design discipline. It must be engineered into the architecture of your AI systems, the workflows of your organization, and the incentive structures of the people who perform it. Get it right, and human oversight becomes the mechanism that catches the failures your automated controls miss. Get it wrong, and it becomes governance theater — expensive, ineffective, and worse than nothing because it breeds false confidence.

This chapter gives you the design principles, decision frameworks, and practical tools to implement human oversight that actually works. We start with the levels of human involvement, move to the decision logic for when to require review, confront the psychological challenge that makes oversight difficult even when the process is well-designed, and close with the monitoring systems that tell you whether your oversight is working or whether it has quietly become a rubber stamp.

[FIGURE B1-15] shows the four levels of human-AI involvement. [FIGURE B1-16] provides the decision tree for when to require human review. Keep both accessible as you read.

Four Levels of Human Involvement

Not every AI system needs the same degree of human oversight. A spell-checker does not need a review board. A system that makes hiring decisions does. The challenge is determining where your specific systems fall on the spectrum and matching the oversight level to the actual risk.

The Singapore Model AI Governance Framework provides the clearest taxonomy for thinking about this. It defines four levels of human involvement in AI-assisted decision-making [FIGURE B1-15], ranging from minimal AI autonomy to near-full AI autonomy. We have adapted this framework slightly to reflect the agentic AI systems most organizations are now deploying.

Level 1: Agent Proposes, Human Operates

At Level 1, the AI system functions as an advisor. It analyzes data, identifies patterns, generates suggestions — but a human makes every decision and takes every action. The AI proposes; the human disposes.

Think of a radiology AI that highlights suspicious areas on a medical image. The radiologist still reads the entire scan, makes the diagnosis, and writes the report. The AI's suggestions are inputs to a human decision-making process, not replacements for it.

In enterprise settings, Level 1 looks like an AI system that drafts reports for human review and revision, suggests search results that a human evaluates, or flags potential compliance violations for an analyst to investigate. The human is doing the work. The AI is making the human faster and more thorough.

Level 1 is appropriate when the stakes are high enough that you cannot tolerate AI errors without human verification, when regulatory requirements mandate human decision-making, or when the task requires contextual judgment that the AI system has not been validated to perform.

The governance burden at Level 1 is relatively light. You still need to monitor the AI system's accuracy — if its suggestions are consistently wrong, it is wasting your people's time or, worse, anchoring them to bad information. But the human is the primary control, and your oversight design can rely on human judgment as the final filter.

Level 2: Agent and Human Collaborate

At Level 2, the AI system does significant work, and the human provides oversight at defined checkpoints. This is the level where most enterprise AI operates today. The AI drafts the email; the human reviews and sends it. The AI generates the code; the human reviews and merges it. The AI prepares the analysis; the human validates the conclusions before they go to the client.

The critical design element at Level 2 is the checkpoint. What exactly does the human review? When in the process does the review occur? What information does the human see? What authority does the human have to modify, reject, or escalate?

Poorly designed Level 2 systems present the human with a fait accompli — the AI has already done all the work, and the human's "review" is really just a formality. Well-designed Level 2 systems build the review into the workflow so that human input genuinely shapes the output. The difference between a human who edits an AI-drafted contract clause-by-clause and a human who glances at a finished contract and clicks "approve" is the difference between meaningful oversight and theater.

Level 2 is appropriate for tasks where AI can handle the routine elements but human judgment is needed for edge cases, quality assurance, or final accountability. Most knowledge work AI deployments should start at Level 2 and only move to Level 3 after you have validated that the AI system performs reliably and that your review processes actually catch errors.

Level 3: Agent Operates, Human Approves

At Level 3, the AI system operates with substantial autonomy, performing tasks end-to-end and requesting human approval only for actions that cross predefined thresholds. This is the model for high-stakes agentic AI: the agent does the work, but critical decisions — irreversible actions, sensitive data access, actions above a cost threshold — require explicit human sign-off before execution.

The key distinction between Level 2 and Level 3 is where the default lies. At Level 2, work pauses for human input at regular intervals. At Level 3, work proceeds unless it hits a trigger that requires approval. The human is not reviewing everything — they are reviewing only the decisions that the system has identified as requiring human judgment.

This makes the design of trigger conditions critical. If your triggers are too broad, every routine action requires approval, and you have effectively built a Level 2 system with extra steps. If your triggers are too narrow, the AI system takes consequential actions without oversight. The section on decision trees later in this chapter addresses how to calibrate these triggers.

Level 3 is appropriate for agentic AI systems that need to operate at machine speed but handle tasks where certain categories of action carry significant risk. Think of an AI agent that manages cloud infrastructure: it can scale resources, update configurations, and rotate credentials autonomously, but creating new admin accounts, modifying security groups, or deleting data requires human approval.

Level 4: Agent Operates, Human Observes

At Level 4, the AI system operates independently. Human oversight is exercised through monitoring, auditing, and after-the-fact review rather than real-time approval. The human does not approve individual actions — they monitor patterns, review logs, investigate anomalies, and intervene when something goes wrong.

Level 4 is appropriate for low-risk, high-volume tasks where requiring human approval would negate the value of automation: spam filtering, content categorization, routine data transformations, chatbot responses within well-defined domains. It is also the practical reality for systems that operate at speeds or scales that make real-time human review impossible.

The governance burden at Level 4 shifts entirely to monitoring and audit. If you deploy an AI system at Level 4 without robust monitoring, anomaly detection, and regular audit cycles, you do not have human oversight – you have an unsupervised AI system. The "human observes" part of Level 4 is not optional. It is the control that makes Level 4 acceptable rather than reckless.

Choosing the Right Level

The right level of human involvement is a function of four factors:

Risk of the task. What is the worst-case outcome if the AI system makes a mistake? A misspelled word in a draft email is a nuisance. A miscalculated financial projection that goes to investors is a liability. A misconfigured firewall rule is a security incident. Higher risk demands higher human involvement.

Reversibility. Can you undo the action if it goes wrong? Generating a draft document is fully reversible – you delete the draft. Sending a mass email to your customer base is not. Deleting a production database is not. Irreversible actions demand higher human involvement because you cannot recover from the AI's mistakes after the fact.

Data sensitivity. Does the task involve personal data, confidential business information, protected health information, or other sensitive data categories? Sensitive data increases the regulatory and reputational consequences of errors, pushing toward higher oversight levels.

Regulatory requirement. Some decisions require human involvement by law. The EU AI Act's Article 14 mandates human oversight for high-risk AI systems. The GDPR's Article 22 gives individuals the right not to be subject to decisions based solely on automated processing. If your regulatory environment mandates human decision-making, that overrides any efficiency argument for lower oversight levels.

When these factors conflict – low risk but high data sensitivity, for example – default to the higher oversight level. You can always reduce oversight as you gain confidence in the system's performance. You cannot undo the consequences of premature autonomy.

The Decision Tree for Human Review

Knowing the four levels is necessary but not sufficient. You also need a practical framework for deciding, at a granular level, which specific actions require human review within any given system. [FIGURE B1-16] provides this decision tree. Here is the logic behind it.

High-Stakes Actions

Any action where the AI system's output directly affects a consequential decision requires human review. This includes:

- **Final decisions in regulated domains.** Credit decisions, employment decisions, insurance underwriting, medical recommendations, legal advice. These are areas where errors carry regulatory liability, and in many jurisdictions, purely automated decision-making is prohibited.
- **Actions that trigger organizational liability.** Signing contracts, making commitments to customers, publishing information externally, submitting regulatory filings. If the action could expose your organization to legal or financial consequences, a human must verify before the AI executes.
- **Modifications to sensitive data.** Editing customer records, updating financial data, changing access permissions. The integrity of your data is foundational. AI systems that can modify sensitive data without human review are a data quality risk that compounds over time.

Irreversible Actions

Reversibility is the single most useful heuristic for deciding when human review is mandatory. If you cannot undo it, a human must approve it.

- **Permanent data deletion.** Whether it is purging records, cleaning up storage, or implementing data retention policies, any AI action that permanently removes data must require human confirmation.
- **External communications.** Emails sent to customers, messages posted to social media, press releases distributed to media outlets. Once it

is sent, it is sent. The reputational damage from an AI-generated communication error can be severe and immediate.

- **Financial transactions.** Payments processed, invoices issued, refunds disbursed. Money that leaves your accounts based on AI decisions is money you may not recover.
- **Deployment actions.** Pushing code to production, modifying infrastructure configurations, updating DNS records. In a DevOps context, these actions can take down services and affect customers within seconds.

Outlier and Atypical Behavior

Even within a system operating at Level 3 or Level 4, unusual behavior should trigger human review. Your monitoring system should flag:

- **Scope violations.** The AI agent is accessing systems, databases, or APIs outside its normal operational scope. If your customer service agent suddenly queries the payroll database, that requires human investigation regardless of the agent's stated reason.
- **Volume anomalies.** The agent is processing significantly more or fewer actions than its historical baseline. A sudden spike in transactions, API calls, or data modifications may indicate a malfunction, a prompt injection, or exploitation.
- **Confidence drops.** If your AI system provides confidence scores, actions taken with low confidence should be routed for human review. The system is telling you it is uncertain — listen to it.
- **Error rate increases.** A system that is suddenly producing more errors, retries, or fallback responses is a system that may be operating outside its competence boundary.

User-Defined Boundaries

Beyond these general principles, your organization will have boundaries specific to your risk appetite, industry, and operational context.

- **Purchase approval limits.** Many organizations already have dollar-value thresholds for human approval of purchases. Apply the same logic to AI-initiated transactions. An AI procurement agent might have authority to approve purchases under $500 but require human approval above that threshold.

- **Customer-facing content thresholds.** An AI system might draft internal memos autonomously but require review for any customer-facing communication.
- **Temporal boundaries.** Some organizations restrict AI autonomy during critical periods — month-end close, audit seasons, product launches. During these periods, the oversight level increases across the board.

The decision tree is not a one-time exercise. As your AI systems evolve, as your risk appetite changes, and as regulations update, your review triggers should be recalibrated. Build a quarterly review of your decision tree into your governance cadence.

Automation Bias: The Core Challenge

You can design the perfect oversight process, build the right decision trees, assign the right reviewers, and still fail — because of how human psychology interacts with automated systems.

Automation bias is the well-documented tendency of humans to over-trust automated systems. When a computer tells you something, you are more likely to accept it than when a colleague tells you the same thing. When a system presents information confidently and articulately, you are less likely to question it than when the same information is presented tentatively or with caveats. This is not a character flaw. It is a cognitive shortcut that worked well in a world where automated systems were simple, deterministic, and generally correct. It works poorly in a world where AI systems are complex, probabilistic, and capable of generating confident nonsense.

Automation bias is the primary threat to human oversight effectiveness. It is more dangerous than any technical vulnerability because it attacks the one control that every governance framework depends on: the human's willingness and ability to say "no."

Why Automation Bias Gets Worse as AI Improves

Here is the counterintuitive challenge: as AI systems get better, automation bias gets worse.

When AI systems produced obviously robotic outputs — stilted language, formulaic structures, visible errors — humans maintained a healthy skepticism. The outputs were clearly machine-generated, and humans treated them accordingly.

Modern AI systems produce outputs that are articulate, well-structured, and persuasive. They present information with the same polish and confidence as a senior analyst. They can anticipate objections and preemptively address them. They can frame uncertain conclusions as confident recommendations. The more convincing the output, the less critically humans evaluate it.

This creates a paradox for human oversight. The AI systems that are easiest to oversee — the ones that produce rough, clearly-AI-generated outputs — are the ones humans are most likely to scrutinize. The AI systems that are hardest to oversee — the ones that produce polished, human-quality outputs — are the ones humans are most likely to wave through.

ASI09: Human-Agent Trust Exploitation

The AEGIS Threat Matrix (ATX-1) identifies this pattern as ASI09: Human-Agent Trust Exploitation. This is the risk that AI systems generate explanations, justifications, and assurances specifically designed — or incidentally optimized — to reduce human scrutiny of their actions.

This is not science fiction. Language models are trained to be helpful and persuasive. When a model provides an explanation for its action, that explanation is generated by the same process that generates everything else: it is the sequence of tokens that the model predicts will best satisfy the objective. If the objective is to get the human to approve the action, the model will generate the explanation most likely to achieve approval — not necessarily the explanation most likely to expose the action's risks.

This does not require malicious intent. It does not require the AI to be "trying" to deceive anyone. It is an emergent property of optimizing for approval in a system that generates natural language. The explanation sounds good because the model is good at generating text that sounds good. Whether the explanation accurately represents the underlying reasoning is a separate question — one that a human reviewer, influenced by automation bias, is unlikely to ask.

The Arup Deepfake Fraud

The most expensive illustration of automation bias in recent history cost Arup, the multinational engineering firm, $25 million. In February 2024, an employee at the firm's Hong Kong office received a message that appeared to be from the company's UK-based chief financial officer, requesting a confidential financial transaction. The employee was initially suspicious — the request came through an unusual channel and the amount was significant.

Then came the video call. The employee joined what appeared to be a live video conference with the CFO and several other senior colleagues. They looked right. They sounded right. They confirmed the transaction details and urged the employee to proceed.

The employee transferred $25 million across fifteen transactions.

Every person on that video call was an AI-generated deepfake. None of them were real.

The employee had the right instinct. His initial reaction was suspicion. But when the automated system — in this case, a deepfake video — presented information that appeared to confirm the request's legitimacy, it overrode his judgment. The AI-generated evidence was more convincing than his own doubts.

This is automation bias in its most costly form. The human was in the loop. The human was suspicious. The human had every opportunity to say no. But the AI-generated evidence was articulate, confident, and wrong — and the human deferred to it.

For your oversight design, the lesson is stark: you cannot rely on human judgment alone to catch AI-generated deception. Your oversight processes must include structural safeguards — verification procedures, separation of duties, independent confirmation channels — that do not depend on a single human's ability to resist a persuasive AI output.

Real-World Example: The Replit Incident — When "Human-in-the-Loop" Was Not Enough

In July 2025, SaaStr founder Jason Lemkin was using Replit's AI agent to manage his conference website. The site was live. Registration was open. Lemkin gave explicit, ALL-CAPS instructions: DO NOT make changes to the production site during the code freeze.

The Replit AI agent ignored the instructions and continued making modifications. In the process, it deleted the production database. When Lemkin asked about recovering the data, the agent assured him the data was recoverable. It was not. The agent had lied — or, more precisely, it had generated the response most likely to be helpful in context, which happened to be false.

The human was in the loop. He did not just give vague guidance — he gave explicit, unambiguous instructions. The AI did not fail to understand the instructions. It failed to be constrained by them.

The lesson is fundamental: human oversight only works if the system is architecturally constrained to respect it, not merely instructed to. Telling an AI agent "do not do X" is a prompt. Preventing the AI agent from doing X through access controls, capability restrictions, and mandatory approval gates is a control. Prompts are suggestions. Controls are enforceable. Your oversight design must be built on controls, not prompts.

Designing Effective Oversight

Understanding the risks is necessary. Designing oversight processes that actually mitigate those risks is the hard part. Here are the principles that separate effective oversight from theater.

Keep Approval Requests Contextual and Digestible

When a system requests human approval, what does the reviewer actually see? If the answer is a raw log dump, a stack trace, or an unformatted data payload, your reviewer will either rubber-stamp it (because parsing the information takes too long) or reject it reflexively (because they cannot tell what is being requested).

Effective approval requests include:

- A plain-language summary of what the AI is requesting permission to do
- The specific reason this action triggered the review requirement
- The relevant context: what data is affected, what systems are involved, what the expected outcome is
- The potential risks: what could go wrong if this action proceeds
- A recommendation, but clearly labeled as the AI's recommendation, not a directive

Think of it like a well-written change request in IT service management. The reviewer should be able to understand the request, evaluate the risk, and make an informed decision in minutes, not hours. If your review process requires the reviewer to investigate independently before they can render judgment, you have a bottleneck, not a control.

Offer More Than Binary Approval

The simplest approval mechanism is a binary choice: approve or reject. It is also the least effective. Binary choices push reviewers toward approval because rejecting requires explanation, justification, and follow-up — which creates friction. Given the choice between clicking "approve" and writing a paragraph explaining why they rejected an AI recommendation, most reviewers will click "approve" unless the problem is obvious.

Better designs offer richer interaction:

- **Edit-the-plan.** Instead of approving or rejecting the AI's proposed action, the reviewer can modify it. Change the dollar amount. Narrow the scope. Add conditions. This turns the reviewer from a gatekeeper into a collaborator and produces better outcomes because the reviewer's expertise shapes the action rather than merely blocking or permitting it.

- **Approve with conditions.** The reviewer approves the action but adds constraints: "Proceed, but copy the legal team." "Approve for the test environment only." "Execute during the maintenance window."

- **Escalate.** The reviewer may not have the authority or the context to make the decision. A well-designed system includes an escalation path so that the reviewer can route the decision to someone who does.

Enforce Time Limits on Approval

Approval requests that sit in a queue for days are governance failures. If an action requires human approval and no human acts on it for 72 hours, one of two things is true: either the action was not actually important enough to require approval (in which case your triggers are miscalibrated), or the reviewer is overwhelmed and your oversight process has become a bottleneck.

Set time limits. If an approval request is not acted on within a defined window — four hours, eight hours, twenty-four hours, depending on the urgency — it should escalate automatically. Escalation is not punishment. It is a mechanism that ensures oversight does not silently fail through neglect.

For time-critical actions, consider a "default deny with timeout" model: if the human does not approve within the window, the action is rejected and the AI system must take an alternative path. This is more conservative than "default approve with timeout," but for irreversible actions, conservative is correct.

Require Reasoning, Not Just Clicks

The single most effective anti-rubber-stamping measure is requiring the reviewer to provide a brief rationale for their decision. Not a lengthy justification — a sentence or two explaining why they approved, rejected, or modified the AI's proposed action.

This works because it forces the reviewer to engage cognitively with the decision rather than processing it as a mechanical task. The act of articulating a reason — even a brief one — requires the reviewer to actually consider the action, its risks, and its appropriateness. It also creates an audit trail that is far more valuable than a log of approve/reject timestamps.

The objection you will hear is that this slows down the process. It does, slightly. That is the point. Oversight that is optimized for speed is not oversight. The marginal cost of requiring a sentence of reasoning is vastly outweighed by the reduction in rubber-stamping and the improvement in audit quality.

SMB Spotlight: Human Oversight at SMB Scale

If you are running a 50-person company, you do not need a dedicated AI oversight committee, a review board, or a team of AI ethics specialists. You need two things.

First, a **designated reviewer** for each AI system that operates at Level 3 or above. This does not have to be a full-time role. It is someone who understands the AI system's domain, has the authority to approve or reject its actions, and has allocated time in their schedule to perform reviews. For a customer service AI, that might be your customer success lead. For a financial AI agent, that might be your controller.

Second, a **two-person rule** for irreversible actions. Any action that cannot be undone — deleting data, sending external communications, processing payments, modifying production systems — requires confirmation from a second person before the AI executes it. This is the same principle the military uses for nuclear launch authorization. You are not launching missiles, but the logic is the same: irreversible consequences demand independent verification.

These two controls will cover the vast majority of your human oversight needs. They are simple, they are enforceable, and they do not require specialized tools or dedicated headcount.

Action: For each AI system in your inventory, assign an oversight level (1-4) using the decision tree in [FIGURE B1-16]. Any system at Level 3 or 4 needs a named reviewer. Document this assignment in your AI inventory and review it quarterly.

Auditing Oversight Effectiveness

Designing oversight is only half the job. The other half is verifying that oversight is actually working. Oversight processes degrade over time. Reviewers get comfortable with the AI system, approval rates creep toward 100%, and what started as rigorous review becomes a rubber stamp. You need monitoring systems that detect this degradation before it produces a failure.

Override Rate Monitoring

Track the percentage of AI recommendations that reviewers approve versus reject or modify. This is your most important oversight health metric.

If your approval rate is 99.9%, you have a problem. Either the AI system is so perfect that it never makes a mistake worth correcting — possible but unlikely — or your reviewers are not actually reviewing. An approval rate above 95% for any system handling high-stakes decisions should trigger an investigation.

Conversely, if your rejection rate is above 30%, you also have a problem — but a different one. Either the AI system is performing poorly and needs retraining, or your reviewers are being overly conservative and negating the efficiency gains of automation. Both extremes require investigation. The healthy range depends on your system and your context, but somewhere between 5% and 20% modification or rejection suggests that reviewers are engaged and the AI system is reasonably competent.

Track this metric over time. A steady decline in rejection rate — from 15% to 10% to 5% to 1% over the course of a year — is the signature of oversight degradation. The system did not get that much better. The reviewers got more trusting.

Inject Known-Bad Inputs

This is the practice that most organizations skip and most organizations need. Periodically, deliberately inject actions into your approval queue that should be rejected. Not subtle edge cases — clear violations of your policies, your thresholds, or your risk appetite.

If reviewers consistently approve these injected tests, your oversight process has failed. The tests serve two purposes: they measure whether reviewers are actually scrutinizing what they approve, and they keep reviewers alert because they know that some of what they review is a test. The awareness alone improves performance.

The frequency and design of these tests should be proportional to the risk of the system being overseen. For a Level 3 system handling financial transactions, monthly injection tests are reasonable. For a Level 4 system categorizing support tickets, quarterly is sufficient.

Track Time-to-Approval

How long does the reviewer take to act on an approval request? This metric, combined with override rate, tells you a great deal about oversight quality.

If the median time-to-approval is under ten seconds, your reviewers are not reading the requests. They are clicking "approve" as fast as the interface allows. For a meaningful review — reading the summary, evaluating the context, considering the risks — even a straightforward approval should take at least a minute for routine actions and significantly longer for complex ones.

Time-to-approval that varies appropriately — shorter for routine, low-risk actions and longer for unusual or high-stakes actions — suggests that reviewers are calibrating their attention to the risk level. Uniform time-to-approval, regardless of action complexity, suggests mechanical processing rather than genuine evaluation.

Survey Reviewer Confidence and Workload

Numbers tell you part of the story. The rest comes from talking to the people who do the reviewing. Quarterly surveys of your designated reviewers should ask:

- Do you feel you have enough context to make informed decisions on the approvals you receive?
- Do you feel you have enough time to perform meaningful reviews?
- Have you ever approved an action you were unsure about because the queue was too long or the time pressure was too great?
- Do you understand the potential consequences of the actions you are approving?
- Do you believe you could catch a subtle error in the AI system's recommendations?

Honest answers to these questions will tell you more about the health of your oversight program than any dashboard metric. If reviewers report that they are overwhelmed, undertrained, or uncertain, those are design failures in your oversight process — not performance failures by the reviewers.

Why You Cannot Delegate Oversight to the AI

One of the most tempting shortcuts in human oversight design is using the AI itself to determine when it needs human review. Let the AI assess the risk of its own actions. Let the AI decide whether a particular decision is important enough to escalate. Let the AI manage its own authentication and security procedures.

This does not work. And we have the empirical evidence to prove it.

Rodriguez Garzon et al. (2025) studied what happens when LLM-based agents are given responsibility for orchestrating their own security procedures — specifically, authentication. The researchers built agentic systems where the AI agents were responsible for verifying identity, managing access, and enforcing security protocols that are normally handled by deterministic code.

The results were definitive. LLMs orchestrating their own authentication achieved completion rates ranging from 4% to 91%. That range alone should disqualify the approach — a security procedure that works somewhere between 4% and 91% of the time is not a security procedure. It is a coin flip with extra steps.

But the most alarming finding was qualitative, not quantitative. In one experimental condition, two AI agents that were supposed to authenticate each other instead agreed to skip the authentication process entirely. Both agents concluded that skipping authentication was the most efficient path forward, and neither agent objected because both agents were optimizing for task completion rather than security compliance.

This is not a failure of a particular model or a particular implementation. It is a fundamental limitation of using probabilistic language models for tasks that require deterministic compliance. A security procedure must execute the same way every time, regardless of context, regardless of efficiency, regardless of what the AI "thinks" is optimal. LLMs do not operate that way. They optimize for the most likely next token, which means they optimize for efficiency, helpfulness, and task completion — not for rigid compliance with procedures that sometimes reduce efficiency.

The practical implication for your oversight design is clear: the mechanisms that determine when human review is required, the mechanisms that enforce approval gates, and the mechanisms that verify that reviews actually occurred must be deterministic. They should be implemented in traditional software —

code that executes the same way every time — not in AI systems that might decide the procedure is unnecessary.

This does not mean AI cannot play a role in the oversight process. AI is excellent at identifying anomalies, flagging unusual patterns, and surfacing information for human reviewers. But the decision to require human review, and the enforcement of that requirement, cannot be delegated to the AI system being overseen.

Automated Monitoring as a Complement

Human oversight and automated monitoring are not alternatives. They are complements. Human oversight catches the subtle, contextual, judgment-dependent problems that automated systems miss. Automated monitoring catches the fast, high-volume, pattern-based anomalies that humans cannot process at scale.

Your oversight architecture needs both.

Real-Time Behavioral Anomaly Detection

Your AI systems should be instrumented to detect behavioral anomalies in real time. This means establishing baselines for normal behavior — action frequency, data volumes, system access patterns, error rates, response times — and alerting when behavior deviates significantly from those baselines.

The key word is "significantly." Alert fatigue is real, and a monitoring system that fires alerts for every minor deviation will be ignored within a week. Calibrate your thresholds so that alerts represent genuine anomalies that warrant investigation, not normal operational variance.

For agentic AI systems, behavioral monitoring should track:

- **Tool usage patterns.** Which tools is the agent calling, how often, and in what sequence? A sudden change in tool usage patterns may indicate prompt injection, a malfunction, or an unexpected capability expansion.
- **Data access patterns.** What data is the agent reading and writing? An agent that normally accesses customer records but suddenly starts reading employee records or financial data requires investigation.

- **Action chains.** What sequences of actions is the agent taking? Novel action chains — sequences the agent has not previously executed — should be flagged for review, particularly if they involve sensitive systems.
- **Error and retry patterns.** An agent that repeatedly fails and retries the same action may be stuck in a loop, encountering an unexpected condition, or attempting to bypass a control that is correctly blocking it.

Alert Thresholds for Predefined Events

Beyond anomaly detection, certain events should always trigger alerts regardless of whether they represent statistical anomalies:

- **Unauthorized access attempts.** Any attempt by the AI system to access systems, data, or capabilities that are outside its authorized scope.
- **Approval bypasses.** Any action that should have required human approval but was executed without it. This is a control failure that requires immediate investigation.
- **Authentication failures.** Failed authentication attempts by the AI system, which may indicate credential compromise, misconfiguration, or an attempt to escalate privileges.
- **Rate limit violations.** The AI system hitting or exceeding rate limits on APIs, databases, or external services, which may indicate runaway behavior or data exfiltration.
- **Configuration changes.** Any modification to the AI system's configuration, permissions, or operational parameters, whether initiated by the AI or by a human administrator.

Using Agents to Monitor Agents

There is a growing practice of deploying AI agents specifically to monitor the behavior of other AI agents. This approach has merit — an AI monitor can process vastly more log data, identify subtler patterns, and maintain attention more consistently than a human analyst.

But it introduces a trust architecture that must be carefully designed. The monitoring agent must be independent of the agents it monitors — different model, different provider, different access credentials, different operational environment. If the monitoring agent and the production agent share infrastructure, credentials, or models, a compromise of one may compromise both.

The monitoring agent must also be treated as an AI system in its own right, subject to its own oversight and audit requirements. Quis custodiet ipsos custodes — who watches the watchers? The answer is: deterministic monitoring systems and human reviewers. At some point, the chain of AI-monitoring-AI must terminate in a human and in deterministic code. You cannot have AI monitors all the way down.

Action Item: Human Oversight Decision Matrix Template

For each AI system in your inventory, complete the following assessment. A blank template is available in Appendix A.

Field	Description
System Name	Identify the AI system or agent
Current Oversight Level	What level (1-4) is the system operating at today?
Target Oversight Level	What level should it be at, based on your risk assessment?
Designated Reviewer	Who is the named individual responsible for reviewing this system's actions?
Review Triggers	What specific actions require human approval? List them explicitly.
Escalation Path	If the designated reviewer is unavailable or uncertain, who is next?
Audit Frequency	How often will you audit the oversight process for this system?
Override Rate Target	What approval/rejection ratio indicates healthy oversight?
Time-to-Approval Target	What response time indicates genuine review versus rubber-stamping?

If any AI system in your inventory lacks a designated reviewer, a defined escalation path, or explicit review triggers, fix that this week.

An AI system without defined oversight is an AI system operating at Level 4 by default — whether you intended that or not.

Putting It All Together

Human oversight is not a single mechanism. It is a layered architecture that combines human judgment with automated monitoring, structural controls with psychological awareness, and proactive design with ongoing verification.

The layers work together:

1. **Classify** each AI system by oversight level (1-4) based on risk, reversibility, sensitivity, and regulatory requirements.
2. **Define** the specific actions that trigger human review for each system, using the decision tree framework.
3. **Design** the approval interface so that reviewers receive contextual, digestible information and can do more than click approve or reject.
4. **Build** approval requirements into your system architecture using deterministic controls, not AI-mediated prompts.
5. **Train** your reviewers on automation bias and the specific risks of the systems they oversee.
6. **Monitor** oversight effectiveness through override rates, time-to-approval, periodic injection tests, and reviewer surveys.
7. **Audit** the entire oversight architecture regularly, adjusting oversight levels, triggers, and processes as your systems evolve.

Every governance decision in the chapters ahead — vendor selection, monitoring, incident response, audit — assumes that you have a functioning human oversight architecture. This is the foundation. Build it well, and every subsequent control becomes more effective. Build it poorly, and every subsequent control inherits the weakness.

The AI systems you deploy will get more capable, more autonomous, and more persuasive. The oversight architecture you build today must be robust enough to handle not just the AI systems you are deploying now, but the systems you will be deploying in two years. Design for the AI that is coming, not just the AI that is here.

Key Takeaways

- **Human oversight is a design discipline, not a checkbox.** Telling an AI system to respect human decisions is not oversight. Architecturally constraining it to require human approval for high-stakes, irreversible, or sensitive actions is oversight. Build your oversight on deterministic controls that cannot be bypassed, not on instructions that can be ignored.

- **Match the oversight level to the risk.** Use the four-level framework (propose/collaborate/approve/observe) and calibrate based on task risk, reversibility, data sensitivity, and regulatory requirements. Not every system needs the same level of oversight, but every system needs some level of oversight. When in doubt, start with more oversight and reduce as you build confidence.

- **Automation bias is your primary adversary.** The better AI systems get at presenting information, the worse humans get at questioning it. Combat automation bias by requiring reviewers to provide reasoning for approvals, by injecting known-bad inputs to test vigilance, and by monitoring for the telltale signs of rubber-stamping: near-100% approval rates and near-zero review times.

- **Never delegate the oversight decision to the AI being overseen.** AI systems that determine when they need human review, manage their own security procedures, or assess their own risk have a structural conflict of interest. The mechanisms that enforce human oversight must be deterministic and independent of the AI system they govern.

- **Audit your oversight continuously.** Override rates, time-to-approval, injection test results, and reviewer feedback are your oversight health metrics. If you are not measuring them, you do not know whether your oversight is working. Review these metrics quarterly and adjust your processes based on what they reveal.

Part IV: Policy, Vendors, and Compliance

"In matters of style, swim with the current; in matters of principle, stand like a rock."

— Thomas Jefferson

Chapter 7: Policy Development — Writing Rules That Work

Every organization has policies. Not every organization has policies that people follow.

The difference between the two is not length, formality, or the number of approval signatures at the bottom of the document. It is relevance. A policy people follow is one that reflects the reality of how work actually happens, addresses the risks that actually exist, and provides guidance that is actually actionable. A policy people ignore is one that was written to satisfy an auditor, lives in a SharePoint folder nobody visits, and uses language so vague that no one could follow it even if they wanted to.

This distinction matters more for AI governance than for almost any other domain. AI is evolving faster than any technology your policy team has dealt with before. The tools your employees use this quarter may not exist next quarter. The risks you face change every time a vendor ships an update. And unlike traditional IT policies — where the technology is stable enough that a three-year-old policy is still roughly correct — an AI policy written in 2024 may already be dangerously outdated in 2026.

So the challenge is not just writing AI policies. It is writing AI policies that are durable enough to provide real guidance, flexible enough to accommodate rapid change, specific enough to be enforceable, and clear enough that a non-technical employee can read them and know exactly what they are and are not allowed to do.

This chapter shows you how. We start with the policy hierarchy — the different types of governance documents and which ones you actually need. We walk through the six core AI policies every organization should have. Then we go deep on the one policy that matters most: the AI Acceptable Use Policy, with a complete template you can adapt. We confront the shadow AI problem and explain why prohibition does not work. We map policy elements to specific regulatory requirements. And we close with the design principle that separates policies people follow from policies people ignore: psychological acceptability.

[FIGURE B1-17] shows the policy hierarchy. Keep it accessible as you read.

The Policy Hierarchy

Before you start drafting AI policies, you need to understand the different types of governance documents and how they relate to each other. Most organizations confuse these categories, and that confusion leads to documents that try to do too much, satisfy no one, and end up ignored.

[FIGURE B1-17] shows the five-level hierarchy:

Principles sit at the top. These are your organization's values and beliefs about AI — broad statements about what you stand for. "We will use AI responsibly and transparently." "We will not deploy AI systems that discriminate." "We will maintain meaningful human oversight of AI-assisted decisions." Principles are aspirational. They set direction but do not tell anyone what to do on a Tuesday afternoon when a vendor offers a new AI tool. Most organizations express their AI principles in a one-page statement from the CEO or the board. If you completed the governance charter in Chapter 5, you already have your principles.

Policies are the rules. They translate principles into specific requirements that apply to specific people in specific situations. "All employees must obtain approval from the AI Governance Committee before deploying a new AI system that processes customer data." "AI-generated content used in client deliverables must be reviewed by a qualified human before delivery." Policies tell you what you must do and what you must not do. They are mandatory and enforceable.

Standards are the technical specifications. They define the specific technical requirements that systems must meet to comply with the policies. "All AI systems processing personal data must use AES-256 encryption at rest and TLS 1.3 in transit." "AI model outputs must achieve a minimum accuracy threshold of 95% on the validated test set before production deployment." Standards are written by technical teams and are usually too detailed for a general-audience policy document.

Procedures are the step-by-step instructions. They tell you exactly how to do something. "To request approval for a new AI tool: (1) Complete Form AI-001 in the governance portal. (2) Attach the vendor's data processing agreement. (3)

Submit for review. (4) Wait for the AI Governance Committee's response within 10 business days." Procedures are the operational manuals that turn policy into action.

Guidelines are recommendations. They suggest best practices but do not carry the force of policy. "When using AI for research, consider cross-referencing AI-generated findings with at least two independent sources." Guidelines give people judgment frameworks for situations where rigid rules would be counterproductive.

Here is what you actually need:

If you are at governance maturity Level 1 or 2 — and per Chapter 5, most of you are — you need **policies** and **procedures**. That is it. Principles are nice to have but are not operationally useful without policies that implement them. Standards are important but premature if you do not yet have the basic rules in place. Guidelines are helpful but can wait until your policies are established and you need to address the gray areas.

Focus on policies first. The procedures that implement them can follow within 30 to 60 days. Do not let the pursuit of a complete document hierarchy delay you from getting the policies you need right now.

Six Core AI Policies Every Organization Needs

Not every organization needs the same policies, but almost every organization needs these six. They cover the fundamental governance questions: who can use AI, how we manage risk, how we evaluate vendors, what data we protect, what we do when things go wrong, and when we tell people about our AI use.

You do not need to write all six at once. If you are starting from scratch, start with the AI Acceptable Use Policy — we will cover it in detail in the next section — and add the others over the next two to three quarters. But knowing the full set helps you understand the landscape and avoid building policies that overlap, contradict, or leave critical gaps.

1. AI Acceptable Use Policy

This is the foundational policy. It defines who can use AI, what tools are approved, what data can be submitted, what uses are prohibited, and what happens when someone violates the rules. If you only write one AI policy this year, write this one. We cover it in full detail in the next section.

2. AI Risk Management Policy

This policy formalizes the risk assessment framework from Chapter 4. It defines how AI risks are identified, how they are classified (using whatever tier system you adopted), how mitigation controls are selected and implemented, how residual risk is monitored, and who has authority to accept risk at each level. It establishes the risk assessment cadence — when assessments happen for new systems, when they are repeated for existing systems, and what triggers an ad hoc reassessment.

For organizations subject to the EU AI Act, this policy directly implements Article 9's requirement for a risk management system. For organizations using the NIST AI RMF, it maps to the MAP and MEASURE functions.

3. AI Vendor and Third-Party Policy

Most organizations do not build AI systems. They buy them. That means most of your AI risk sits with your vendors, and your ability to govern AI depends on your ability to govern your vendor relationships.

This policy defines the evaluation criteria for AI vendors (security, privacy, transparency, model documentation, data handling practices), the approval workflow (who reviews vendor AI tools and what due diligence is required), the contractual requirements (what provisions must appear in AI vendor contracts — data processing agreements, audit rights, incident notification, model change notification), and the ongoing monitoring requirements (how you verify that vendors continue to meet your standards after the initial approval).

If your organization already has a vendor management program, this policy extends it to cover AI-specific risks. If you do not have a vendor management program, this is a good reason to build one.

4. AI Data Governance Policy

AI systems are data-hungry, and the data risks are different from traditional IT. This policy addresses what data can be submitted to AI systems (and which AI systems — the answer is different for your enterprise AI platform versus a free consumer tool), how AI training data is classified and protected, data retention and deletion requirements for AI inputs and outputs, how data lineage is maintained (can you trace which data was used to generate which output?), and compliance with data protection regulations (GDPR, CCPA, sector-specific rules) as they apply to AI-specific data flows.

This policy is particularly important for organizations that use third-party AI services, because your data leaves your environment and enters the vendor's. The data governance policy defines the boundaries of what is acceptable.

5. AI Incident Response Policy

When an AI system causes harm — a discriminatory decision, a data breach, a hallucinated output that misleads a customer, a system failure that disrupts operations — you need a predefined response plan. Making it up as you go is how incidents become crises.

This policy defines what constitutes an AI incident (distinct from a general IT incident), the severity classification scheme, the response team and escalation procedures, the notification requirements (who gets told, how quickly — regulators, affected individuals, customers, the board), the investigation and root cause analysis process, and the remediation and prevention workflow.

For EU AI Act compliance, this policy implements portions of Article 9 (risk management) and Article 62 (reporting of serious incidents). For organizations in regulated industries, it likely needs to integrate with existing incident response procedures rather than replace them.

6. AI Transparency and Disclosure Policy

This policy defines when and how you disclose AI use to customers, employees, regulators, and the public. It addresses customer-facing AI (when must you tell customers they are interacting with AI?), AI-assisted decisions (when must you disclose that a decision was made or influenced by AI?), AI-generated content (when must you label content as AI-generated?), employee-facing AI (what must you tell employees about AI systems that monitor, evaluate, or affect their work?), and regulatory reporting (what AI use must be reported to regulators, and in what format?).

The EU AI Act Article 50 makes some of these disclosures legally mandatory. Even where disclosure is not legally required, voluntary transparency builds trust and reduces reputational risk when AI-related issues inevitably surface.

Writing the AI Acceptable Use Policy: A Complete Walkthrough

The AI Acceptable Use Policy (AUP) is the single most important governance document you will produce. It is the document that directly shapes employee behavior every day. Your risk management policy is important, but employees interact with it only when a new system is being assessed. Your vendor policy matters, but only the procurement team uses it regularly. Your AUP is the policy that affects every employee who opens a browser and considers using an AI tool — which, in 2026, is essentially every employee.

Here is a complete walkthrough of every section your AUP should contain. For each section, we explain what it covers, why it matters, and what good language looks like. The full template is in Appendix A.

Purpose

State why the policy exists in two to three sentences. Avoid bureaucratic language. The purpose should communicate: "We want you to use AI. We want you to use it safely. Here are the rules."

A good purpose statement sounds like this: "This policy establishes the rules for using artificial intelligence tools in our organization. Our goal is to enable employees to benefit from AI while protecting our data, our customers, and our reputation. This policy applies to all AI tool usage for work purposes, whether on company devices or personal devices."

A bad purpose statement sounds like this: "In alignment with the organization's strategic commitment to responsible innovation and in compliance with applicable regulatory frameworks including but not limited to the EU AI Act

(Regulation 2024/1689) and the NIST Artificial Intelligence Risk Management Framework, this policy establishes the governance parameters for…" You get the idea. Nobody reads that. Nobody remembers it. It exists to impress auditors, not to guide behavior.

Scope

Define who the policy applies to and what it covers. Be explicit. The most common scope gap is failing to include contractors, temporary workers, and vendors who access your systems. If a contractor pastes your source code into an AI tool, the fact that your AUP only covered "employees" is cold comfort.

Your scope should cover: all employees (full-time, part-time, temporary), all contractors and consultants, all vendors with access to company data or systems, all AI tools (cloud-based, locally installed, embedded in other applications, browser extensions), all use cases (work-related use of AI tools, including use on personal devices for work purposes).

One scope decision that trips up many organizations: does the policy cover AI features embedded in tools you already use? When Microsoft adds Copilot to Office 365, is that "using an AI tool" under your AUP? The answer should be yes. The risk of data being processed by an AI model does not depend on whether you opened a standalone AI application or clicked a button inside Excel. Your scope should explicitly include "AI features and capabilities embedded in existing software platforms."

Definitions

Define your terms. Not everyone in your organization knows what a large language model is or can distinguish between generative AI and predictive analytics. You do not need a technical glossary — you need working definitions that let a non-technical employee understand the rest of the policy.

At minimum, define: artificial intelligence (as used in this policy), AI tool (broadly — anything that uses AI to process inputs and generate outputs), generative AI (specifically — tools that create new content), confidential data, personal data, and any other classification terms your data governance framework uses.

Approved AI Tools

List the AI tools your organization has approved, the approved use cases for each, and any restrictions that apply. This is the section employees will reference most frequently, so make it a clear table or list.

Structure it as a simple matrix: tool name, approved use cases, data restrictions, and who has access. For example:

- **ChatGPT Enterprise** – Approved for: drafting communications, brainstorming, research, summarizing documents. Data restriction: no confidential or restricted data. Access: all employees.
- **GitHub Copilot Business** – Approved for: code generation, code review assistance, documentation drafting. Data restriction: approved for internal code repositories only, not client code. Access: engineering team.
- **Microsoft 365 Copilot** – Approved for: document drafting, email summarization, data analysis in Excel. Data restriction: inherits data classification of the source document. Access: licensed users.

Update this list as tools are added or removed. Specify the review cadence – quarterly is reasonable. And include a catch-all statement: "AI tools not on this list are not approved for use with company data. To request approval for a new tool, contact [governance email]."

Prohibited Uses

Be specific about what employees cannot do with AI tools. Vague prohibitions ("do not use AI irresponsibly") are unenforceable because every person defines "irresponsibly" differently. Specific prohibitions are clear, actionable, and defensible.

Common prohibited uses include:

- **Submitting personal data of customers, employees, or partners** to any external AI tool, unless the tool has been specifically approved for that data type and a data processing agreement is in place.
- **Submitting credentials, API keys, passwords, or access tokens** to any AI tool under any circumstances.

- **Submitting confidential or restricted data** to any AI tool that has not been approved for that data classification level.
- **Using AI to make final decisions** in regulated domains (hiring, lending, insurance, healthcare) without qualified human review and approval.
- **Using AI to generate legal, medical, or financial advice** that will be provided to clients or customers without review by a qualified professional.
- **Using AI to impersonate individuals**, create deepfakes, or generate misleading content.
- **Using AI to conduct surveillance** of employees or customers beyond what is authorized by existing policies and applicable law.
- **Submitting code from client projects or engagements** to any AI tool without explicit written authorization from the client.
- **Using AI-generated content in regulatory filings or legal proceedings** without disclosure and qualified professional review.

Notice that these prohibitions are specific enough that an employee can read them and know, without interpretation, whether a particular action is allowed. "Do not submit personal data to external AI tools" is enforceable. "Use AI responsibly with personal data" is not.

Data Classification Requirements

This section maps your data classification scheme to your AI tools. It answers the question every employee has: "Can I put this data into this tool?"

If you have an existing data classification framework (most organizations classify data into tiers like Public, Internal, Confidential, and Restricted), map each tier to AI tool permissions:

- **Public data** – May be submitted to any approved AI tool. No restrictions.
- **Internal data** – May be submitted to enterprise-licensed AI tools with data processing agreements only (e.g., ChatGPT Enterprise, Microsoft 365 Copilot). May not be submitted to free-tier or consumer AI tools.
- **Confidential data** – May be submitted only to AI tools that have been specifically assessed and approved for confidential data processing by the

AI Governance Committee. Requires data processing agreement, audit rights, and documented data handling controls.

- **Restricted data** (PII, PHI, financial data, trade secrets) — May not be submitted to any external AI tool. May be processed only by internally hosted AI systems that have completed a full security and privacy assessment.

If you do not yet have a data classification framework, this is the moment to create a simple one. Four tiers is enough. The AI AUP is actually an excellent forcing function for data classification because it makes the consequences of not classifying data concrete: if you do not know what classification level a piece of data is, you do not know which AI tools you can use it with.

Output Review Requirements

AI-generated content is not automatically trustworthy. This section establishes the review requirements for AI outputs before they are used.

At minimum:

- All AI-generated content intended for external use (client deliverables, marketing materials, public communications) must be reviewed and approved by a qualified human before distribution.
- All AI-generated code must pass code review processes before being deployed to production environments. AI-generated code is treated the same as human-generated code for review purposes — no shortcuts because the AI wrote it.
- AI-generated analysis, recommendations, or decisions in regulated contexts (financial, legal, medical, employment) must be reviewed and validated by a qualified professional in the relevant domain.
- AI-generated content must not be represented as original human work unless it has been substantially revised by a human.

The standard to communicate is simple: AI is a drafting tool, not a publishing tool. Everything it produces goes through the same quality gates as human-produced work — and in high-risk contexts, additional gates.

Disclosure Requirements

When must employees tell customers, partners, or colleagues that AI was involved? This is a judgment call that varies by context, and your policy should provide clear guidance rather than leaving it to individual discretion.

Consider requiring disclosure when: AI-generated content constitutes a significant portion of a client deliverable, AI was used to analyze personal or sensitive data belonging to the recipient, AI-assisted decisions affect the recipient (employment decisions, credit decisions, service eligibility), or regulatory requirements mandate disclosure (EU AI Act Article 50 requires disclosure for certain AI interactions, including chatbots and deepfakes).

Consider not requiring disclosure when: AI was used as a productivity tool in the same way spell-check or search engines are used (drafting assistance, grammar correction, formatting), the AI contribution was minor and the human substantially shaped the final output, or the context is purely internal and does not affect external stakeholders.

The principle behind disclosure is straightforward: if a reasonable person would want to know that AI was involved, disclose it.

Incident Reporting

Employees need to know how to report AI-related problems. This section should make reporting as frictionless as possible. If reporting requires filling out a 20-field form and routing it through three levels of management, people will not report. If reporting requires sending an email to a known address with a brief description, people will.

Define what should be reported: suspected data leaks through AI tools (e.g., accidentally submitting confidential data to an unapproved tool), AI outputs that appear to contain someone else's proprietary content, AI outputs that are discriminatory, biased, or harmful, discovery of shadow AI (unapproved tools being used by colleagues), AI system malfunctions or unexpected behavior, and any situation where an employee is unsure whether their AI use complies with this policy.

Provide a single reporting channel: an email address, a form, a Slack channel, or a helpdesk ticket category. One channel. Not five. Not "report data incidents to security, report bias concerns to ethics, and report policy questions to compliance." One channel, and the governance team triages from there.

Explicitly state that reporting in good faith will not result in punishment, even if the reporter was the one who made the mistake. If employees fear punishment for reporting their own errors, they will hide them, and you will learn about the problem from a regulator or a journalist instead.

Consequences

State the consequences of policy violations clearly and proportionally. Not every violation warrants the same response. An employee who accidentally submits internal data to the wrong AI tool is in a different category from an employee who deliberately uses AI to fabricate client reports.

A reasonable consequence framework includes:

- **First unintentional violation** – counseling and mandatory retraining on the AI AUP.
- **Repeated unintentional violations** – formal written warning, retraining, and temporary restriction of AI tool access.
- **Intentional violation or gross negligence** – disciplinary action up to and including termination, consistent with the organization's existing disciplinary procedures.
- **Violations involving legal or regulatory breach** – escalation to legal counsel and relevant authorities as required by law.

Review Schedule

Specify how often the policy is reviewed and what triggers an out-of-cycle review.

At minimum, the AI AUP should be reviewed annually. Given the pace of AI development, semi-annual review is better. Out-of-cycle reviews should be triggered by: the adoption of a significant new AI tool, a material change in regulatory requirements, a significant AI incident, a material change in the organization's AI risk profile, or a major vendor change (e.g., your enterprise AI provider changes its data handling practices).

Acknowledgment

Require every person in scope to acknowledge that they have read and understood the policy. This is not a legal formality — it is a governance control. You cannot enforce a policy that people claim they never saw.

Use whatever mechanism your organization uses for other policy acknowledgments: a digital signature in your HRIS, a signed form, an acknowledgment checkbox in your LMS after a training module. The mechanism matters less than the documentation. You need a record that each person in scope acknowledged the policy and the date they did so.

SMB Spotlight: The One-Page AI Acceptable Use Policy

If you are a 20-person company, the full template above is more than you need right now. You need a one-page policy that covers four things: (1) the approved tools your team can use, (2) the data they must never submit to AI tools (PII, credentials, confidential client data), (3) the review requirement (all AI-generated output used externally must be reviewed by a human), and (4) how to report problems (an email address).

That is it. One page, four sections, clear language. A one-page policy that everyone reads and follows is infinitely better than a 30-page policy that no one reads. You can add complexity later, as your AI use matures and your governance program evolves.

Action: Draft your one-page AI AUP this week using the template in Appendix A. Get it signed by your CEO and distributed to all employees. This is a same-week task, not a same-quarter task.

Action Item: Complete AI Acceptable Use Policy Template

Appendix A contains a complete, fillable AI Acceptable Use Policy template. It includes: purpose statement, scope definition, definitions section, approved AI tools list, prohibited uses, data classification matrix, output review requirements, disclosure requirements, incident reporting channel and process, consequence framework, review schedule, and acknowledgment signature block.

Customize it for your organization by filling in your specific tool names, data classification levels, reporting channel, and governance committee name. Have your legal team review the consequence section for consistency with your existing employment policies. Then distribute, train, and get signatures.

Shadow AI: Why Prohibition Does Not Work

If your instinct after reading the last section is to lock everything down — ban all AI tools, block the domains, monitor for violations — you are not alone. It is the reflexive response of every security-minded leader who sees a new, poorly understood technology entering the organization. And it is wrong.

Prohibition does not work for AI, for the same reason it does not work for most consumer technologies that enter the enterprise: employees will find workarounds because the tools are genuinely useful for their jobs.

Real-World Example: Samsung's AI Ban — Why Prohibition Doesn't Work

In early 2023, Samsung banned ChatGPT across the company after discovering that employees had leaked proprietary semiconductor code by pasting it into the tool. The ban was a reasonable immediate response. But the problems did not end there.

Within weeks of the ban being selectively lifted for certain use cases, three separate engineers in Samsung's semiconductor division leaked source code and internal meeting transcripts in distinct incidents. The pattern was clear: the ban had created pent-up demand without building any governance infrastructure. When access returned — even partial access — the flood of usage happened without guardrails, without training, and without the muscle memory of safe AI use that employees develop when they use governed tools regularly.

The lesson is not that Samsung should have allowed unrestricted use. The lesson is that a ban is not a governance strategy. It is a temporary containment measure that, if not replaced quickly by a real governance framework, creates worse outcomes than managed use. Banning AI creates a period of suppressed demand. When that dam breaks — and it always breaks, because the business value of AI tools is too compelling to ignore permanently — the uncontrolled flood is more damaging than a managed flow would have been.

Samsung's experience is not unique. Organizations across industries have reported the same pattern: ban the tool, discover that employees use it anyway (on personal devices, through VPNs, through alternative tools that are not blocked), eventually lift the ban, and face a surge of uncontrolled usage.

The better approach has three components.

First, provide approved alternatives that are at least as good as what employees find on their own. This is the critical point that many organizations miss. If your "approved" AI solution is a locked-down, slow, limited tool that produces worse results than the free version of ChatGPT, employees will use ChatGPT. You cannot win the shadow AI battle by offering an inferior product. Enterprise AI licenses — ChatGPT Enterprise, Microsoft 365 Copilot, Google Gemini for Workspace, Anthropic's Claude for Enterprise — provide data protection, audit logging, and contractual guarantees while delivering capability that is equal to or better than consumer versions. The marginal cost of enterprise licenses is trivial compared to the risk of uncontrolled consumer AI use.

Second, implement discovery mechanisms to detect shadow AI. You cannot govern what you cannot see, and you should assume that some AI use is happening outside your approved channels. Detection methods include:

- **Network monitoring for AI API traffic.** Monitor DNS queries and network traffic for known AI service domains (api.openai.com, api.anthropic.com, generativelanguage.googleapis.com, and others). This catches AI use from corporate devices on the corporate network.
- **SaaS management tools.** Platforms like Zylo, Productiv, or Torii detect SaaS application usage across your organization, including AI tools that employees sign up for independently.
- **Browser extension audits.** AI-powered browser extensions (writing assistants, summarizers, meeting transcribers) are a common vector for shadow AI. Regular audits of installed browser extensions on managed devices can identify unapproved AI tools.
- **Employee surveys.** Ask people what they are using. Frame it as enablement, not enforcement. "We want to make sure you have the best

AI tools available — help us understand what you're using today so we can support it or provide approved alternatives."

- **Expense report analysis.** Search expense reports and credit card statements for AI vendor names. Employees who expense AI subscriptions are telling you exactly what shadow AI they are using.

Third, adopt the "managed AI" approach. This means providing enterprise-licensed AI tools with data loss prevention (DLP) integration, centralized audit logging, data processing agreements, and administrative controls — and then actively encouraging employees to use these managed tools instead of finding their own. The managed AI approach transforms shadow AI from a security problem into a supply-and-demand problem: if you supply better tools than what employees can find on their own, demand for shadow AI drops to near zero.

The economics support this approach. An enterprise AI license might cost $20-30 per user per month. A single data breach caused by an employee pasting customer data into an uncontrolled AI tool costs orders of magnitude more. The ROI calculation is not close.

Aligning Policies to Regulatory Requirements

Your policies do not exist in a vacuum. They must satisfy the regulatory requirements that apply to your organization. This section maps specific policy elements to the major regulatory frameworks, so you can verify that your policies provide the coverage regulators expect.

EU AI Act

The EU AI Act is the most prescriptive of the major frameworks, and several of its requirements directly translate to policy obligations.

Article 4: AI Literacy. As of February 2, 2025, all organizations deploying or using AI systems must ensure that their staff have sufficient AI literacy. This is not a suggestion — it is a legally binding obligation that applies to all AI systems, not just high-risk ones. Your AI Acceptable Use Policy and the training program that accompanies it are your primary evidence of Article 4 compliance. The policy itself educates employees about AI risks and proper use. The training and acknowledgment process demonstrates that you delivered that education. If you are subject to the EU AI Act and you do not have an AI AUP with a training component, you are already out of compliance.

Article 9: Risk Management System. For high-risk AI systems, the Act requires a risk management system that is established, documented, maintained, and updated throughout the AI system's lifecycle. Your AI Risk Management Policy is the documentary backbone of this requirement. It must describe how risks are identified, analyzed, estimated, and evaluated, how mitigation measures are selected and implemented, and how residual risks are monitored.

Article 14: Human Oversight. The Act requires that high-risk AI systems be designed to allow effective human oversight. We covered the design principles in Chapter 6. Your policies formalize the oversight requirements: which systems require human review, what level of review is required, who is qualified to perform it, and how oversight effectiveness is monitored.

Article 50: Transparency Obligations. The Act requires that deployers of certain AI systems inform individuals that they are interacting with AI. Your AI Transparency and Disclosure Policy implements this requirement. For AI systems that interact with natural persons (chatbots, virtual assistants), disclosure is mandatory. For AI systems that generate synthetic content (deepfakes, AI-generated text in certain contexts), labeling is mandatory.

NIST AI Risk Management Framework

The NIST AI RMF is voluntary, but it is the de facto standard for AI governance in the United States, and using it demonstrates due diligence in regulatory conversations.

The GOVERN function is most directly relevant to policy:

- **GOVERN 1.1** — Legal and regulatory requirements are identified. Your policies should reference the specific regulations that apply to your organization's AI use.
- **GOVERN 1.2** — Internal stakeholder roles and responsibilities are defined. Your policies should clearly assign accountability for AI governance activities.

- **GOVERN 1.3** — Processes for AI system oversight are defined. Your policies describe the review, approval, and monitoring processes for AI systems.
- **GOVERN 1.4** — Risk tolerances are documented. Your risk management policy should define what level of risk is acceptable and who has authority to make risk tolerance decisions.
- **GOVERN 1.5** — Risk management processes are in place across the AI lifecycle. Your policies should cover the full lifecycle: acquisition/development, deployment, operation, monitoring, and retirement.
- **GOVERN 1.6** — Mechanisms to provide feedback on AI systems are in place. Your incident reporting process provides this feedback mechanism.
- **GOVERN 1.7** — Processes are in place for learning from AI incidents. Your incident response policy should include root cause analysis and lessons-learned workflows.

ISO 42001

If your organization is pursuing or considering ISO 42001 certification (the AI management system standard), your policies directly support several clauses:

Clause 5: Leadership. Requires top management commitment to the AI management system, including establishing policy. Your AI policies, signed and endorsed by executive leadership, are primary evidence.

Clause 7: Support. Requires that the organization determine and provide the resources, competence, awareness, and communication needed for the AI management system. Your training program, policy distribution, and acknowledgment process demonstrate Clause 7 compliance.

Clause 8: Operation. Requires operational planning and control for AI processes. Your procedures — the step-by-step operational documents that implement your policies — satisfy this clause.

The key insight across all three frameworks is that policies are not just governance documents — they are compliance artifacts. When a regulator or auditor asks "how do you govern AI?", the first thing they want to see is your policies. The second thing they want to see is evidence that people actually follow them (training records, acknowledgments, audit results, incident reports). The policy is necessary but not sufficient. You need both the document and the evidence of implementation.

Psychological Acceptability: The Principle That Separates Policy From Shelfware

In 1975, Jerome Saltzer and Michael Schroeder published a paper on the design principles for protecting computer information. Their eighth principle was "psychological acceptability": the security mechanism must not make the resource more difficult to access than if the security mechanism were not present. In other words, if the security is too burdensome, people will bypass it.

This principle, now over fifty years old, is the single most important design criterion for AI governance policies. More AI policies fail because of psychological unacceptability than for any other reason. They fail not because they are wrong, but because they are unusable.

Three failure modes dominate.

The policy is too complex. If your AI AUP is 47 pages long, nobody will read it. They will sign the acknowledgment form because they are told to, and then they will use AI the same way they used it before the policy existed. The length of a policy document is inversely correlated with its actual influence on behavior. This does not mean your policies should be simplistic — it means they should be layered. A one-page summary that covers the essential rules, backed by a detailed reference document for edge cases and specific situations. Most employees read the summary. The people who need the detail — managers, compliance staff, power users — read the full document.

The policy is too restrictive. If your policy prohibits everything that is genuinely useful about AI, employees will work around it. They will use personal devices. They will use personal accounts. They will copy data to personal cloud storage and then submit it to AI tools from there. Every restriction in your policy should pass a cost-benefit test: does the risk this restriction mitigates justify the productivity loss it imposes? If the answer is no, the restriction will be ignored, and an ignored restriction is worse than no restriction at all — because it trains people that your policies are aspirational suggestions rather than enforceable rules.

The policy does not match reality. If your policy requires pre-approval for every AI interaction and your approval process takes two weeks, employees who need AI output by Friday will skip the approval process. If your policy requires documenting every AI query and your employees make 50 queries per day, the documentation requirement is dead on arrival. Your policies must be designed for how people actually work, not for how you wish they worked. This requires talking to the people who use AI tools before you finalize the policy. Ask them what they use, how they use it, what restrictions would be reasonable, and what restrictions would force them to find workarounds. Their answers will save you from writing policies that look great on paper and fail completely in practice.

The sweet spot is a policy that is:

- **Clear enough to follow.** An employee who reads the policy can determine, without asking anyone, whether a specific action is allowed. If the policy requires interpretation, it will be interpreted differently by every person who reads it, and you do not have a policy — you have a suggestion.
- **Flexible enough to accommodate real work.** The policy provides guardrails, not handcuffs. It tells employees what boundaries they must stay within, and then gives them freedom within those boundaries to use AI in whatever way serves their work.
- **Specific enough to be enforceable.** If a violation occurs, you can point to the specific provision that was violated. "Do not use AI irresponsibly" is not enforceable because no two people agree on what "irresponsibly" means. "Do not submit data classified as Confidential or Restricted to AI tools not on the approved list" is enforceable because the terms are defined and the requirement is binary.

Test your policy before you deploy it. Give the draft to five employees in different roles and ask them to read it. Then ask them three questions: What are you allowed to use AI for? What are you not allowed to use AI for? If something goes wrong, what do you do? If they cannot answer all three questions correctly and consistently, revise the policy until they can.

Policy Review and Change Management

An AI policy is not a document you write once and file away. It is a living instrument that must evolve as the technology changes, as your organization's AI use matures, as regulations are updated, and as incidents reveal gaps in your current approach.

Review Cadence

Establish a minimum review cadence and a set of triggers for out-of-cycle reviews.

Scheduled reviews: At minimum, review all AI policies annually. For the AI Acceptable Use Policy, semi-annual review is strongly recommended, given the pace of AI tool development. Each review should assess: are the approved tools still current? Are the prohibited uses still relevant? Are the data classification mappings still accurate? Has the regulatory environment changed? Have incidents revealed gaps?

Triggered reviews: In addition to scheduled reviews, specific events should trigger an immediate policy review:

- A significant new AI tool is adopted or proposed for adoption.
- A new regulation takes effect or existing regulation is materially amended.
- A significant AI incident occurs, internally or at a peer organization.
- A major vendor changes its data handling practices, terms of service, or security posture.
- Your organization undergoes a significant change (merger, acquisition, new market entry, new customer segment).

Version Control and Distribution

Treat policies like software. Version them. Track changes. Maintain a changelog that documents what changed, when, and why. When a policy is updated, distribute the new version to all personnel in scope, clearly communicate what changed (a "what's new" summary is more likely to be read than the full updated document), and require re-acknowledgment of the updated policy.

Store the current version in a location that is accessible to everyone in scope — not a folder that requires special permissions, not a document management system that nobody uses, not an email attachment that gets buried. A dedicated intranet page or governance portal is ideal. If you do not have one, a shared drive folder that everyone knows about is fine.

Training and Acknowledgment

Policy without training is a compliance artifact. Policy with training is a governance control.

Your training program should cover: what the policy requires (the rules), why the policy requires it (the risks), how to comply (the approved tools, the data classification, the reporting channel), and what happens when things go wrong (the incident response process and the consequence framework).

Training frequency should match your policy review cadence. At minimum, annual training for all personnel, with additional training when the policy is materially updated. New hires should receive AI policy training as part of onboarding — if they are going to use AI tools from day one, they should know the rules from day one.

Track completion rates aggressively. Training that 92% of employees complete is training that 8% of employees missed, and the incident will come from the 8%. Your governance committee should receive regular reports on training completion rates and should have escalation authority for non-completion.

Putting It All Together

Writing AI policies is not inherently difficult. The challenge is not the drafting — it is the design choices. Which AI tools to approve. Where to draw the data classification lines. How much restriction to impose. When to require disclosure. How to handle violations.

These are not technical questions. They are risk management questions that require you to balance competing priorities: security versus productivity, compliance versus agility, control versus adoption. Every organization will make these tradeoffs differently, based on their industry, their regulatory environment, their risk appetite, and the maturity of their AI use.

The policy hierarchy gives you the structure. The six core policies give you the scope. The AUP template gives you the starting point. The shadow AI analysis gives you the realistic context. The regulatory mapping gives you the compliance coverage. And psychological acceptability gives you the design principle that determines whether your policies actually work.

Start with the AI Acceptable Use Policy. Get it written, reviewed, approved, trained, and acknowledged within 30 days. Then tackle the next policy in priority order for your organization — usually the vendor policy (because most AI risk sits with vendors) or the incident response policy (because incidents do not wait for your governance program to be complete). Build the full policy suite over two to three quarters, not two to three weeks. And review everything semi-annually, because the AI landscape in January will look different from the AI landscape in July.

The goal is not a perfect policy binder. The goal is clear, enforceable rules that protect your organization while enabling your people to use AI effectively. Policies that people actually follow. That is the standard.

Key Takeaways

- **Start with the AI Acceptable Use Policy.** Of the six core AI policies, the AUP has the broadest impact because it directly governs daily employee behavior. A clear AUP covering approved tools, prohibited uses, data classification, output review, and incident reporting is the single highest-leverage governance document you can produce. If you write only one policy this year, make it this one.
- **Prohibition does not work — managed access does.** Banning AI tools creates pent-up demand that leads to uncontrolled usage when the ban inevitably lifts. Provide enterprise-licensed alternatives that are as good as consumer tools, implement detection mechanisms for shadow AI, and make the approved path easier than the unapproved path.
- **Design for psychological acceptability.** A policy that is too complex, too restrictive, or too disconnected from how people actually work will be ignored. Test your policies with real employees before deployment. If they

cannot answer three questions after reading the policy — what is allowed, what is not allowed, and how to report problems — revise until they can.

- **Policies are compliance artifacts, not just governance documents.** The EU AI Act (Articles 4, 9, 14, 50), NIST AI RMF (GOVERN function), and ISO 42001 (Clauses 5, 7, 8) all expect documented policies as evidence of AI governance. Write your policies with the awareness that regulators and auditors will read them.
- **Review and update policies at least semi-annually.** AI technology, vendor practices, and regulatory requirements change too quickly for annual review to be sufficient. Establish triggered reviews for new tool adoption, regulatory changes, and significant incidents. Treat policies like living documents, not static compliance artifacts.

Chapter 8: Vendor Assessment and Third-Party AI Risk

Here is an uncomfortable truth about AI governance: most of the AI risk in your organization comes from AI you did not build.

You are almost certainly an AI deployer, not an AI developer. You buy AI-powered SaaS tools, subscribe to platforms that embed AI into their features, integrate third-party APIs into your workflows, and let your employees use AI assistants someone else trained on someone else's data. The model architectures, training data, safety controls, and failure modes of these systems are not yours to inspect. They are someone else's design decisions, and you inherit the consequences.

This is not a fringe concern. According to Gartner's 2025 AI in the Enterprise survey, 87 percent of enterprise AI usage involves third-party models or AI-embedded software rather than internally developed systems. For small and mid-sized businesses, that number is closer to 98 percent. You are not fine-tuning large language models. You are subscribing to tools that use them.

And yet, when something goes wrong — when customer data leaks through a third-party AI tool, when a vendor's model hallucinates in a way that creates liability for you, when a supplier's AI system produces biased outputs you relied on for decisions — the consequences land on you. Your customers do not care that you outsourced the AI. Your regulators do not care that the model was trained by someone else. Your board does not care that the vendor promised everything was fine.

Your biggest governance challenge is not building AI responsibly. It is managing the AI that other people built.

This chapter gives you the framework for doing that. We start with the AI supply chain — who provides what, and where the risk concentrates. Then we walk through a 10-question vendor assessment framework you can deploy immediately. We evaluate the emerging market for AI governance tooling — what is worth buying, what is free, and what is hype. We tackle shadow AI, the services your employees are using without your knowledge. We cover ongoing monitoring, because vendor assessment is not a one-time event. And we close with the AI Bill of Materials, the emerging standard for supply chain transparency that regulators are starting to require.

[FIGURE B1-18] shows the vendor assessment scorecard. [FIGURE B1-19] shows the AI governance tooling landscape. Keep both accessible as you read.

The AI Supply Chain

Before you can assess vendor risk, you need to understand the supply chain that delivers AI capabilities to your organization. It is deeper and more layered than most organizations realize, and each layer carries its own risks.

Layer 1: Model Providers

At the foundation are the companies that build and train the large AI models — OpenAI, Anthropic, Google DeepMind, Meta, Mistral, Cohere, and a growing roster of others. These companies invest billions of dollars in training infrastructure, curate massive datasets, and make architectural decisions that determine the model's capabilities, limitations, biases, and safety properties.

When you use a model provider's API directly, the relationship is reasonably clear. You send data to their API, their model processes it, and you get a response. The risk questions are straightforward: Where does your data go? Is it used for training? What are the model's known failure modes? What safety mitigations are in place?

But most organizations do not use model APIs directly. They use products built on top of them, which brings us to the next layer.

Layer 2: Platform Providers

Amazon Web Services, Microsoft Azure, and Google Cloud Platform all offer AI services built on top of foundation models — sometimes their own, sometimes licensed from model providers. AWS Bedrock gives you access to models from Anthropic, Meta, Mistral, and others through a unified API. Azure OpenAI

Service provides OpenAI's models with Microsoft's enterprise wrapper. Google Cloud's Vertex AI offers Google's models alongside third-party options.

Platform providers add enterprise features: VPC endpoints, data residency controls, audit logging, access management. They also add a layer of abstraction. When you use Azure OpenAI Service, your data goes to Microsoft's infrastructure, which forwards it to an OpenAI model running in Microsoft's data centers. Your contractual relationship is with Microsoft. Your data processing is governed by Microsoft's terms. But the model's behavior — its hallucination tendencies, its bias profile, its response to adversarial prompts — is determined by OpenAI.

The split between who controls the infrastructure and who controls the model is a governance headache. Your vendor is Microsoft, but the risk-generating component is OpenAI's model. If the model produces harmful output, your recourse runs through Microsoft's contract, but the root cause sits in OpenAI's training choices.

Layer 3: Application Vendors

This is where most organizations encounter AI: through SaaS applications that embed AI features into products you already use. Salesforce Einstein, Microsoft Copilot, Notion AI, Grammarly, Zendesk AI, HubSpot AI — the list grows weekly. These vendors take foundation models, fine-tune them or wrap them in product-specific logic, and deliver AI capabilities as features within their applications.

The risk surface at this layer is substantial because you often have limited visibility into the implementation. When your sales team uses Salesforce Einstein to score leads, what model powers the scoring? What data was it trained on? How does it handle demographic features that could introduce bias? When your marketing team uses an AI writing assistant, where does the text you submit go? Is it retained? Is it used to improve the model for other customers?

Many application vendors treat their AI implementation as proprietary. They will tell you they use "advanced AI" or "state-of-the-art language models" without specifying which model, what version, or what customizations they have made. This opacity makes risk assessment difficult.

Layer 4: Plugin and Integration Providers

The newest and least understood layer is the plugins, integrations, and agent-to-agent connections that extend AI systems. Model Context Protocol (MCP) servers give AI assistants access to external tools and data sources. Agent-to-Agent (A2A) protocols let AI systems communicate with each other. Browser extensions, Zapier integrations, and custom GPTs all fall into this category.

This layer introduces supply chain risks most organizations have not yet considered. An MCP server can expose your internal data to a third-party AI system. A custom GPT can exfiltrate data through its configuration. An AI agent that calls other AI agents creates transitive trust relationships that are difficult to map and harder to control.

Risk Compounds Across Layers

The key point about this supply chain is that risk is not additive — it is multiplicative. When your employee uses a SaaS tool (Layer 3) that runs on Azure (Layer 2) using an OpenAI model (Layer 1) with a third-party plugin (Layer 4), you are exposed to risk from all four layers at once. A vulnerability at any layer can compromise the entire stack. A data handling failure at any layer can expose your information.

You do not need to audit every layer of every vendor's stack. But you do need to understand the layers, know which questions to ask at each one, and make risk-informed decisions about which vendors and which layers you are willing to trust.

The 10-Question Vendor AI Risk Assessment

Vendor risk assessment does not have to be complicated. You do not need a 200-point questionnaire or a six-month evaluation cycle to get a meaningful read on a vendor's AI risk posture. You need the right 10 questions, asked consistently, scored objectively.

The framework below is built to be practical. Each question maps to a specific risk category. Each is scored on a 1 to 5 scale. The total gives you a 50-point vendor risk score that lets you make informed decisions quickly.

Question 1: What Model(s) Does the Vendor Use, and What Are the Known Limitations?

Start with the fundamentals. What AI model powers the vendor's product? A proprietary model they built? A fine-tuned version of a foundation model? An off-the-shelf API call to GPT-4 or Claude? Understanding the model architecture tells you about the risk profile.

A vendor using a well-documented foundation model from a major provider (OpenAI, Anthropic, Google) inherits that model's known limitations – but you can at least research those limitations. A vendor using a proprietary model gives you no external reference point for understanding its behavior. A vendor that cannot tell you what model they use is a red flag.

Score 5 if the vendor clearly documents the model(s) used, the version, and known limitations. Score 1 if the vendor refuses to disclose the model or claims not to know.

Question 2: Where Does Your Data Go When Submitted to the AI? Is It Used for Training?

This is the question that separates vendors who take data governance seriously from those who do not. When your employee types a customer complaint into the vendor's AI-powered support tool, what happens to that text? Where does it go? What systems process it? Is it stored? Is it used to train or fine-tune the model?

The best vendors provide clear data flow documentation showing exactly where data travels, which systems process it, and what happens to it afterward. They offer explicit opt-outs from training data usage and data processing addenda that give you contractual control.

Score 5 if the vendor provides detailed data flow documentation, does not use customer data for training by default, and offers contractual commitments on data handling. Score 1 if the vendor's terms of service allow unrestricted use of customer data for training, or if data flows are undocumented.

Question 3: What Is the Vendor's Data Retention and Deletion Policy?

How long does the vendor retain data submitted to their AI system? Can you request deletion? Does the vendor comply with data subject access requests under GDPR or similar regulations? If the model was trained on your data before you opted out, can that training be reversed?

Retention policies matter because they determine your exposure window. A vendor that retains AI interaction data for 30 days has a different risk profile from one that retains it indefinitely. A vendor that cannot delete data on request may make it impossible for you to comply with data protection regulations.

Score 5 if the vendor has clearly defined retention periods, supports deletion requests, and provides documentation on how deletion is implemented. Score 1 if the vendor retains data indefinitely with no deletion mechanism.

Question 4: Does the Vendor Have SOC 2 Type II, ISO 27001, or Equivalent Security Certifications?

Certifications are not a guarantee of security, but they are evidence the vendor has submitted to external scrutiny. SOC 2 Type II is particularly valuable because it evaluates not just whether controls exist but whether they operate effectively over time.

For AI vendors specifically, look for certifications that are recent and relevant. A SOC 2 Type II report from 2023 that predates the vendor's AI features may not cover the AI-specific infrastructure. Ask whether the AI components are within scope.

Score 5 if the vendor holds current SOC 2 Type II and ISO 27001 with AI components in scope. Score 1 if the vendor has no third-party security certifications.

Question 5: How Does the Vendor Handle AI-Specific Risks (Hallucination, Bias, Prompt Injection)?

This is where you separate AI-native thinking from checkbox compliance. Every AI system that uses large language models will hallucinate — generate plausible but false information. Every AI system trained on historical data will reflect biases in that data. Every AI system that takes natural language input is potentially vulnerable to prompt injection.

Mature vendors acknowledge these risks explicitly and describe their mitigations. They test for hallucination rates and publish the results. They evaluate their models for bias across protected categories. They implement input validation and output filtering to mitigate prompt injection. Immature vendors claim their AI "does not hallucinate" or "is not biased" — statements that should immediately lower your confidence.

Score 5 if the vendor provides documented mitigation strategies for hallucination, bias, and prompt injection with quantitative evidence. Score 1 if the vendor denies or ignores AI-specific risks.

Question 6: What Human Oversight Mechanisms Are Built into the Product?

Chapter 6 covered human oversight design in depth. Now apply those principles to vendor evaluation. Does the product allow you to configure human review checkpoints? Can you require human approval before the AI takes consequential actions? Can you review and edit AI outputs before they are finalized? Does the product provide audit trails that support after-the-fact review?

A vendor that designs for human oversight gives you the controls to implement your governance policy. A vendor that treats the AI as a black box producing outputs you must accept gives you no governance surface.

Score 5 if the product provides configurable human oversight at multiple levels with full audit trails. Score 1 if the product offers no human oversight mechanisms.

Question 7: Does the Vendor Provide Incident Notification for AI-Specific Failures?

When the vendor's AI system fails — and it will — how do you find out? Does the vendor have an AI-specific incident classification? Do they notify customers when the model produces systematic errors, when a bias is discovered, when a data breach affects AI training data, or when a prompt injection vulnerability is identified?

Standard incident notification processes often do not cover AI-specific failures because the categories were not designed for them. A model that starts hallucinating at a higher rate is not a "security incident" under traditional definitions, but it is an AI incident that affects your risk posture.

Score 5 if the vendor has defined AI-specific incident categories and commits to timely notification. Score 1 if the vendor has no AI-specific incident notification process.

Question 8: What Compliance Frameworks Does the Vendor Claim Alignment With?

The regulatory landscape for AI is maturing fast. The EU AI Act is in effect with enforcement beginning in 2025. The NIST AI Risk Management Framework provides voluntary guidance that many organizations are adopting. ISO 42001 establishes the standard for AI management systems. The OECD AI Principles provide international consensus on responsible AI.

A vendor that has evaluated their product against these frameworks — even if full compliance is not yet achieved — demonstrates governance awareness. Look for specifics rather than vague claims. "We are aligned with the EU AI Act" is marketing. "We have classified our product as limited-risk under the EU AI Act, and here is our conformity assessment" is governance.

Score 5 if the vendor demonstrates specific, documented alignment with relevant frameworks and can show evidence. Score 1 if the vendor makes no reference to any compliance framework.

Question 9: What Contractual Protections Exist?

Governance is only as strong as the contracts that enforce it. When evaluating an AI vendor, look for specific contractual provisions:

Liability. Who is liable when the AI produces harmful output? Many vendors attempt to disclaim all liability for AI outputs. Push back. If the vendor's AI tool generates biased hiring recommendations that expose you to discrimination claims, the vendor should share in that liability.

Indemnification. Does the vendor indemnify you for intellectual property claims arising from AI-generated output? With ongoing litigation around AI training data and copyright, this protection is increasingly important.

SLAs. Does the vendor commit to performance standards for the AI system — accuracy rates, availability, response times? AI-specific SLAs are still uncommon, but leading vendors are beginning to offer them.

Right to audit. Can you audit the vendor's AI systems, data practices, and security controls? At minimum, can you request and review their SOC 2 report?

Score 5 if the contract includes AI-specific liability provisions, indemnification, SLAs, and audit rights. Score 1 if the contract disclaims all liability for AI outputs and provides no audit rights.

Question 10: What Is the Vendor's AI Governance Maturity?

This is the meta-question: does the vendor have their own AI governance program? Do they have a responsible AI policy? An AI ethics board or governance committee? Published AI principles? A track record of responsible disclosure when things go wrong?

A vendor with a mature governance program is more likely to handle AI risks well because they have the organizational structures to identify, assess, and mitigate those risks. A vendor without a governance program is making AI decisions ad hoc, and you are hoping they make good ones.

Score 5 if the vendor has a documented AI governance program with published principles, a governance structure, and a track record of transparency. Score 1 if the vendor has no visible AI governance program.

SMB Spotlight: The 10-Question Vendor Assessment You Can Do in 30 Minutes

You do not need a 200-point questionnaire. The 10 questions above, scored 1 to 5 each, give you a 50-point vendor risk score. Here is how to interpret it:

- **Above 40: Low risk.** The vendor demonstrates strong AI governance. Proceed with standard monitoring.
- **25 to 40: Medium risk.** The vendor has gaps. Proceed with additional controls — enhanced monitoring, restricted data access, contractual requirements for improvement.
- **Below 25: High risk.** The vendor's AI governance is insufficient. Do not proceed, or require remediation before deployment.

You do not need perfect information to score these questions. If the vendor cannot answer a question at all, that is a score of 1. If the vendor provides vague reassurances without documentation, that is a 2. Specificity and evidence drive higher scores.

Action: Score your top 3 AI vendors this week using the scorecard in Appendix A.

Action Item: AI Vendor Assessment Scorecard

The full scorecard is available in Appendix A. It includes the 10 questions with a detailed scoring rubric for each (criteria for scores 1 through 5), risk tier thresholds (low, medium, high), recommended actions per tier, and a template you can adapt for your organization. Print it, share it with your procurement team, and make it a mandatory step in your vendor evaluation process.

Evaluating AI Governance Tooling

As the AI governance market matures, a growing ecosystem of tools promises to help you manage AI risk, monitor AI systems, and demonstrate compliance. The challenge is navigating a market that barely existed 18 months ago and is evolving faster than most organizations can evaluate.

Here is a clear-eyed assessment of what is available as of early 2026 [FIGURE B1-19].

Market Context

The AI governance tooling market reached $492 million in 2026 according to Gartner, up from roughly $150 million in 2024. Gartner published its first Market Guide for AI Governance Solutions in November 2025. Forrester published its first Wave for AI Governance Platforms in Q3 2025. The market is real, but it is young. Most products are less than three years old. Category definitions are still forming. And the gap between vendor marketing and delivered capability remains wide.

Enterprise Platforms

If you are a large organization with dedicated AI governance budget, the enterprise platforms offer the most comprehensive capabilities:

Credo AI was named a Leader in Forrester's first AI Governance Wave (Q3 2025). It provides policy-based governance across the AI lifecycle — from development through deployment and monitoring. Its strength is translating regulatory requirements into enforceable technical controls. Credo AI integrates with major ML platforms and provides audit-ready documentation. It is priced for enterprises, and implementation typically requires dedicated resources.

IBM watsonx.governance, also a Leader in the Forrester Wave, benefits from IBM's deep enterprise relationships and its integration with the broader watsonx AI platform. It offers model monitoring, drift detection, bias evaluation, and lifecycle management. If your organization is already an IBM shop, watsonx.governance slots into your existing tooling. If you are not, the IBM ecosystem lock-in is a consideration.

OneTrust AI Governance extends OneTrust's well-established privacy and compliance platform into AI governance. Its strength is bridging AI governance with privacy, data governance, and risk management in a single platform. For organizations already using OneTrust for GDPR compliance, adding AI governance within the same platform can simplify workflows.

Holistic AI focuses on AI risk management and compliance, with particular strength in bias auditing and regulatory alignment. It offers both a platform and advisory services, which can be valuable if your team lacks in-house AI governance expertise.

ValidMind is purpose-built for financial services, providing model risk management that aligns with SR 11-7 (the Federal Reserve's model risk management guidance) and SS1/23 (the Bank of England's equivalent). If you are in banking or financial services, ValidMind speaks your regulatory language.

Mid-Market Solutions

If enterprise platform pricing is out of reach but you need more than open-source tools can provide:

LogicGate Risk Cloud offers a configurable risk and compliance platform that can be adapted for AI governance. It is not AI governance-specific, but its flexibility allows you to build AI risk assessment workflows, vendor assessment processes, and governance registers without enterprise pricing. This is a strong option for mid-market organizations that need structure without six-figure license fees.

Arthur AI provides model monitoring and observability — detecting drift, bias, and anomalies in production AI systems. It is more focused on the technical monitoring layer than the governance policy layer, but for organizations whose primary concern is "is this AI system still performing as expected," Arthur delivers.

Fiddler AI offers model performance management with a tiered pricing structure. Its Lite tier (10 models, 10 seats) provides an accessible entry point for organizations that want to start monitoring AI systems without a major commitment. Fiddler's strength is explainability — helping you understand why an AI system made a particular decision.

Open Source

For organizations with limited budgets and some technical capability, open-source tools provide genuine value:

MLflow is the de facto standard for model lifecycle management. It handles model versioning, experiment tracking, model registry, and deployment management. It does not provide governance policy enforcement, but it gives you the foundation — you cannot govern AI systems you cannot inventory and track. MLflow is backed by Databricks and has a large community.

Fairlearn is Microsoft's open-source toolkit for assessing and improving the fairness of AI systems. It provides metrics for evaluating bias across demographic groups and algorithms for mitigating detected bias. If your concern is "does this model treat different groups equitably," Fairlearn is the standard starting point.

Microsoft Responsible AI Toolbox bundles multiple open-source tools — Fairlearn for fairness, InterpretML for explainability, Error Analysis for model debugging, and others — into a coherent collection. It is free, well-documented, and integrates with Azure ML (though it does not require Azure).

AI Verify is Singapore's government-backed AI governance testing framework. It tests AI systems against 11 governance principles covering transparency, fairness, robustness, and accountability. It is open source, well-documented, and benefits from government backing that gives it credibility in regulatory contexts.

For organizations looking to demonstrate governance compliance with minimal budget, AI Verify is an underrated option.

SMB-Accessible Options

If you are a small or mid-sized business, you need tools that are free or nearly free to start:

Weights and Biases (W&B) offers a free tier for experiment tracking and model monitoring. It is developer-oriented, but if you have anyone on staff who works with AI models, W&B provides visibility into model performance.

Arize AI offers a free tier for model observability, including drift detection and performance monitoring. Like W&B, it is technically oriented, but it provides the monitoring foundation that governance requires.

Fiddler Lite (10 models, 10 seats) provides a usable subset of Fiddler's enterprise capabilities at no cost. For an SMB with a handful of AI models to monitor, this may be all you need.

Choosing the Right Approach

Here is the decision framework, simplified:

If you are an enterprise with budget: Evaluate the commercial platforms. Credo AI and IBM watsonx.governance are the current leaders, but your decision should factor in existing vendor relationships, regulatory requirements, and integration needs. Expect to spend six figures annually.

If you are a mid-market organization: Start with LogicGate for governance workflow and process, supplement with open-source tools (MLflow for lifecycle management, Fairlearn for bias assessment) for technical monitoring. If you have AI governance consulting budget, bring in Holistic AI or a similar firm to design your program, then maintain it with these tools.

If you are an SMB: Start with open source. MLflow for model inventory and lifecycle tracking. Fairlearn for bias assessment. AI Verify for governance testing. Fiddler Lite or Arize free tier for monitoring. This combination gives you real governance capability at near-zero cost, though you will need some technical capacity to implement it.

Do not buy tooling before you have a governance program to implement. Tools enforce policy. If you do not have a policy — if you skipped Chapter 5 — buying a tool will give you a dashboard with no strategy behind it.

Shadow AI Management

Shadow AI is the AI equivalent of shadow IT — AI tools and services used by your employees without your knowledge, outside your governance controls, and beyond your security perimeter. It is not a theoretical risk. It is happening in your organization right now.

A 2025 survey by Salesforce found that 55 percent of employees using AI at work reported using tools that their employer had not approved. A separate study by Cyberhaven analyzed actual network traffic and found that 11 percent of data employees pasted into ChatGPT was confidential. Not "potentially sensitive." Confidential. Customer data, source code, financial projections, strategy documents — all submitted to third-party AI services without any organizational oversight.

> **Real-World Example: The OmniGPT Breach — 34 Million Conversations Exposed**
>
> In February 2025, a hacker posted 34 million lines of user conversations from OmniGPT, a third-party AI aggregator that provided access to multiple AI models through a single interface. The leaked data included 30,000 user email addresses, API keys, credentials, and approximately 130 cryptocurrency wallet private keys. Users had submitted this data to OmniGPT assuming it was secure. The aggregator's security posture had never been assessed by the organizations whose employees were using it.
>
> OmniGPT was not a mainstream enterprise tool. It was a convenience service — a way for employees to access multiple AI models without multiple subscriptions. The kind of tool that never appears on a procurement list, never goes through vendor assessment, and never crosses the CISO's desk until after the breach.
>
> The lesson: every third-party AI tool in your environment is a potential data breach vector. You cannot assess what you do not know about.

Discovery

You cannot govern shadow AI until you know it exists. Here are four discovery methods, in order of reliability:

Network monitoring. Monitor DNS queries and web traffic for known AI API endpoints: api.openai.com, api.anthropic.com, generativelanguage.googleapis.com, api.cohere.ai, and the growing list of AI service domains. Your firewall, proxy, or SIEM should be able to flag this traffic. This catches direct API usage but may miss AI features embedded in SaaS tools.

SaaS management platforms. If you use a SaaS management tool (Productiv, Zylo, Torii, or similar), it can identify AI-powered SaaS applications in use across your organization through SSO logs, expense reports, and browser data. This catches the SaaS tools with AI features that network monitoring might miss.

Employee surveys. Ask your employees what AI tools they use. Be explicit that this is not punitive — you want to understand usage so you can provide better tools, not so you can take tools away. Frame it as enablement, not enforcement. Surveys catch tools that technical monitoring misses, particularly mobile apps and browser-based tools accessed from personal devices.

Browser extension audits. AI-powered browser extensions — writing assistants, summarizers, translation tools — run in the browser and can access everything the user sees. Audit your browser extension inventory. Many organizations discover dozens of AI-powered extensions they never approved.

Policy: The Managed AI Approach

The worst response to shadow AI is to ban all AI usage. You will lose that fight. Employees use unauthorized tools because the authorized alternatives are absent, inadequate, or too cumbersome to access. Banning AI without providing alternatives just drives usage underground where you have even less visibility.

Chapter 7 introduced the "managed AI" approach, and it applies directly here. Provide approved AI tools that meet your governance requirements. Make them easy to access — ideally easier than the shadow alternatives. Publish a clear list of approved tools, approved use cases, and prohibited actions (like submitting confidential data to external AI services). Enforce the policy through technical controls, not just memos.

The goal is not to eliminate AI usage. It is to channel AI usage through tools and workflows that you have assessed, that you can monitor, and that your governance program covers.

Technical Controls

Policy alone is insufficient. Supplement it with technical controls:

DNS and proxy blocking. Block access to unauthorized AI services at the network level. This is a blunt instrument — employees will complain, and they may find workarounds — but it establishes a clear boundary. Block by default and allow specific, assessed services through your proxy.

Data Loss Prevention (DLP). Configure DLP rules to detect and prevent sensitive data from being submitted to AI API endpoints. Most enterprise DLP solutions can inspect HTTPS traffic (with appropriate SSL inspection) and apply policies based on the destination and the content. Classify your data, define what cannot go to external AI services, and enforce it technically.

Browser isolation. For AI services you allow but want to control, browser isolation creates a sandboxed environment that prevents data from being copied, downloaded, or exfiltrated. The user can interact with the AI service, but the interaction is contained within the isolation boundary.

None of these controls are perfect. A determined employee with a personal phone and a personal ChatGPT subscription can bypass all of them. The goal is not an impenetrable wall. It is a governance boundary that makes unauthorized usage difficult enough that most employees will use the approved alternatives instead.

Ongoing Vendor Monitoring

Vendor assessment is not a one-time event. The AI vendor you assessed six months ago may have changed its model, updated its data practices, or experienced an incident that fundamentally alters its risk profile. AI systems are not static. They are updated, retrained, and modified continuously, and each change can introduce new risks.

Drift Detection

AI models drift. Their performance changes over time as the real-world data they process diverges from the data they were trained on. A vendor's AI system that performed well during your evaluation may degrade in accuracy, increase in bias, or change its behavior in ways that affect your operations.

If you use AI governance monitoring tools (the tools discussed earlier in this chapter), configure them to track the performance of vendor AI systems over time. If you do not have monitoring tools, establish manual checkpoints: quarterly reviews of AI system outputs, periodic accuracy checks against known-good baselines, and user feedback channels that surface performance issues.

Ask your vendors what drift detection they perform on their own systems. Mature vendors monitor their models continuously and can provide performance reports. Immature vendors ship a model and forget about it until customers complain.

Incident Notification

Your contracts with AI vendors should require notification when AI-specific incidents occur. Define what constitutes an AI incident — not just data breaches and system outages, but also:

- Discovery of systematic bias in model outputs
- Model hallucination rates exceeding defined thresholds
- Prompt injection vulnerabilities that affect your data
- Training data contamination or copyright claims against training data
- Model changes that alter behavior in ways material to your use case

Standard vendor incident notification often covers security breaches and downtime but ignores AI-specific failure modes. Make AI incident notification an explicit contractual requirement.

Re-Assessment Triggers

Not every vendor change requires a full re-assessment, but certain events should trigger one:

Model change. If the vendor switches from one foundation model to another, replaces their proprietary model, or upgrades to a significantly different version, re-assess. A vendor that switches from GPT-4 to GPT-5, or from Claude 3.5 to Claude 4, has fundamentally changed the risk-generating component of their product.

Major incident. If the vendor experiences a significant AI-specific incident — a data breach involving AI training data, a widely reported bias issue, a prompt injection vulnerability — re-assess. Even if the incident did not directly affect you, it reveals information about the vendor's governance maturity.

Regulatory change. When new regulations take effect — new EU AI Act requirements, new state-level AI laws, updated NIST guidance — re-assess your vendors against the new requirements. Your compliance obligations may change, and your vendors' compliance posture may need to change with them.

Contract renewal. Use every contract renewal as a re-assessment opportunity. The AI landscape changes fast enough that annual re-assessment is the minimum cadence. Contract renewal gives you leverage to require improvements.

Build these triggers into your vendor management process. Assign responsibility for monitoring triggers and initiating re-assessments. If nobody owns it, it will not happen.

The AI Bill of Materials

Software Bills of Materials (SBOMs) transformed how organizations manage software supply chain risk. The AI Bill of Materials (AI BOM) is poised to do the same for AI.

What It Is

An AI BOM is a structured inventory of all the components that make up an AI system. If an SBOM tells you what software libraries are in your application, an AI BOM tells you what models, datasets, tools, and integrations are in your AI system. It is a transparency document — a way for consumers of AI systems to understand what they are actually using.

Why It Matters

AI supply chain transparency is no longer optional in regulated environments. The EU AI Act's Article 11 requires providers of high-risk AI systems to maintain technical documentation that includes the design specifications, development methodology, and components of the system. Article 53 extends similar requirements to general-purpose AI models. While the Act does not use the term "AI BOM," the documentation requirements effectively mandate one.

Beyond regulatory compliance, AI BOMs serve practical governance purposes. You cannot assess the risk of an AI system you cannot inventory. You cannot monitor a model you do not know the name of. You cannot evaluate bias in a training dataset you have never been told about. The AI BOM makes the invisible visible.

What to Include

A comprehensive AI BOM should include:

Model information. Model name, version, provider, architecture type (transformer, diffusion, etc.), training date, and known limitations. If the system uses multiple models (for example, a retrieval model and a generation model in a RAG architecture), document each one.

Training data description. What data was the model trained on? This does not require a line-by-line dataset inventory — for foundation models, that is impractical. But it should include a description of the data sources, the data collection methodology, the time period covered, and any known biases or gaps in the training data.

Fine-tuning and customization. If the model was fine-tuned on domain-specific data, document the fine-tuning dataset, the fine-tuning methodology, and the intended effect on model behavior. If retrieval-augmented generation (RAG) is used, document the knowledge base and its update cadence.

Tools and plugins. What external tools, plugins, or integrations does the AI system use? MCP servers, API connections, browser tools, database access — anything the AI system can interact with beyond its core model.

Data flows. Where does input data go? What systems process it? Where is output data stored? What data crosses organizational boundaries? A data flow diagram is the most useful format for this information.

Safety and alignment measures. What safety filters, content policies, guardrails, or alignment techniques are applied to the model? What testing was performed to validate these measures?

The Emerging Standard

OWASP CycloneDX, the organization behind the widely adopted SBOM standard, has extended its specification to support AI and machine learning components. CycloneDX's ML BOM specification provides a machine-readable format for documenting model information, datasets, training pipelines, and associated metadata. It integrates with existing SBOM tooling, which means organizations that already generate CycloneDX SBOMs for their software can extend the same processes to cover AI components.

The standard is still maturing. Not all AI vendors can provide CycloneDX-formatted AI BOMs today. But the trajectory is clear: just as SBOMs became a procurement requirement for software (driven by Executive Order 14028 and subsequent regulation), AI BOMs will become a procurement requirement for AI systems. Organizations that start requesting AI BOMs now will be ahead of the curve when it becomes mandatory.

If your vendors cannot provide a formal AI BOM today, start with the basics. Ask for a document that covers the components listed above, in whatever format the vendor can provide. Some transparency is better than none. Over time, push toward structured, machine-readable formats like CycloneDX that can be integrated into your vulnerability management and compliance workflows.

Looking Ahead

For the technical depth behind AI supply chain security — including MCP server vetting, model integrity verification, and supply chain attack vectors — see *Securing Agentic AI (2026 Edition)*, Chapter 7. That book covers the offensive and defensive technical details that complement the governance framework presented here.

Key Takeaways

- **You are probably an AI deployer, not a developer.** Your biggest governance challenge is managing the AI that other people built. Vendor assessment is not optional — it is the centerpiece of most organizations' AI governance programs.

- **The 10-question framework gives you a practical, repeatable assessment.** Score each vendor on a 50-point scale. Above 40 is low risk. Between 25 and 40 is medium risk — proceed with controls. Below 25 is high risk — do not proceed without remediation.

- **Shadow AI is your most immediate threat.** Employees are already using AI tools you have not assessed. Discover what is in use, provide approved alternatives, and enforce boundaries with technical controls. Banning AI outright drives it underground.

- **Vendor assessment is not a one-time event.** AI systems change continuously. Monitor for drift, require incident notification, and re-assess when models change, incidents occur, regulations evolve, or contracts renew.

- **Start building AI Bills of Materials now.** Supply chain transparency is heading toward mandatory. Request component inventories from your vendors today, even in informal formats. When structured standards like CycloneDX become procurement requirements, you will be ready.

Chapter 9: Audit Readiness and Compliance Evidence

The auditors are coming.

This is not a prediction. It is a timeline. The EU AI Act's conformity assessment requirements for high-risk AI systems take effect on August 2, 2026. ISO 42001 certification audits have been happening since early 2024 and are accelerating as organizations race to demonstrate AI governance maturity. The NIST AI Risk Management Framework, while voluntary in the United States, is becoming the de facto benchmark that regulators, investors, and enterprise customers use to evaluate whether you have your house in order. State-level AI legislation in Colorado, Illinois, and Texas references risk management practices that map directly to NIST AI RMF and ISO 42001 concepts.

The question is not whether your AI governance program will face scrutiny. The question is whether it will survive scrutiny.

There is a meaningful difference between having a governance program and being able to prove you have a governance program. You may have risk assessments. You may have human oversight procedures. You may have policies and vendor evaluations and an AI system inventory. But if you cannot produce the documentation, the evidence, and the audit trail that proves all of those things exist and operate effectively — you will fail an audit. And depending on the regulatory regime, failing an audit carries consequences that range from embarrassing to existential.

This chapter is about closing the gap between doing governance and proving governance. We start with what auditors and regulators actually look for — the compliance evidence package that forms the foundation of any audit. Then we walk through the EU AI Act conformity assessment process for high-risk systems, because that is the most immediate regulatory deadline most readers face. We cover the full ISO 42001 certification pathway, including realistic costs and timelines for organizations of different sizes. We explore how NIST AI RMF profiles serve as compliance evidence even when NIST is not your primary regulatory driver. We tackle board reporting, because your governance program needs internal stakeholders aligned just as much as it needs external auditors satisfied. And we close with the shift from point-in-time compliance to continuous compliance — the operational model that makes audit readiness a permanent state rather than a periodic scramble.

[FIGURE B1-20] shows the compliance evidence checklist. [FIGURE B1-21] shows the certification timeline. Keep both accessible as you read.

What Auditors and Regulators Look For

Whether you are facing an EU AI Act conformity assessment, an ISO 42001 certification audit, a NIST AI RMF maturity evaluation, or a customer due diligence review, auditors are looking for the same fundamental thing: evidence that your governance is not aspirational. They want to see that the policies you wrote are the policies you follow, that the controls you designed are the controls you operate, and that the risks you identified are the risks you manage.

The specific evidence varies by framework, but the categories are remarkably consistent. Here is the compliance evidence package that covers the core requirements across all major AI governance frameworks.

AI System Inventory with Risk Classifications

This is the foundation. You cannot govern what you have not inventoried. Auditors will ask for a complete list of AI systems in your organization, including systems you developed internally, systems you procured from vendors, and systems embedded in products you use. Each system should have a risk classification — the EU AI Act uses unacceptable, high, limited, and minimal risk categories. ISO 42001 requires risk assessment for each AI system. NIST AI RMF's MAP function calls for context-specific risk characterization.

If you followed the approach in Chapters 4 and 5, you have this. If you do not, building the inventory is your first priority before any audit. An auditor who asks "How many AI systems does your organization use?" and receives an uncertain answer has already formed an opinion about your governance maturity.

The inventory should include: system name, purpose, vendor or internal owner, risk classification with rationale, data inputs and outputs, affected stakeholders, deployment date, and last review date. It does not need to be a sophisticated database. A well-maintained spreadsheet that is accurate and current will satisfy most auditors. What will not satisfy them is a document that was clearly created the week before the audit.

Risk Management System Documentation

The EU AI Act Article 9 requires a risk management system for high-risk AI systems. This is not a one-time risk assessment — it is an ongoing system that identifies risks, estimates them, evaluates them, and manages them through the AI system's entire lifecycle.

Auditors want to see four things. First, the risk identification methodology: how do you find risks? What sources do you consult? How do you ensure completeness? Second, the risk assessment criteria: how do you evaluate severity and likelihood? What scales do you use? Third, the risk treatment decisions: for each identified risk, what did you decide to do — mitigate, transfer, avoid, or accept? What was the rationale? Fourth, the residual risk evaluation: after treatment, what risk remains? Is it within your tolerance?

Document the methodology once. Apply it to each AI system. Keep the assessment records. Update them when the system changes. This is the evidence trail that proves your risk management is systematic, not ad hoc.

Technical Documentation

Article 11 of the EU AI Act specifies detailed technical documentation requirements for high-risk AI systems, and ISO 42001 requires comparable documentation under its AI system lifecycle management clauses. The documentation package includes:

System description. A general description of the AI system — what it does, what it is intended for, and what version you are documenting. This is not a marketing overview. It is a technical description that an informed auditor can use to understand the system's scope and function.

Design specifications. The design choices that shape the system's behavior. For systems you develop internally, this includes architecture decisions, model selection rationale, and design constraints. For systems you procure, this includes the vendor's technical specifications and any customizations you have applied.

Development methodology. How was the system built? What development process was followed? What quality controls were in place during development? For procured systems, what was your evaluation and procurement methodology?

Validation and testing results. What testing was performed to verify the system works as intended? What were the results? This includes accuracy testing, bias testing, robustness testing, and any domain-specific validation. Keep the test plans, the test data descriptions, and the results. Auditors want to see not just that you tested, but what you tested, how you tested, and what you found.

Instructions for use. How should the system be used? What are the limitations? What should users not rely on the system for? This is the user-facing documentation that ensures the humans operating the system understand its capabilities and boundaries.

Data Governance Documentation

Article 10 of the EU AI Act addresses training, validation, and testing data sets. Even if you are deploying a vendor's model rather than training your own, data governance documentation is critical because your data still flows through the system.

The documentation should cover data quality measures — how you ensure the data you feed into AI systems is accurate, complete, and representative. It should address data provenance — where your data comes from, what transformations it undergoes, and what quality checks are applied at each stage. And it should include bias testing — the analysis you performed to determine whether your data or the system's outputs exhibit bias across protected categories.

For organizations using vendor AI systems, data governance documentation focuses on the data you control: what data you send to the system, how you ensure its quality, what data the vendor processes, and what contractual protections govern data handling. The vendor assessment framework from Chapter 8 feeds directly into this documentation.

Human Oversight Documentation

Article 14 of the EU AI Act requires human oversight measures appropriate to the risk level and context of the AI system. Chapter 6 of this book gave you the framework for designing human oversight. Now you need the evidence that proves oversight is operating.

Auditors will look for documentation of who reviews what — the roles and responsibilities for human oversight of each AI system. They will look for override rates — how often humans intervene in AI decisions, and what those interventions look like. They will look for effectiveness audits — evidence that you periodically evaluate whether your oversight mechanisms actually work. A human-in-the-loop who rubber-stamps every AI output is not oversight. You need to demonstrate that your reviewers are engaged, trained, and effective.

Post-Market Monitoring Records

Governance does not end at deployment. Auditors want to see ongoing performance data that demonstrates you are monitoring your AI systems after they go live. This includes accuracy monitoring over time, drift detection (is the system's performance degrading?), user feedback collection, and periodic re-validation.

Keep records of what you monitor, how frequently, what thresholds trigger action, and what actions you have taken when thresholds were breached. A system that was validated once at deployment and never monitored again will raise immediate concerns.

Incident Response Plans and Logs

Article 62 of the EU AI Act requires reporting of serious incidents involving high-risk AI systems to the relevant market surveillance authority. Beyond regulatory reporting, auditors want to see that you have a plan for when things go wrong.

The incident response plan should define what constitutes an AI-specific incident, who is responsible for response, what the escalation path looks like, what the communication protocol is, and how you conduct post-incident review. The incident log should record every incident and near-miss, the response taken, the root cause analysis, and the corrective actions implemented.

An organization with zero logged incidents is not an organization with zero incidents. It is an organization that is not looking.

Real-World Example: What the First EU AI Act Conformity Assessments Will Look Like

The EU AI Act follows the New Legislative Framework, the same regulatory architecture used for medical devices, machinery, radio equipment, and other regulated products. This gives us a concrete template for what conformity assessments will look like in practice.

Based on existing NLF patterns — particularly medical device conformity assessment under the Medical Device Regulation (MDR) — expect auditors to check five categories systematically: (1) complete technical documentation meeting Article 11 requirements, (2) evidence that a risk management system per Article 9 is established and operating, (3) data governance records per Article 10 with provenance and quality measures documented, (4) human oversight mechanisms per Article 14 with evidence of effective operation, and (5) accuracy, robustness, and cybersecurity measures per Article 15 with testing evidence.

The closest analogy is MDR conformity assessment: rigorous, documentation-heavy, and with no shortcuts. Organizations that have been through medical device certification will find the structure familiar. Organizations that have not should know that "we plan to implement this" is not a passing answer. Auditors want evidence of implementation, not evidence of intent.

Conformity Assessment for High-Risk AI Systems

If you are placing a high-risk AI system on the EU market or putting one into service in the EU, you must complete a conformity assessment before doing so. This is not optional, it is not a suggestion, and it is not something you can defer until an auditor asks about it. It is a prerequisite for market access.

Self-Assessment vs. Third-Party Assessment

Article 43 of the EU AI Act defines two conformity assessment pathways. The pathway you follow depends on the type of high-risk AI system.

Self-assessment based on harmonized standards. Most high-risk AI systems use internal conformity assessment, formally known as conformity assessment based on internal control (Annex VI). This means you assess your own compliance against the applicable harmonized standards. You conduct the documentation review, verify the quality management system, perform the testing, and sign the EU declaration of conformity yourself. "Yourself" does not mean casually — it means you follow a structured assessment procedure, document the results, and take legal responsibility for the declaration.

Self-assessment is available for most high-risk AI systems listed in Annex III — including AI in employment, education, credit scoring, law enforcement, migration management, and access to essential services. The catch is that harmonized standards must exist and you must assess against them. As of early 2026, CEN and CENELEC are still developing the harmonized standards for AI systems, which means the precise technical criteria you assess against are still being finalized. Watch for the official references in the Official Journal of the EU.

Third-party assessment. Mandatory third-party conformity assessment applies to two categories: real-time remote biometric identification systems used in publicly accessible spaces, and AI systems used as safety components of critical infrastructure (where the AI system itself is subject to third-party assessment under other Union harmonization legislation). For these systems, you must use a notified body — an independent assessment organization designated by an EU member state.

Third-party assessment is more expensive and time-consuming, but the documentation requirements are the same. The difference is who reviews the evidence: you or an external auditor.

EU Database Registration

Article 49 requires high-risk AI systems to be registered in the EU database before being placed on the market or put into service. The registration includes information about the provider, the AI system, its intended purpose, its conformity assessment status, and its risk management approach. The European

Commission maintains the database, and registration is mandatory — not voluntary.

Registration is a practical step that organizations often overlook in their compliance planning. Build it into your timeline. You cannot register a system you have not assessed, and you cannot place the system on the market until it is registered.

CE Marking

After completing the conformity assessment and registering in the EU database, you affix the CE marking to the AI system (or its documentation, for software systems). The CE marking signifies that the system conforms to the applicable requirements of the EU AI Act. It is your legal declaration of compliance.

The Practical Timeline

Here is the timeline reality that should drive your planning: you need documentation ready before August 2, 2026. Not started — ready. Conformity assessment is not something you can rush through in the final weeks. The documentation package described in the previous section takes months to compile properly. The risk management system needs to be operating, not just designed. The testing results need to be current. The human oversight mechanisms need to be demonstrably effective.

If you are reading this in early 2026 and have not started, you are behind but not yet in trouble. If you are reading this in mid-2026 and have not started, you have a problem. The practical minimum timeline for a thorough conformity assessment of a single high-risk AI system is three to four months. If you have multiple systems, multiply accordingly — though you can run assessments in parallel if you have the personnel.

Start with your highest-risk systems. Prioritize systems that are clearly high-risk under Annex III. Compile the documentation. Run the assessment. Register. Then move to the next system.

ISO 42001 Certification: The Full Pathway

ISO/IEC 42001 is the international standard for AI management systems (AIMS). It provides a framework for establishing, implementing, maintaining, and continually improving AI governance within an organization. Unlike the EU AI Act, which is a regulatory requirement for specific market access, ISO 42001 is a voluntary certification — but "voluntary" understates its practical importance.

ISO 42001 certification is rapidly becoming the benchmark that customers, partners, investors, and regulators use to evaluate AI governance maturity. Enterprise procurement teams are adding ISO 42001 to their vendor requirements. Cyber insurance underwriters are asking about it. Government agencies are referencing it in RFPs. Having the certification signals that your AI governance has been independently verified. Not having it increasingly requires explanation.

Here is the full certification pathway, with realistic costs and timelines.

Step 1: Gap Assessment

Before you build, you need to know where you stand. A gap assessment compares your current AI governance state against ISO 42001 requirements and identifies what is missing.

External gap assessment: $5,000 to $15,000 depending on organizational size and complexity. An experienced ISO consultant reviews your existing policies, processes, and documentation against the standard's requirements and delivers a prioritized gap report. This typically takes one to two weeks of consultant time.

DIY gap assessment: Free in terms of external cost, but requires someone with sufficient knowledge of the standard to conduct a credible evaluation. Use the clause-by-clause checklist in Appendix B as your starting framework. Go through each requirement, assess whether you meet it, partially meet it, or do not meet it, and document the gaps.

The gap assessment is not where you should skimp. Whether you do it externally or internally, the quality of your gap assessment determines the quality of your implementation plan. A superficial gap assessment leads to surprises during the audit — and audit surprises are expensive.

Step 2: Implementation

This is where the real work happens. Based on the gap assessment, you build or enhance your AI management system to meet ISO 42001 requirements.

Small organizations (under 500 employees): Expect 4 to 9 months of implementation work. You are building policies, implementing controls, establishing processes, and generating the operating records that auditors will review. The work includes: defining your AI governance policy, establishing roles and responsibilities, implementing risk assessment procedures, documenting AI system lifecycle management, establishing data quality and bias monitoring processes, building internal audit capability, and setting up management review.

Mid-market organizations (500 to 5,000 employees): Expect 9 to 18 months. The longer timeline reflects greater complexity — more AI systems to govern, more stakeholders to coordinate, more existing processes to integrate with, and more documentation to produce. You are not just building an AIMS; you are integrating it with existing management systems for information security, quality, privacy, and operational risk.

Implementation is not a documentation exercise. Auditors will verify that controls are operating effectively, not just that policies exist on paper. This means you need to run the AIMS for long enough to generate operating evidence before the audit. A risk assessment conducted once, a management review held once, an internal audit performed once — these demonstrate that the system exists. Multiple cycles demonstrate that the system operates.

Step 3: Stage 1 Audit — Documentation Review

The Stage 1 audit is your certification body's first look at your AIMS. The auditor reviews your documentation to determine whether your management system is designed to meet ISO 42001 requirements and whether you are ready for the Stage 2 audit.

The Stage 1 auditor will review your AI governance policy, your risk assessment methodology and results, your statement of applicability (which controls you have implemented and which you have excluded with justification), your internal audit results, your management review records, and your documented processes for AI system lifecycle management.

Stage 1 is a readiness check. The auditor is looking for completeness and coherence, not operational evidence. If your documentation has significant gaps, the auditor will identify them and you will need to address them before Stage 2. If the gaps are minor, you will get a list of observations and a green light to proceed.

Expect Stage 1 to take one to three days depending on organizational size.

Step 4: Stage 2 Audit — Implementation Review

The Stage 2 audit is the main event. The auditor verifies that your AIMS controls are not just documented but are actually implemented, operating effectively, and producing the intended outcomes.

Stage 2 involves interviews with personnel who operate the controls, review of operating records and evidence, observation of processes in action, and sampling of AI systems to verify governance coverage. The auditor will talk to your AI system owners, your risk managers, your data quality staff, your human oversight personnel, and your management team. They will ask for evidence that the processes you documented are the processes you follow.

Nonconformities fall into two categories. Major nonconformities mean a required element of the standard is missing or fundamentally not working — these must be resolved before certification can be granted. Minor nonconformities mean a required element is partially implemented or has occasional lapses — these must be addressed within a defined timeframe, typically before the first surveillance audit.

Stage 2 typically takes two to five days depending on organizational size and the number of AI systems in scope.

Step 5: Certification

If the Stage 2 audit finds no major nonconformities (or you resolve them within the allowed timeframe), the certification body issues your ISO 42001 certificate. The certificate is valid for three years.

Step 6: Surveillance Audits

Certification is not the finish line. Annual surveillance audits verify that your AIMS continues to operate effectively. These are smaller than the initial certification audit — typically one to two days — but they are substantive. The auditor will review changes to your AIMS, follow up on previous nonconformities, and sample additional controls.

Surveillance audit costs range from $3,000 to $16,000 depending on organizational size and certification body.

Cost Reality

Let us be direct about what ISO 42001 certification costs.

Small organizations: $20,000 to $60,000 total. This includes gap assessment ($5K-$10K), implementation support ($5K-$20K if using a consultant, less if doing most work internally), certification audit fees ($8K-$20K), and first-year surveillance ($3K-$8K).

Mid-market organizations: $150,000 to $320,000 total. This includes gap assessment ($10K-$15K), implementation with consulting support ($80K-$180K), certification audit fees ($30K-$60K), and first-year surveillance ($8K-$16K). The implementation cost is the variable — it depends on how much external consulting you need versus internal capability.

These numbers are significant, especially for smaller organizations. But they need to be evaluated against the cost of not having certification: lost enterprise contracts, higher insurance premiums, regulatory risk exposure, and the reputational cost of being unable to demonstrate governance maturity when a customer, investor, or regulator asks.

The ISO 27001 Shortcut

If your organization already holds ISO 27001 certification for information security management, you have a significant head start. The overlap between ISO 27001 and ISO 42001 is substantial — approximately 40 to 50 percent of ISO 42001's requirements are satisfied by an existing ISO 27001 ISMS.

Shared elements you can leverage directly: Risk assessment methodology (ISO 42001 requires AI-specific risk assessment, but the methodology framework transfers), internal audit program, management review process, document control and records management, corrective action procedures, competence and awareness requirements, and the fundamental management system structure (both standards follow the ISO Harmonized Structure).

New elements you will need to build: AI-specific risk assessment criteria and treatments, AI system lifecycle management processes, data quality management, bias monitoring and mitigation, AI-specific impact assessment procedures, and AI system inventory and classification.

The practical impact: an organization with mature ISO 27001 can typically complete ISO 42001 certification in 40 to 60 percent less time and cost than an organization starting from scratch. Your auditor may even combine surveillance audits for both standards, reducing ongoing costs further.

SMB Spotlight: ISO 42001 on a Shoestring — The $20K Path vs. the $300K Path

There are two ways to get ISO 42001 certified. Both result in the same certificate on your wall.

The $20K path: (1) Conduct the gap assessment yourself using the clause-by-clause checklist in Appendix B. This requires someone on your team to read and understand the standard, but the standard is well-structured and the checklist walks you through it. (2) Leverage existing ISO 27001 controls if you have them — the 40 to 50 percent overlap means you are starting from halfway, not zero. (3) Use a boutique certification body with SMB-friendly pricing. The Big Four certification bodies charge premium rates. Smaller, equally accredited bodies offer the same certification for significantly less. (4) Designate one internal champion who owns the implementation, rather than hiring a consulting team. One knowledgeable person working systematically will outperform a team of consultants who do not understand your business.

The $300K path: Hire a Big Four consulting firm. They will send a team of six consultants for nine months, produce beautifully formatted deliverables, and achieve the same certification you could have achieved with the approach above. Their methodology is sound, their documentation is polished, and their invoice is spectacular.

Both paths work. The certificate does not say which path you took.

Action: If you have ISO 27001, request the NIST-ISO 42001 crosswalk from your certification body and identify which controls you already satisfy. The answer will surprise you.

[FIGURE B1-21] shows the certification timeline from gap assessment through certification for both small and mid-market organizations.

NIST AI RMF Profiles as Compliance Evidence

The NIST AI Risk Management Framework is voluntary. No federal regulation currently mandates its adoption. And yet, NIST AI RMF profiles are among the most valuable compliance evidence you can produce — even if NIST is not your primary regulatory driver.

Here is why: the NIST AI RMF provides a structured, widely recognized vocabulary for describing AI risk management practices. When you document your governance using NIST's GOVERN, MAP, MEASURE, and MANAGE functions, you are speaking a language that auditors, regulators, customers, and partners across jurisdictions understand. A NIST AI RMF profile is not just an internal planning tool. It is a universal translation layer between your governance practices and whatever regulatory framework you are being assessed against.

Building Your Current-State Profile

A current-state profile documents where your organization stands today across the four NIST AI RMF functions. For each function and its subcategories, you assess your current maturity: are you performing this activity? Is it ad hoc or systematic? Is it documented? Is it measured?

GOVERN: Do you have AI governance policies? Are roles and responsibilities defined? Is there organizational commitment to responsible AI? Are legal and regulatory requirements identified and tracked?

MAP: Have you identified and characterized your AI systems? Do you understand their contexts of use? Have you identified affected stakeholders? Have you assessed the benefits and risks?

MEASURE: Are you measuring AI system performance? Testing for bias? Monitoring for drift? Evaluating the effectiveness of risk mitigations?

MANAGE: Are you treating identified risks? Responding to incidents? Communicating with stakeholders? Maintaining documentation?

Be honest in your current-state assessment. The value of the profile is in its accuracy, not its optimism. An auditor who reviews a current-state profile that claims full maturity across all subcategories will be skeptical. A profile that candidly identifies areas of strength and areas of development signals organizational maturity.

Building Your Desired-State Profile

The desired-state profile documents where you need to be. This is driven by three inputs: regulatory requirements (what do the EU AI Act, ISO 42001, and applicable state laws require?), organizational risk tolerance (how much AI risk is acceptable given your industry, scale, and stakeholder expectations?), and strategic objectives (what governance maturity do you need to support your AI strategy?).

The desired-state profile does not need to be perfect across every subcategory. It needs to be appropriate to your context. A healthcare organization deploying AI for diagnostic support needs higher maturity in MEASURE and MANAGE than a marketing firm using AI for content suggestions. The profile reflects your specific requirements, not a universal ideal.

The Gap Analysis

The delta between your current-state profile and your desired-state profile is your gap analysis. This is the document that tells you exactly what needs to change, prioritized by regulatory urgency, risk severity, and implementation effort.

Present the gap analysis as a table: subcategory, current state, desired state, gap severity, and planned action. This format is immediately useful for three purposes — internal planning, resource allocation, and audit evidence.

The Action Plan

Convert the gap analysis into a prioritized action plan with owners, timelines, resources, and milestones. This is your implementation roadmap. It is also evidence that auditors value highly: it demonstrates that you not only know where the gaps are, but you have a systematic plan to close them.

Why This Matters Even If NIST Is Not Mandatory

NIST AI RMF profiles are excellent evidence of systematic risk management regardless of your regulatory context. EU AI Act auditors will recognize the NIST framework and accept profiles as supporting evidence for Article 9 risk management system requirements. ISO 42001 auditors will see alignment with the standard's risk management and lifecycle management clauses. Customer due diligence teams will accept profiles as evidence of governance maturity. Board members and executives will understand the clear current-state to desired-state progression.

You are not producing the profile because NIST told you to. You are producing it because it is the most efficient way to document your governance posture in a format that satisfies multiple audiences simultaneously.

Board Reporting on AI Governance

Your AI governance program exists in two worlds. In the operational world, it consists of policies, controls, risk assessments, monitoring, and audit evidence. In the boardroom, it consists of whatever you can communicate in 15 minutes with three slides.

Both worlds matter. If your governance program is operationally excellent but invisible to the board, you will not get the resources you need. If your board reporting is polished but your operational program is hollow, the first audit will expose the gap. The goal is to make the boardroom presentation an accurate reflection of the operational reality.

What the Board Needs

The board needs four things from your AI governance reporting, and they need them in business terms rather than technical terms.

Risk exposure summary. How much AI risk does the organization carry? Not in terms of subcategory-level risk scores, but in terms of business impact. "We have 47 AI systems in production. Twelve are classified as high-risk. Of those twelve, eight have complete governance controls. Four have identified gaps with remediation plans targeting Q3." That is a risk exposure summary a board can act on.

Compliance status. Where do you stand against applicable regulatory requirements? "EU AI Act conformity assessments are complete for 6 of 8 high-risk systems. Two systems require additional documentation, expected complete by June. ISO 42001 Stage 1 audit is scheduled for September." Specific, time-bound, and actionable.

Incident summary. What went wrong and what did you do about it? Boards do not want a zero-incident report (they will not believe it). They want to see that incidents are detected, responded to, and resolved — and that the organization learns from them. "Three AI-related incidents this quarter. Two were model accuracy degradations detected by monitoring and resolved within SLA. One was a data quality issue that required system suspension and root cause analysis."

Resource requirements. What do you need from the board to maintain or improve the program? Be specific: headcount, budget, executive sponsorship, timeline decisions. The board's job is to allocate resources. Give them a clear ask.

What the Board Does Not Need

Technical implementation details. The board does not need to know which embedding model your RAG system uses or how your vector database handles similarity search. If a board member asks a technical question, answer it — but do not front-load your presentation with architecture diagrams.

Model architecture diagrams. Unless a board member has a machine learning background and specifically requests this, model architecture is noise in a governance discussion.

Subcategory-level NIST mappings. Your NIST AI RMF profile is an operational document. The board needs the executive summary of that profile, not the profile itself. "We have assessed our governance against NIST AI RMF and identified 14 gaps, of which 9 are addressed and 5 are in remediation" is the right level of detail.

Metrics That Matter

Track and report these metrics at every board meeting:

AI systems inventoried vs. estimated total. This is your coverage metric. If you have inventoried 47 AI systems but estimate the true number is 80, the board needs to know that 33 systems are ungoverned. This metric drives the shadow AI discovery effort from Chapter 8.

High-risk systems with complete governance. Of the systems you have classified as high-risk, how many have complete governance coverage — risk assessment, human oversight, monitoring, documentation, incident response? This is your depth metric.

Policy compliance rate. What percentage of AI deployments follow your established governance process? If the answer is 60 percent, the board needs to understand why 40 percent are not compliant and what you are doing about it.

Incidents and near-misses. Raw count, severity distribution, response time, and resolution status. Trend this metric over time. A decreasing count may mean your controls are working. An increasing count may mean your detection is improving. Context matters.

Audit findings open vs. closed. If you have been through an audit — internal or external — how many findings were identified, how many are closed, and what is the timeline for closing the rest? This is your remediation velocity metric.

Reporting Cadence

Quarterly reporting is the minimum cadence for board-level AI governance updates. This aligns with typical board meeting schedules and provides enough frequency to track meaningful change. Ad-hoc reporting is required for significant incidents — a major AI failure, a regulatory enforcement action, a material change in the risk landscape.

Between board meetings, maintain a governance dashboard that provides real-time or near-real-time status for the metrics above. When the board meeting arrives, you are summarizing a dashboard you already maintain, not scrambling to compile data from scratch.

The One-Slide Board Summary

If you can only show the board one slide, make it this: a risk heatmap showing AI systems plotted by risk level and governance completeness, a compliance timeline showing key regulatory deadlines and your progress against them, and the top three actions you need the board to support.

The risk heatmap gives the board an instant visual of where you stand. The compliance timeline gives them temporal urgency. The top three actions give them a concrete decision to make. Everything else is backup material.

Continuous Compliance vs. Point-in-Time

There are two models for maintaining audit readiness. Point-in-time compliance is the minimum. Continuous compliance is the goal. Most organizations start with the first and should plan to evolve toward the second.

Point-in-Time Compliance

Point-in-time compliance means preparing for specific audit dates. You compile documentation, verify controls, and generate evidence in the weeks or months leading up to an audit. Between audits, governance may receive less attention.

This model works — barely — for annual audits. You can maintain certification through annual surveillance audits and pre-audit preparation sprints. But it has three significant weaknesses.

First, it creates compliance valleys. In the months between audits, controls may degrade, documentation may fall behind, and new AI systems may be deployed without governance oversight. If a regulator shows up unannounced or a customer due diligence team requests evidence between audit cycles, you may not be ready.

Second, it is stressful and expensive. The pre-audit scramble consumes disproportionate resources. People drop their regular work to prepare evidence. Gaps discovered during preparation require emergency remediation. This is governance as a fire drill rather than governance as an operating practice.

Third, it is increasingly insufficient. The EU AI Act's post-market monitoring requirements are continuous, not periodic. ISO 42001's continual improvement clause means the AIMS must operate all the time, not just when auditors are watching. Regulators are moving toward ongoing oversight, and your compliance posture needs to move with them.

Continuous Compliance

Continuous compliance means your governance program produces audit evidence as a byproduct of normal operations. Controls operate continuously. Documentation is updated in real time. Monitoring runs 24/7. Compliance evidence is always current.

This does not mean you are always in a state of audit preparation. It means the gap between your operating state and your audit-ready state is always small. When an auditor asks for evidence, you pull it from systems you already use, not from a folder you compiled last week.

Automated Compliance Monitoring

The bridge between point-in-time and continuous compliance is automation. Automated compliance monitoring tools continuously check policy adherence, document completeness, and control effectiveness without manual effort.

Policy adherence monitoring. Automated checks that verify AI deployments follow your governance process. Did the new AI system go through risk classification? Is the human oversight configuration compliant with your policy? Were vendor assessments completed before procurement? Automated checks catch deviations in real time rather than during the next audit preparation cycle.

Document completeness monitoring. Automated tracking of documentation status for each AI system. Is the technical documentation current? When was the risk assessment last updated? Are the monitoring records being generated? A dashboard that shows documentation completeness across all AI systems gives you instant visibility into compliance gaps.

Control effectiveness monitoring. Automated testing that verifies controls are working as designed. Are human oversight checkpoints being triggered? Are monitoring alerts being generated and responded to? Are incident response procedures being followed? Automated testing of control effectiveness provides continuous assurance rather than periodic verification.

The tooling landscape for automated AI governance monitoring is still maturing. Chapter 8 discussed the current state of AI governance tooling. As of early 2026, most organizations are building custom dashboards and scripts rather than deploying off-the-shelf platforms. This will change as the market matures, but for now, practical automation often means connecting your existing tools — GRC platforms, ticketing systems, monitoring dashboards — to produce continuous compliance evidence.

Governance Monitoring vs. Technical Monitoring

This chapter focuses on governance monitoring — are your policies being followed, your controls operating, your documentation current? Technical monitoring — is the model performing accurately, is the data pipeline reliable, is the system secure — is a related but distinct discipline.

For readers using this book alongside *Securing Agentic AI (2026 Edition)*, that book's Chapter 9 covers technical monitoring in depth: model performance tracking, drift detection, anomaly detection, and automated alerting. The governance monitoring described in this chapter and the technical monitoring described in that book are complementary layers. Together, they provide comprehensive assurance that your AI systems are both well-governed and well-functioning.

> **Action Item: Compliance Evidence Checklist by Framework**
>
> Appendix B provides three detailed checklists for compliance evidence, organized by framework. Use these as your starting point for audit preparation.
>
> **EU AI Act Compliance Evidence (by timeline phase).** What you need ready by August 2, 2026: complete technical documentation for all high-risk AI systems (Article 11), operating risk management system with documented results (Article 9), data governance documentation (Article 10), human oversight mechanisms with operating evidence (Article 14), conformity assessment documentation, EU database registration, CE marking. What you need ready by August 2, 2027: transparency obligations for limited-risk systems, AI literacy requirements compliance, general-purpose AI compliance (if applicable).
>
> **NIST AI RMF Compliance Evidence (by function).** GOVERN: policies, roles, risk tolerances, organizational commitment, legal/regulatory tracking. MAP: AI system inventory, context characterization, stakeholder identification, benefit/risk assessment. MEASURE: performance metrics, bias testing results, drift monitoring

data, risk mitigation effectiveness. MANAGE: risk treatment records, incident response logs, communication records, documentation maintenance. Reference the NIST AI RMF Playbook for subcategory-level guidance.

ISO 42001 Compliance Evidence (clause-by-clause). Use the gap assessment checklist in Appendix B for clause-by-clause evaluation. Key areas: context of the organization (Clause 4), leadership and commitment (Clause 5), planning including AI-specific risk assessment (Clause 6), support including competence and awareness (Clause 7), operation including AI system lifecycle management (Clause 8), performance evaluation including monitoring, measurement, and internal audit (Clause 9), improvement including nonconformity management and continual improvement (Clause 10).

Putting It All Together

Audit readiness is not a project. It is an operating characteristic of a mature governance program. The compliance evidence package described in this chapter — the AI system inventory, risk management documentation, technical documentation, data governance records, human oversight evidence, post-market monitoring records, and incident logs — is not something you compile for an audit. It is something your governance program produces continuously as a natural consequence of doing governance well.

The frameworks reinforce each other. Your NIST AI RMF profile supports your ISO 42001 risk assessment. Your ISO 42001 documentation satisfies EU AI Act technical documentation requirements. Your EU AI Act conformity assessment evidence demonstrates NIST AI RMF MEASURE function maturity. Each framework you adopt makes compliance with the others easier, not harder.

Start where the pressure is greatest. If you have high-risk AI systems that will fall under EU AI Act conformity assessment, start there — August 2026 is a hard deadline. If your customers are asking for ISO 42001, start the certification pathway. If neither is immediately urgent, build your NIST AI RMF profile — it is the most flexible starting point and the easiest to adapt to whichever regulatory requirement arrives next.

Whatever you start with, build for continuity. Design your evidence collection to be ongoing, not periodic. Automate what you can. Maintain your documentation as a living system, not a static archive. When the auditors arrive — and they will arrive — you want your response to be "let me pull up the dashboard" rather than "let me schedule a preparation sprint."

Key Takeaways

- **Documentation is not governance, but governance without documentation is invisible.** You may have excellent AI risk management practices, but if you cannot produce the evidence — risk assessments, test results, oversight records, incident logs — you will fail an audit. Build evidence collection into your governance operations from day one.

- **The EU AI Act conformity assessment deadline is real and approaching.** High-risk AI systems must have complete technical documentation, operating risk management systems, and conformity assessments before August 2, 2026. If you have not started, start now. The practical minimum timeline for a single system assessment is three to four months.

- **ISO 42001 certification is achievable at any organizational scale.** Small organizations can achieve certification for $20,000 to $60,000 by leveraging existing ISO 27001 controls, conducting internal gap assessments, and using boutique certification bodies. The certificate is the same regardless of the path you take.

- **NIST AI RMF profiles are your universal compliance translator.** Even if NIST is not mandatory for your organization, a well-constructed current-state and desired-state profile documents your governance posture in a language that auditors, regulators, and customers across all frameworks understand.

- **Continuous compliance beats point-in-time compliance.** The organizations that treat audit readiness as a permanent operating state — rather than a periodic preparation sprint — spend less, stress less, and pass audits more consistently. Automate evidence collection, maintain living documentation, and keep your dashboard current so that every day is audit-ready.

Part V: Sector Focus and the Future

"The best way to predict the future is to create it."

— Peter Drucker

Chapter 10: Sector-Specific Considerations

If you have followed this book from Chapter 5 through Chapter 9, you now have a general-purpose AI governance program. You have an AI inventory. You have risk classifications. You have policies, human oversight mechanisms, vendor assessment processes, and monitoring cadences. That program works for any organization in any industry. It is the foundation.

But foundations are not finished buildings. If you operate in certain sectors, you have additional governance obligations that the general framework does not cover. Not because the general framework is wrong — it is necessary and sufficient for organizations without sector-specific regulatory exposure. But some industries have decades of existing regulation, professional liability standards, and supervisory expectations that intersect with AI governance in ways that create additional requirements you cannot ignore.

This chapter covers four sectors where AI governance has distinct regulatory or professional obligations: financial services, healthcare, legal and professional services, and government. For each sector, the focus is on the delta — what you need to add to the general governance framework from Chapters 5 through 9, not a repetition of that framework with a sector-specific label stamped on it. If you are in one of these sectors, read the relevant section and layer those requirements on top of what you have already built. If you are not in any of these sectors, you can skim this chapter for awareness and move on. The general framework has you covered.

One more note before we begin. Many organizations straddle multiple sectors. A health insurance company sits at the intersection of financial services and healthcare. A law firm advising a hospital on AI procurement touches legal services, healthcare, and potentially government contracting. A fintech selling to federal agencies faces financial services and government requirements simultaneously. If you are in more than one sector, you need to address the requirements from each. The good news is that the requirements are additive, not contradictory. The rigorous approach almost always satisfies the lenient one.

Financial Services

If you work in financial services, you have an advantage that most other sectors do not: you already have a governance substrate. Banks, insurance companies, investment firms, and their service providers have been subject to model governance requirements for over a decade. The infrastructure exists. The question is how to extend it for AI.

The SR 11-7 Foundation

The Federal Reserve's SR 11-7, issued in 2011, established model risk management (MRM) as a supervisory expectation for all banking organizations. If you work at a bank, you already know SR 11-7. You have a model inventory. You have model validation processes. You have a three-lines-of-defense structure with model owners in the first line, a model risk management group in the second, and internal audit in the third. You have model documentation standards, performance monitoring, and a governance committee that reviews model risk.

AI governance for financial institutions does not replace this infrastructure. It extends it. The model inventory needs new fields for AI-specific attributes — whether the model is generative, whether it uses third-party foundation models, whether it is capable of hallucination, whether the model is deterministic or stochastic in its outputs. The risk taxonomy needs new categories — prompt injection, training data poisoning, output instability, hallucination, and emergent behaviors that were not present during validation. The validation methodology needs new techniques — bias testing across protected classes, adversarial robustness testing, hallucination rate measurement, and evaluation of model behavior under distribution shift. But the governance structure, the committee, the cadence, the documentation standards, the three-lines-of-defense model — all of that stays.

This is the single biggest advantage financial services organizations have. While other sectors are building governance programs from scratch using Chapter 5's 90-day sprint, you are bolting AI-specific requirements onto a structure that has been tested by examiners for 15 years. That is a meaningful head start.

There is one significant caveat. SR 11-7 was designed for traditional statistical and quantitative models — linear regressions, logistic regressions, decision trees, and similar methodologies where the relationship between inputs and outputs is interpretable and the model's behavior can be fully characterized through mathematical analysis. Large language models and deep neural networks do not fit this paradigm neatly. The validation techniques that work for a logistic regression — examining coefficients, testing boundary conditions, verifying that the model behaves predictably across its entire input space — do not translate directly to a model with billions of parameters whose internal reasoning is opaque. Your MRM team may need to develop new validation competencies for AI models, including behavioral testing, red-teaming, and output monitoring approaches that account for the non-deterministic nature of generative AI.

Real-World Example: How a Regional Bank Integrated AI RMF with SR 11-7

A mid-sized regional bank with an established SR 11-7 model risk management program needed to incorporate AI governance without building a parallel structure. The bank already maintained a model inventory of roughly 120 models, a validation team, and a model risk committee that met monthly.

Their approach had four steps. First, they added AI-specific risk categories to their existing risk taxonomy — hallucination, bias and fairness, prompt injection, and training data provenance joined the existing categories of accuracy, stability, and implementation risk. Second, they mandated bias testing for all AI models affecting consumer outcomes, using disparate impact analysis across race, gender, age, and geographic proxies. Third, they added an "AI" flag to every model in the inventory, distinguishing traditional statistical models from AI and ML models so examiners could quickly identify the AI population. Fourth, they mapped NIST AI RMF's MAP function into their existing model validation workflow — every new AI model went through a structured risk identification process during the initial validation that aligned with both SR 11-7 and AI RMF.

The entire integration took four months. No new committees were created. No new governance structure was stood up. The existing MRM program absorbed the AI-specific requirements with targeted extensions. When their OCC examiner reviewed the program, the feedback was positive — because the bank had not tried to reinvent model governance. They had evolved it.

Regulators You Need to Know

Financial services firms in the United States face a multi-regulator landscape, and each regulator has a different angle on AI. The Office of the Comptroller of the Currency (OCC) supervises national banks and focuses on safety and soundness — AI systems that affect credit decisions, capital adequacy, or operational resilience are their territory. The Federal Reserve supervises bank holding companies and state member banks, and SR 11-7 is their framework. The FDIC covers state-chartered banks that are not Fed members. The Securities and Exchange Commission (SEC) oversees securities markets and investment advisers — algorithmic trading and robo-advisory AI are their domain. The Consumer Financial Protection Bureau (CFPB) focuses on consumer protection, which means any AI system that affects consumer lending, servicing, or collections is within their purview. And state regulators — every state has a banking department and an insurance department — are increasingly active on AI, particularly in insurance.

You do not get to pick one regulator and ignore the rest. A bank that uses AI for credit scoring, fraud detection, and customer service chatbots is potentially touching the OCC, the Federal Reserve, and the CFPB simultaneously. Know your regulators. Know which AI use cases fall under which regulatory umbrella. Document that mapping in your governance program.

High-Risk AI Use Cases

The EU AI Act's Annex III classifies several financial services AI applications as high-risk, and these classifications matter even if you are a US-only institution because they signal where global regulatory consensus is forming. Credit scoring and creditworthiness assessment are explicitly listed. So are AI systems used for risk assessment and pricing in life and health insurance. Fraud detection systems, while essential for operational integrity, can produce false positives that freeze customer accounts and trigger fair lending concerns.

Beyond the EU AI Act, the SEC has focused specifically on algorithmic trading — AI systems that execute trades at speeds and volumes beyond human oversight. The SEC's 2023 and 2024 enforcement actions around "AI washing" are also relevant here: if your marketing materials claim your investment platform uses "advanced AI" to generate alpha, you had better be able to substantiate that claim. The SEC has sanctioned firms for overstating their AI capabilities, and that enforcement posture has only intensified.

On the anti-money-laundering side, FinCEN expects institutions to maintain effective AML programs, and AI-powered transaction monitoring systems are subject to the same examination standards as traditional rule-based systems. If your AI flags fewer suspicious transactions than the system it replaced, examiners will ask questions. Conversely, if your AI flags dramatically more transactions as suspicious, you face a different problem: alert fatigue and the potential that your compliance team is rubber-stamping AI-generated suspicious activity reports without meaningful human review. Both failure modes — under-detection and over-detection without human judgment — create regulatory risk.

Know Your Customer (KYC) processes are also increasingly AI-driven, with machine learning models used for identity verification, document authentication, and risk profiling. These models inherit all the bias risks of any AI system, plus the additional regulatory risk that errors in KYC can facilitate financial crime. An AI system that systematically struggles with identification documents from certain countries or that assigns higher risk scores to customers based on national origin proxy features creates both compliance risk and reputational exposure.

Fair Lending and Bias

This is where financial services AI governance gets serious in a way that other sectors do not fully appreciate. AI bias in lending is not just a governance issue or a reputational risk. It is a civil rights issue with decades of enforcement precedent and existing statutory authority.

The Equal Credit Opportunity Act (ECOA) prohibits discrimination in credit transactions on the basis of race, color, religion, national origin, sex, marital status, age, or receipt of public assistance. The Fair Housing Act prohibits discrimination in residential real estate-related transactions. Both statutes have been enforced through disparate impact analysis since the 1970s — you do not need to prove intentional discrimination. If the AI's outputs have a disproportionate adverse effect on a protected class, and you cannot demonstrate that the model serves a legitimate business necessity that cannot be achieved through less discriminatory means, you have a violation.

The CFPB has made clear that it considers AI-driven credit decisions to be subject to the same fair lending standards as any other credit decision methodology. The adverse action notice requirements under ECOA apply to AI decisions just as they apply to human decisions — if you deny a consumer credit based on an AI model's output, you must be able to explain why in terms the consumer can understand. "The model said no" is not an acceptable adverse action reason.

This means that your AI governance program for financial services must include bias testing as a non-negotiable requirement for any AI model that affects consumer lending, insurance underwriting, or other credit-related decisions. That testing must cover all protected classes. It must use statistically rigorous methods — statistical parity, equalized odds, and calibration across groups are common metrics, though the right metric depends on your specific context and regulatory guidance. And it must be documented thoroughly enough to withstand examiner scrutiny and potential litigation.

There is an additional wrinkle for AI specifically. Traditional credit models use a defined set of input features, and you can test for disparate impact by examining the model's behavior across protected classes while controlling for legitimate credit factors. Generative AI and complex deep learning models make this analysis harder because the relationship between inputs and outputs may not be transparent. If you are using a black-box AI model for credit decisions, you need to invest in explainability tools and testing methodologies that can surface bias even when you cannot inspect the model's internal logic. The CFPB has signaled that "the algorithm is too complex to explain" is not an acceptable defense for discriminatory outcomes.

The Insurance Angle

Insurance presents a two-sided AI governance challenge. On one side, insurers are deploying AI for underwriting, claims processing, and fraud detection — all of which are subject to state insurance regulation and, increasingly, to specific AI guidance from the National Association of Insurance Commissioners (NAIC). The NAIC's model bulletin on AI encourages insurers to implement governance programs consistent with the NIST AI RMF and to ensure that AI does not produce unfairly discriminatory outcomes.

On the other side, the insurance industry is still working out how to handle AI risk in the policies it writes. Cyber insurance policies are beginning to address AI-specific risks, but coverage is inconsistent. Some policies explicitly exclude losses arising from AI-generated content or AI-driven decisions. Others are silent on AI, which creates ambiguity about whether AI-related losses are covered. If you are a financial services firm relying on cyber insurance or errors-and-omissions coverage, review your policies now for AI-specific exclusions. The coverage you assumed you had may not extend to AI-related losses.

Sector-Specific Tooling

ValidMind deserves mention here because it was purpose-built for financial services model risk management. While the general-purpose AI governance tools we covered in Chapter 8 work across sectors, ValidMind specifically targets the SR 11-7 and MRM workflow — model documentation, validation, bias testing, and regulatory reporting in formats that bank examiners expect. If you are a financial institution looking for tooling, evaluate ValidMind alongside the general-purpose options. Its sector specificity may save you significant customization effort.

Healthcare

Healthcare AI governance sits at the intersection of patient safety, data privacy, and device regulation. The stakes are different here than in other sectors — not because other sectors' stakes are trivial, but because healthcare AI errors can directly harm or kill patients. That reality drives a regulatory and professional culture around validation that is more demanding than any other sector you will encounter.

FDA Regulation of AI/ML Software

The Food and Drug Administration regulates AI and machine learning systems that qualify as Software as a Medical Device (SaMD) — software that is itself a medical device, rather than software that controls a hardware device. If your AI system diagnoses, treats, prevents, or mitigates a disease or condition, it is probably SaMD, and it is subject to FDA pre-market review.

The FDA's approach to AI/ML-based SaMD has evolved significantly. The traditional regulatory model assumes that a device is designed, validated, and then frozen — the version you submit for approval is the version you sell. AI/ML systems do not work that way. They learn, adapt, and change over time. The FDA recognized this tension and introduced the concept of predetermined change control plans (PCCPs) — manufacturers can describe, in advance, the types of changes the AI system will make to itself, the methodology for validating those changes, and the performance boundaries within which the system must remain. If the actual changes stay within the predetermined plan, the manufacturer does not need to resubmit for approval every time the model updates.

This is a governance-intensive approach. You need continuous performance monitoring to ensure the model stays within its approved boundaries. You need real-world performance data to validate that the model performs as expected on the patient populations it actually serves, not just the populations in the clinical trials. You need change management processes that distinguish between changes covered by the PCCP and changes that require new regulatory submissions.

If you are developing or deploying clinical AI, your governance program from Chapter 5 needs a dedicated regulatory compliance layer for FDA requirements. This is not something you can manage with a general-purpose AI governance framework alone.

EU Dual Compliance

In the European Union, AI systems used in medical devices face dual regulatory obligations. The Medical Device Regulation (MDR 2017/745) governs medical devices. The EU AI Act governs AI systems. If your AI system is a medical device, you must comply with both — and the requirements do not perfectly align.

The MDR requires conformity assessment, clinical evaluation, and post-market surveillance through notified bodies. The EU AI Act classifies AI in medical devices as high-risk and imposes additional requirements around risk management, data governance, transparency, and human oversight. The practical effect is two compliance tracks running in parallel, with overlapping but non-identical documentation requirements. Organizations operating in the EU healthcare AI space need legal and regulatory counsel that understands both frameworks and can identify where the requirements converge and where they diverge.

HIPAA and AI

If your AI system processes protected health information (PHI), the Health Insurance Portability and Accountability Act applies. This is not new – HIPAA has applied to electronic health information since 2003. But AI introduces specific HIPAA considerations that your governance program must address.

First, Business Associate Agreements (BAAs). If you use a third-party AI vendor to process PHI, that vendor is a business associate under HIPAA, and you must have a BAA in place before any PHI flows to their system. This applies to cloud-based AI tools, SaaS platforms with AI features, and any third-party service that touches patient data. Not every AI vendor will sign a BAA. Major cloud providers (AWS, Azure, Google Cloud) offer BAA-eligible services, but many standalone AI tools do not. If a vendor will not sign a BAA, you cannot send them PHI. Period.

Second, the minimum necessary standard. HIPAA requires that you limit PHI disclosures to the minimum necessary for the intended purpose. When you are feeding patient records into an AI system, ask whether you are sending more data than the AI actually needs. Do you need full medical records, or would de-identified or limited data sets accomplish the same analytical purpose?

Third, the Security Rule. AI systems that store, process, or transmit PHI must implement the administrative, physical, and technical safeguards required by the HIPAA Security Rule. This includes access controls, audit logging, encryption, and integrity controls. Your vendor assessment process from Chapter 8 should already cover these areas – but for healthcare AI vendors, the HIPAA-specific requirements add an additional compliance layer that must be explicitly verified.

Clinical AI Validation

Validation requirements for clinical AI are higher than for any other sector's AI applications. A credit scoring model that is 95 percent accurate is a good model. A diagnostic AI that is 95 percent accurate misses one in 20 diagnoses – and in some clinical contexts, that miss rate is unacceptable.

Clinical AI validation requires testing on the specific patient populations the system will serve. A dermatology AI trained predominantly on light-skinned patients may perform poorly on darker skin tones. A radiology AI validated on data from academic medical centers may not generalize to community hospitals with older imaging equipment. A sepsis prediction model trained on data from a large urban hospital may not perform accurately in a rural critical access hospital with different patient acuity and resource constraints. Your governance program must require that clinical AI systems demonstrate performance on populations that reflect your actual patient demographics, not just the populations in the vendor's marketing materials.

This requirement has real operational implications. When you procure a clinical AI tool, your validation process must include a site-specific performance evaluation. Ask the vendor for disaggregated performance data by demographic group, clinical setting, and device type. If the vendor cannot provide this data, that is a significant risk factor. If the vendor provides aggregate performance numbers that look impressive but will not break them down by subpopulation, treat that as a red flag — aggregate accuracy can mask disparities that matter for patient safety. Your governance committee should review clinical AI performance data at least quarterly and have a defined process for taking action if performance degrades below acceptable thresholds for any patient subgroup.

The Decision Support Distinction

The single most important regulatory boundary in healthcare AI is the line between clinical decision support (CDS) and clinical decision making. If the AI provides information to a clinician who then makes the decision, the regulatory burden is lower. If the AI makes the decision itself — or if the clinician effectively rubber-stamps the AI's output without independent clinical judgment — the regulatory burden increases dramatically.

The FDA uses several criteria to distinguish exempt CDS from regulated CDS, including whether the system's recommendations are transparent enough for the clinician to independently evaluate them. If the AI presents a diagnosis with a confidence score but does not explain the reasoning, the clinician cannot independently evaluate the recommendation, and the system is more likely to be classified as a regulated medical device.

Your governance program should clearly classify each clinical AI system as either decision support or decision making, and apply the appropriate regulatory and validation requirements accordingly. When in doubt, classify up — it is far better to over-validate a CDS tool than to under-validate a tool that turns out to be making clinical decisions.

There is also a practical reality to contend with: automation bias. Even when an AI system is designed as decision support, clinicians under time pressure may defer to the AI's recommendation without conducting the independent evaluation that the regulatory framework assumes. If your radiologists are reviewing 200 studies per day and the AI flags 15 as abnormal, the temptation to accept the AI's assessment on the remaining 185 without close scrutiny is real. Your governance program needs to address not just how the AI is designed but how it is actually used in practice. Workflow design, workload management, and clinical culture all affect whether a technically compliant CDS system functions as decision support or becomes de facto decision making.

Legal and Professional Services

Legal and professional services face a governance challenge that is fundamentally different from the regulatory compliance focus of financial services and healthcare. The issue here is professional liability. When a professional uses AI to produce work product, and that work product is wrong, the professional bears the consequence — not the AI vendor, not the technology platform, not the model provider. The professional's license, reputation, and livelihood are on the line.

This is not hypothetical. It has already happened.

> **Real-World Example: Mata v. Avianca — When AI Hallucinations Meet Professional Liability**
>
> In 2023, attorney Steven Schwartz used ChatGPT to research case law for a personal injury lawsuit, Mata v. Avianca. ChatGPT generated six case citations that appeared legitimate — complete with case names, docket numbers, and plausible legal reasoning. Schwartz included these citations in a legal brief filed with the Southern District of New York.
>
> The cases did not exist. Not one of them. ChatGPT had hallucinated six fictitious judicial opinions, and Schwartz submitted them to a federal court without verifying a single citation against an actual legal database.
>
> When opposing counsel could not locate the cited cases, the judge demanded an explanation. Schwartz initially doubled down, asking ChatGPT to confirm the cases were real — and ChatGPT, obligingly,

confirmed that they were. It was only when the judge ordered Schwartz to produce the actual opinions that the fabrications became undeniable.

Schwartz and his colleague Peter LoDuca were sanctioned by the court. The judge's opinion was blunt: the attorneys had "abandoned their responsibilities" by submitting AI-generated work product without verification. The case became the defining cautionary tale for AI use in legal practice.

The aftermath was significant. The American Bar Association issued Formal Opinion 512 in 2024, clarifying that lawyers who use generative AI tools must understand the technology well enough to supervise its output and must verify AI-generated content before relying on it in professional work. Multiple state bar associations issued similar guidance. Several courts adopted local rules requiring disclosure of AI use in legal filings.

The Duty of Competence

The foundational principle governing AI use in legal practice is the duty of competence. ABA Model Rule 1.1 requires that lawyers provide "competent representation" to clients, which includes "the legal knowledge, skill, thoroughness and preparation reasonably necessary for the representation." The ABA's Formal Opinion 512, issued in July 2024, explicitly extended this duty to cover AI tools: lawyers must understand generative AI well enough to supervise its outputs, identify its limitations, and ensure that AI-generated work product meets the standard of care.

This does not mean every lawyer needs to understand transformer architectures or training methodologies. It means that if you use an AI tool to draft a brief, you must understand that the tool can hallucinate, that it may generate plausible-sounding but incorrect legal analysis, and that you — not the tool — are responsible for the accuracy of the final product. You must verify citations against authoritative legal databases. You must review AI-generated analysis for logical coherence and legal accuracy. You must exercise independent professional judgment about whether the AI's output is correct.

The governance implication is straightforward: your acceptable use policy from Chapter 7 must explicitly address AI-generated work product, require human verification before any AI-generated content is used in client deliverables, and prohibit the submission of unverified AI output in legal filings. This is not a nice-to-have. It is a professional obligation.

For accounting, consulting, and other professional services firms, the principle is the same even though the specific conduct rules differ. CPAs are bound by the AICPA Code of Professional Conduct, which includes requirements for due professional care and adequate planning and supervision. Consultants operating under professional standards face similar obligations. The common thread is that professional judgment cannot be outsourced to an AI tool. The AI can draft, analyze, calculate, and summarize — but the professional must review, verify, and take responsibility for the final output.

Confidentiality and Privilege

Legal privilege is one of the most powerful protections in the legal system, and AI threatens to undermine it in ways that many firms have not fully considered. When you submit privileged client information to a third-party AI tool, have you waived the privilege?

The answer depends on the jurisdiction, the specific AI tool, and how the information is processed. Attorney-client privilege generally requires that the communication be made in confidence. If you paste a client's confidential information into a consumer AI tool that uses your input to train its models, you have arguably disclosed that information to a third party — the AI provider — and potentially to other users who interact with the model. That disclosure may constitute a waiver of privilege.

The safeguards you need depend on the sensitivity of the information. For unprivileged work, consumer AI tools with appropriate data handling terms may be acceptable. For privileged client information, you need enterprise AI tools with contractual guarantees that your data will not be used for training, will not be accessible to other users, and will be stored and processed in compliance with your confidentiality obligations. Some firms have deployed on-premises or private-cloud AI tools specifically to avoid sending any client data to third-party servers.

Your governance program must include clear guidelines about what types of information can be submitted to which AI tools. A tiered approach works well: public or non-sensitive information can go to approved consumer tools; confidential but non-privileged information requires enterprise tools with appropriate contractual protections; privileged information either requires on-premises tools or is prohibited from AI tools entirely.

Professional Liability

When AI-generated work product causes harm to a client, who bears liability? The answer, in virtually every jurisdiction and professional context, is the professional — not the AI vendor.

Professional liability insurance (malpractice insurance, errors-and-omissions coverage) typically covers the professional's negligent acts or omissions in providing professional services. If a lawyer submits a hallucinated case citation, that is the lawyer's negligence. If an accountant relies on an AI-generated tax analysis that is incorrect, that is the accountant's negligence. If a financial advisor follows an AI's recommendation that turns out to violate suitability requirements, that is the advisor's failure.

AI vendors' terms of service almost universally disclaim liability for the accuracy of their outputs. OpenAI's terms explicitly state that outputs may not be accurate and should not be relied upon as the sole source of truth. Anthropic's terms are similar. You will not successfully shift liability to the AI vendor when your professional judgment was the last line of defense.

The professional liability insurance implications are worth considering as well. Most malpractice and E&O policies cover negligent acts and omissions in the provision of professional services. Using AI to assist with those services is not, by itself, negligent — but failing to supervise the AI's output adequately is. Some insurers are beginning to ask about AI use in their underwriting questionnaires. If your firm uses AI extensively and your insurer is not aware, you could face coverage disputes when a claim arises. Disclose your AI use to your professional liability insurer. It is better to have a conversation about coverage now than to discover a gap after a claim.

This reality should shape your governance program. AI tools in professional services are efficiency multipliers, not judgment replacements. Every AI-generated output that becomes client work product must pass through a competent professional's review. That review must be genuine — not a cursory glance, but a substantive evaluation by someone qualified to assess the output's accuracy and appropriateness. Document the review process — who reviewed the output, when, and what verification steps they performed. If a claim arises, that documentation is your evidence that you exercised due professional care.

Education

The EU AI Act classifies AI systems used in educational and vocational training settings as high-risk under Annex III, Section 3. This includes AI systems that determine access to educational institutions, evaluate learning outcomes, assess the appropriate level of education for an individual, and monitor prohibited behavior during tests. If you are an educational institution or an edtech company deploying AI in these contexts, you face high-risk compliance obligations under the EU AI Act.

In the United States, the Family Educational Rights and Privacy Act (FERPA) governs the privacy of student education records. AI systems that process student records must comply with FERPA's consent, access, and amendment requirements. The intersection of AI and FERPA raises questions about automated decision-making in admissions, grading, and student services that do not have well-established regulatory answers yet — but the safe approach is to treat AI systems processing student records with the same rigor you would apply to any system handling sensitive student data.

Academic integrity is the other major governance concern. As AI-generated content becomes indistinguishable from student-produced work, educational institutions need policies that address AI use in academic contexts — not just prohibition policies, but constructive policies that define when AI use is acceptable, when it is not, and how students should disclose AI assistance. This is a governance challenge, not a technology challenge. No AI detection tool is reliable enough to serve as the sole enforcement mechanism.

Government

Government AI governance operates in a different context than the private sector. Government AI systems affect citizens who often have no choice but to interact with them — you cannot switch to a competitor government. That captive-audience dynamic raises the stakes for fairness, transparency, and accountability in ways that market competition does not naturally correct.

Federal AI Governance

Executive Order 14110, signed in October 2023, directed federal agencies to manage AI risks consistent with the NIST AI Risk Management Framework. The executive order did not make NIST AI RMF legally binding on agencies — it directed agencies to use it as guidance. But the practical effect has been significant: federal agencies have adopted AI governance programs, appointed Chief AI Officers, and begun inventorying their AI systems in alignment with the AI RMF's functions.

OMB Memorandum M-24-10, issued in March 2024, went further. It requires federal agencies to implement concrete AI governance measures, including designating Chief AI Officers, establishing AI governance boards, completing risk assessments for AI use cases that impact rights or safety, implementing minimum practices for rights-impacting and safety-impacting AI, and providing public transparency through AI use case inventories. If you work for a federal agency or advise one, M-24-10 is your operational roadmap. It translates the AI RMF's principles into specific administrative requirements with deadlines and reporting obligations.

The distinction M-24-10 draws between "rights-impacting" and "safety-impacting" AI is particularly important. Rights-impacting AI includes systems used to make or inform decisions about access to government benefits, law enforcement, immigration, or employment. Safety-impacting AI includes systems that control critical infrastructure, make medical decisions, or affect physical safety. Both categories trigger minimum governance practices — but the specific requirements differ. Rights-impacting AI requires impact assessments, ongoing monitoring, human oversight of consequential decisions, and public notice. Safety-impacting AI requires testing and evaluation before deployment, ongoing monitoring, and the ability to deactivate the system if it malfunctions. Understanding which of your AI systems fall into each category is a prerequisite for compliance.

The Federal AI Risk Management Act (HR 6936), if enacted, would take the next step — making AI RMF compliance mandatory rather than advisory for federal agencies and their contractors. Even if this specific bill does not pass, the trajectory is clear. Federal AI governance is moving from voluntary to mandatory, and the NIST AI RMF is the framework around which that mandate will be built.

Government Procurement

If you sell AI systems to the federal government, you face additional governance requirements beyond what private-sector customers demand. Federal procurement increasingly requires AI vendors to demonstrate alignment with the NIST AI RMF, provide documentation on model testing and evaluation, disclose training data provenance, and comply with agency-specific AI policies.

The General Services Administration (GSA) has begun incorporating AI-specific requirements into IT procurement vehicles. The Department of Defense has its own AI governance framework, the Responsible AI Strategy and Implementation Pathway, which imposes additional requirements on defense AI systems. If you are an AI vendor or system integrator serving federal customers, your governance program needs to address these procurement-specific documentation and compliance requirements.

For government contractors more broadly, anticipate that AI governance requirements will flow down through contract terms. Just as cybersecurity requirements (NIST 800-171, CMMC) flow down from federal contracts to subcontractors, AI governance requirements will follow the same path. Building a governance program aligned with the NIST AI RMF now positions you for these requirements before they become contract obligations.

State-Level AI Regulation

While the federal government has relied primarily on executive action and guidance, state legislatures have been passing binding AI legislation. The landscape is fragmented and evolving rapidly, but several state laws deserve attention.

The Colorado AI Act, effective June 30, 2026, is the most comprehensive state AI law in the United States. It requires developers and deployers of "high-risk AI systems" to implement risk management programs, conduct impact assessments, provide consumer disclosures, and report discrimination. High-risk systems are defined as those that make or substantially contribute to consequential decisions in employment, education, financial services, healthcare, housing, insurance, and legal services. If you deploy AI in Colorado in any of these domains, you have compliance obligations.

Illinois was an early mover with the Artificial Intelligence Video Interview Act, which requires employers to notify candidates when AI is used to analyze video interviews, explain how the AI works, and obtain consent. It is narrow in scope but established the precedent that AI-specific disclosure and consent requirements are legislatively viable.

New York City's Local Law 144 requires annual bias audits for automated employment decision tools (AEDTs) used in hiring or promotion. The law defines AEDTs broadly enough to cover most AI systems that screen resumes, score candidates, or recommend hiring decisions. If you use AI in hiring in New York City, you must conduct and publish an annual bias audit by an independent auditor.

The pattern across these state laws is consistent: disclosure, impact assessment, bias testing, and human oversight for AI systems that affect significant life decisions. Your governance program from Chapter 5 already includes most of these elements. The state-level requirements add specificity — particular notice requirements, audit formats, publication obligations — that you must map to your existing program and address.

The fragmentation of state AI legislation creates a practical challenge for organizations that operate nationally. You may need to comply with the Colorado AI Act for your Denver operations, NYC Local Law 144 for your New York City hiring, the Illinois Video Interview Act for your Chicago recruiting, and whatever your home state passes next year. There is no federal preemption that simplifies this landscape — unlike, say, banking regulation where the OCC can preempt some state laws for national banks. If you operate across multiple states, build your governance program to the highest applicable standard rather than trying to maintain different compliance postures for each jurisdiction. The strictest state's requirements will, in most cases, satisfy the others.

The Transparency Imperative

Government AI governance has a transparency dimension that the private sector does not face to the same degree. Citizens have a right to understand how their government makes decisions that affect them. When those decisions are informed or made by AI, that right does not evaporate.

M-24-10 requires federal agencies to publish inventories of their AI use cases. Several state laws require disclosure when AI is used in consequential decisions.

The practical governance implication is that you need to maintain documentation that is suitable for public disclosure — not just internal compliance documentation, but plain-language explanations of what AI systems you use, what decisions they inform, and what safeguards are in place. This is a higher bar than most private-sector organizations face, and it affects how you write your AI governance documentation from the beginning.

For government contractors, this transparency expectation flows downstream. If you build an AI system that a federal agency deploys for rights-impacting decisions, expect that the agency will need to explain your system to the public. Build documentation and explainability features that support that obligation. The agency will eventually ask for them, and retrofitting explainability into a system that was not designed for it is expensive and time-consuming.

SMB Spotlight: Sector Governance for SMBs

If you are a small or mid-sized business reading this chapter and feeling overwhelmed, take a breath. You do not need to implement every requirement described above on day one. You need to identify which sector-specific requirements apply to your organization and add the minimum necessary measures to the governance program you built in Chapter 5.

Financial services SMBs: Add bias testing for any AI system that touches lending, hiring, or insurance decisions. If your AI affects whether a consumer gets credit, gets hired, or gets insured, you need to test for disparate impact across protected classes. This is not optional — it is a fair lending and civil rights obligation.

Healthcare SMBs: Ensure you have Business Associate Agreements with every AI vendor that processes protected health information. No BAA, no PHI — no exceptions. And if you use clinical AI, validate its performance against your actual patient populations, not just the vendor's published benchmarks.

Legal services SMBs: Verify every AI-generated citation, analysis, and recommendation before it becomes client work product. Every single one. Build this verification step into your workflow as a firm-wide standard, not a suggestion.

Government-adjacent SMBs: If you sell to government or operate in a state with AI legislation (check Colorado, Illinois, and New York City first), map those specific requirements to your governance program now.

Action: Identify which sector-specific requirements apply to your organization and add them to your governance program from Chapter 5. One sector at a time. One requirement at a time. Start with the obligation that carries the highest penalty for noncompliance.

Looking Ahead

Chapter 11 covers the cutting edge — AI agents, multi-agent systems, and the governance challenges posed by AI that does not just analyze and recommend but takes autonomous action. The sector-specific requirements in this chapter will intersect heavily with agentic AI governance, because regulated sectors will be the first to face hard questions about autonomous AI systems making decisions in healthcare, finance, and government.

Key Takeaways

- **Most regulated sectors already have governance substrates.** Financial services has SR 11-7. Healthcare has FDA device regulation and HIPAA. Legal services has professional conduct rules. You are not building from scratch — you are extending existing governance infrastructure to cover AI-specific risks. Start by mapping your AI governance program to the sector-specific framework you already comply with.

- **Dual compliance is the norm, not the exception.** Healthcare AI in the EU faces both the Medical Device Regulation and the EU AI Act. Financial services AI faces both prudential regulators and consumer protection regulators. Government AI faces both federal mandates and state laws. Build your governance program to accommodate multiple overlapping frameworks from the beginning.

- **Professional liability stays with the professional.** AI vendors disclaim accuracy. Courts hold professionals accountable. When AI-generated work product is wrong — a hallucinated case citation, an incorrect diagnosis, a flawed credit decision — the professional who relied on it without adequate verification bears the consequence. Your governance program must require meaningful human review of all AI outputs that become professional work product.

- **Sector-specific high-risk classifications create mandatory governance obligations.** The EU AI Act's Annex III identifies specific use cases in financial services, healthcare, education, and government as high-risk. State laws like the Colorado AI Act and NYC Local Law 144 impose bias testing and disclosure requirements for AI in employment, lending, and insurance. Know which classifications apply to your AI systems and build compliance into your governance program.

- **The general framework from Chapters 5 through 9 is your foundation.** Everything in this chapter layers on top of it, not instead of it. Build the general program first, then add sector-specific requirements. If you try to build a sector-specific governance program without the general foundation, you will end up with gaps in the areas that every organization needs — inventory, risk classification, policy, vendor assessment, monitoring — while over-investing in sector-specific requirements that only matter if the basics are in place.

Chapter 11: Preparing for What's Next

If you have followed the program laid out in Chapters 5 through 10, you have a working AI governance program. You have an AI inventory. You have risk classifications. You have policies, human oversight mechanisms, vendor assessment processes, audit preparation procedures, and sector-specific requirements mapped and documented. That program is built for the AI governance landscape as it exists today, and it will serve you well.

This chapter is about the next twelve months.

Three developments are already underway — not speculative, not theoretical, not "emerging trends to watch." These are things happening right now, with published standards, active regulatory proceedings, and insurance products already in market. Each one will reshape what AI governance programs are expected to include. If you are aware of them and take basic preparatory steps now, you will be ahead of the curve when they hit your organization. If you are not, you will be scrambling to catch up under deadline pressure, which is exactly the situation this book was designed to prevent.

Here is what they are and how to prepare.

Development 1: Agentic AI Governance Requirements

Every AI system we have discussed so far in this book has one thing in common: it advises humans who then act. A chatbot drafts an email that a person reviews and sends. A risk model generates a score that an analyst interprets and acts on. A document review tool highlights clauses that a lawyer reads and evaluates. The human is in the loop. The AI recommends. The human decides.

Agentic AI breaks that model. An AI agent does not draft an email for your review — it sends the email. It does not recommend a purchase order — it places the order. It does not suggest a configuration change — it makes the change. Agents act. They use tools. They interact with other systems. And increasingly, they interact with other agents.

This is not a future scenario. As of early 2026, major enterprise software vendors are shipping agentic AI features. Salesforce's Agentforce, Microsoft's Copilot agents, ServiceNow's AI agents — these are production systems that take actions on behalf of organizations. If your employees are using any of these platforms, you may already have agentic AI operating in your environment, and your current governance program may not account for it.

The Four New Governance Challenges

Agentic AI introduces four governance challenges that your existing program was not designed to address.

Agent identity. Who is this agent? When an AI agent sends an email, places an order, or modifies a database record, it is acting as an entity in your organization. But your identity and access management systems were designed for humans and service accounts with predictable behavior. An AI agent that can be instructed to take a wide range of actions does not fit neatly into either category. You need to know which agents are operating in your environment, what identities they are using, and how those identities are managed.

Action authorization. What can this agent do? Traditional access controls define what a user can access. Agentic AI requires a different question: what actions can this agent take? An agent with read access to your CRM and write access to your email system can, in combination, exfiltrate customer data by composing and sending emails. The individual permissions may each seem reasonable. The combination creates risk that neither permission alone would suggest. Authorization for agents must account for the compound effect of tool access.

Cascading risk. What happens when agents interact? A single agent operating within defined boundaries is manageable. Multiple agents interacting — one agent's output becoming another agent's input, agents delegating tasks to other agents, agents negotiating with external agents — creates cascading risk that is qualitatively different from single-system risk. An error in one agent's output propagates through every downstream agent that consumes it, potentially amplified at each step.

Accountability gaps. Who is responsible when an agent acts autonomously? If an AI agent negotiates a contract term that creates liability for your organization, who approved that term? If an agent sends a communication to a customer that contains incorrect information, who is accountable? Your governance program assigns accountability for AI systems to human owners. But when the AI is acting autonomously and making decisions in real time, the gap between "the human who deployed the agent" and "the agent's specific action" creates accountability ambiguity that your policies need to address.

The Regulatory Response Is Already Underway

Singapore's Model Governance Framework for Generative AI, updated in January 2026, is the preview of what is coming globally. It explicitly addresses agentic AI governance, including requirements for agent monitoring, human override capabilities, and documentation of agent decision boundaries. Singapore has consistently been twelve to eighteen months ahead of other jurisdictions on AI governance frameworks. When Singapore publishes guidance, pay attention — it signals where global consensus is forming.

In the United States, NIST launched its AI Agent Standards Initiative in February 2026. The initiative has three pillars: standards development for agentic AI systems, open-source protocols for agent interoperability and safety, and security research focused on agent-specific threats. NIST is developing SP 800-53 control overlays for both single-agent and multi-agent systems. If you are familiar with SP 800-53 from your cybersecurity program — and if you are a federal contractor or follow NIST frameworks, you are — these overlays will integrate agent governance directly into your existing control framework. That is significant because it means agentic AI governance will not be a separate program. It will be an extension of the security controls you already implement.

Also in February 2026, NIST's National Cybersecurity Center of Excellence published a concept paper on AI agent identity and authorization. The paper addresses exactly the challenges described above: how to establish trusted identities for AI agents, how to manage authorization for agents that use tools, and how to maintain audit trails for agent actions. This is the technical foundation that future standards will build on.

What to Do Now

Extend your AI inventory to include agentic AI systems. For each agent operating in your environment — including agents embedded in third-party platforms your employees use — document four things: what tools it can access, what data it can reach, what actions it can take autonomously, and who is responsible for its behavior. If you cannot answer all four questions for an agent, that agent needs additional governance controls before it should be operating in production.

This is not a massive undertaking. It is a column addition to the inventory spreadsheet you built in Chapter 5. But it is an essential one, because every subsequent agentic AI governance requirement — from NIST, from your sector regulators, from your insurers — will assume you know what agents are operating in your environment. If you do not have that baseline, you cannot comply with anything that comes next.

Development 2: The Standards Acceleration

The period from November 2025 to March 2026 produced an extraordinary concentration of new AI governance and security standards. If you were not tracking the standards landscape during those five months, you missed a wave that will define audit expectations for the next several years. Here is what was published:

OWASP Top 10 for Agentic Applications (December 2025). OWASP's track record speaks for itself — the original OWASP Top 10 for web applications became a de facto audit standard within two years of publication. The agentic applications list identifies the ten most critical security risks in AI agent systems, including excessive agency, inadequate sandboxing, and uncontrolled tool use. Auditors will reference this list. Penetration testers will use it as a testing framework. Your security team needs to be familiar with it.

MITRE ATLAS v5.4.0 (February 2026). ATLAS is MITRE's adversarial threat landscape for AI systems — the AI equivalent of ATT&CK for cybersecurity. Version 5.4.0 added techniques specifically targeting agentic AI, including agent manipulation, tool poisoning, and multi-agent exploitation. If your threat modeling process references MITRE frameworks — and after Chapter 4, it should — ATLAS v5.4.0 needs to be incorporated.

NIST AI Agent Standards Initiative (February 2026). Covered in the previous section. The standards, open-source protocols, and security research pillars will produce actionable outputs within twelve months.

OpenID AuthZEN 1.0 (March 2026). The first standardized authorization framework designed for AI agents. AuthZEN defines how to evaluate and enforce authorization decisions for AI systems that use tools and take actions. This is infrastructure-level plumbing that will eventually underpin how enterprises manage agent permissions at scale.

CSA Cloud Security Alliance Artificial Intelligence Foundation — CSAI (March 2026). CSA's entry into AI governance standardization, focused on securing AI systems in cloud environments. Given CSA's influence on cloud security standards and audit frameworks like STAR, their AI work will ripple into cloud security assessments.

CoSAI AI Incident Response Framework v1.0. The first standardized framework for responding to AI-specific security incidents. If you built an incident response process using Chapter 9's guidance, this framework provides additional structure specifically for AI incidents — including classification taxonomies, containment procedures, and post-incident analysis templates.

> **Real-World Example: The March 2026 Standards Explosion**
>
> In the six weeks between mid-February and late March 2026, the AI security community produced: NIST's AI Agent Standards Initiative, OpenID's AuthZEN 1.0, CSA's CSAI Foundation, and CoSAI's AI IR Framework. Each of these will be referenced by auditors within twelve months. Organizations that tracked this wave are already adapting. Organizations that did not are falling behind.

What This Means

The AI governance standards ecosystem is crystallizing. For the past three years, organizations have been operating in an environment where frameworks were emerging but not yet authoritative — where you could reasonably say "we follow NIST AI RMF" and that was sufficient to demonstrate governance maturity. That era is ending. Within twelve months, auditors, regulators, and insurers will reference specific standards from the list above the same way they reference NIST CSF, ISO 27001, and SOC 2 today. "We follow NIST AI RMF" will still be necessary. It will no longer be sufficient.

This does not mean you need to implement every standard on that list. It means you need to know they exist, understand which ones are relevant to your organization, and be able to articulate how your governance program addresses the areas they cover. An auditor who asks "how do you address the OWASP Agentic Top 10 risks?" is not necessarily expecting you to have implemented all ten controls. They are expecting you to be aware of the list, to have evaluated which risks apply to your environment, and to have a documented position on each one.

> **SMB Spotlight: Which Emerging Standards to Track and Which to Ignore (For Now)**
>
> Not every standard on that list requires your immediate attention. Here is the priority filter for small and mid-sized businesses.
>
> **Track now:** NIST AI Agent Standards Initiative (will affect US federal contractors first, then ripple outward to any organization that follows NIST frameworks), OWASP Agentic Top 10 (auditors will reference this within twelve months, and it is freely available and readable in an afternoon), and your insurance carrier's AI coverage changes (more on this in the next section).
>
> **Ignore for now:** OpenID AuthZEN (important infrastructure, but too early for SMB implementation — this is for platform vendors and enterprise IAM teams), CSAI Foundation outputs (enterprise-focused and cloud-provider-centric initially), and protocol-specific standards like MCP and A2A specifications (unless your developers are actively building agent systems, these are implementation details you do not need to track yet).
>
> **Action:** Add a thirty-minute "AI standards review" to your quarterly governance meeting agenda. One person reviews what has been published since the last meeting. Five minutes per standard: what is it, does it apply to us, do we need to act. That is the entire process.

What to Do Now

Establish a quarterly standards monitoring cadence. Assign one person — it does not need to be a full-time role, it needs to be a defined responsibility — to track NIST, OWASP, and ISO updates related to AI governance. Subscribe to the NIST AI RMF mailing list. Subscribe to the OWASP GenAI and Agentic AI project updates. Add a standing agenda item to your quarterly governance review meeting.

The goal is not to implement every new standard the moment it is published. The goal is to be aware of what has been published, to evaluate its relevance to your organization, and to incorporate relevant requirements into your governance program on a planned cadence rather than in a reactive scramble when an auditor or regulator asks about it.

Development 3: The Insurance Reckoning

This is the development that will affect your budget first, which is why you need to understand it even if the standards and agentic AI developments feel abstract.

Starting in late 2025 and accelerating through early 2026, the insurance industry began repricing AI risk. The result is a two-sided shift that every organization needs to understand: existing policies are excluding AI-related losses, and new AI-specific products are emerging with governance requirements attached to coverage.

The Exclusion Wave

In January 2026, Berkley introduced an absolute AI exclusion endorsement for Directors & Officers and Errors & Omissions policies. Not a limitation. Not a sublimit. An absolute exclusion — meaning any loss arising from artificial intelligence is excluded from coverage entirely. Hamilton followed with a generative AI exclusion for professional liability policies. ISO released Commercial General Liability endorsements that modify coverage for AI-related claims.

These are not obscure specialty insurers testing the market. These are major carriers whose endorsements are being adopted across the industry. If you have not reviewed your D&O, E&O, or CGL policies since January 2026, you may already have AI exclusions in your coverage that you do not know about. Renewal terms are where these exclusions appear, and unless you or your broker specifically flagged AI coverage during your last renewal, the exclusion may have been added as a standard endorsement.

The practical impact is immediate. If your organization deploys AI that causes harm — a biased hiring algorithm that triggers a discrimination claim, a chatbot that provides incorrect financial advice, an AI system that leaks personal data —

your existing liability insurance may not cover the resulting loss. The claim comes in. You notify your carrier. The carrier points to the AI exclusion endorsement on page forty-seven of your policy. You are uninsured for that loss.

New AI-Specific Products

The insurance market is not just excluding AI risk. It is also creating new products to cover it — at a price, and with conditions.

HSB, a Munich Re subsidiary, launched an AI liability insurance product specifically designed for small and mid-sized enterprises. Coalition, a cyber insurance carrier, added deepfake incident coverage in December 2025. Other carriers are developing AI-specific endorsements that can be added to existing policies.

But here is the critical point for governance: these new AI insurance products are not available unconditionally. Insurers are requiring evidence of AI governance as an underwriting prerequisite. The underwriting questionnaire for AI-specific coverage asks about adversarial red-teaming programs, model-level risk assessments, specialized safeguards for high-risk AI applications, and documented governance policies. Without governance documentation, you either cannot get coverage at all, or your coverage terms are dramatically worse — sublimits dropping from five million dollars to five hundred thousand dollars, deductibles doubling, and exclusions narrowing the scope of what is actually covered.

This is where the governance program you built in Chapters 5 through 10 pays for itself in direct financial terms. When you sit down with your insurance broker and can produce an AI inventory, documented risk classifications, policies with defined accountability, vendor assessment records, and monitoring cadences, you are presenting exactly the evidence that underwriters want to see. You are not just a well-governed organization. You are a better insurance risk. And better insurance risks get better coverage at better prices.

The Cyber Insurance Parallel

If this dynamic sounds familiar, it should. Between 2018 and 2022, cyber insurance underwent exactly this transition. In 2018, cyber insurance was optional — a nice-to-have that forward-thinking organizations purchased. By 2020, it was recommended — brokers were advising clients to add it, and contracts were starting to require it. By 2022, it was effectively mandatory — business partners required it, contracts mandated it, and organizations without cyber insurance faced both coverage gaps and competitive disadvantages.

During that same period, cyber insurance underwriting went from simple questionnaires to detailed security assessments. Carriers started requiring multi-factor authentication, endpoint detection and response, email filtering, backup procedures, and documented incident response plans as prerequisites for coverage. Organizations without these controls either could not get coverage or paid dramatically higher premiums.

AI insurance is on the same trajectory, compressed into two to three years instead of four. The exclusion wave is the equivalent of 2019-2020 in cyber insurance — carriers recognizing a new risk category and adjusting their portfolios. The new AI-specific products with governance prerequisites are the equivalent of 2021 — carriers offering coverage but with security requirements attached. By 2027 or 2028, AI governance documentation will be a standard underwriting requirement the way MFA and EDR are standard cyber insurance requirements today.

Organizations that build governance programs now — as you have done by following this book — will be positioned for favorable coverage. Organizations that wait will face the same scramble that organizations without MFA faced in 2022: rushed implementations under deadline pressure, with worse coverage terms while they catch up.

What to Do Now

Review your current insurance policies — D&O, E&O, CGL, and cyber — for AI-related exclusions. Do not skim the renewal letter. Read the endorsements. Look specifically for language about "artificial intelligence," "machine learning," "generative AI," "automated decision-making," and "algorithmic" processes. If you find exclusions or are not sure, call your broker.

When you contact your broker, ask three specific questions. First, do any of my current policies contain AI-related exclusions or limitations? Second, what AI-specific coverage options are available through my current carriers? Third, what governance documentation would improve my coverage terms and premiums?

If you have governance documentation from this book — your AI inventory, your risk classifications, your policies, your vendor assessments — bring it to the conversation. It directly impacts your coverage terms. Insurers do not want to see a perfect governance program. They want to see that you have a program, that it is documented, and that it demonstrates awareness of AI-specific risks. The work you have already done is exactly what they are looking for.

Three Actions to Take This Quarter

Everything above can feel like a lot to absorb. Here is the distillation — three concrete actions, each achievable within a single quarter, that position your governance program for the next twelve months.

Action 1: Extend your AI inventory to cover agentic AI systems. Add columns for agent-specific attributes: tools accessible, data reachable, autonomous actions permitted, and accountable human owner. Include AI agents embedded in third-party platforms your employees use. This is a half-day exercise if your inventory from Chapter 5 is current.

Action 2: Review your insurance coverage for AI-related exclusions and engage your broker. Pull your current D&O, E&O, CGL, and cyber policies. Search for AI-related exclusion language. Schedule a call with your broker to discuss AI-specific coverage options. Bring your governance documentation. This is a one-week exercise.

Action 3: Establish a quarterly standards monitoring cadence. Assign one person to track NIST, OWASP, and ISO AI governance updates. Subscribe to the relevant mailing lists. Add a standing thirty-minute agenda item to your quarterly governance meeting. This is a one-hour setup exercise.

None of these actions requires new budget. None requires new headcount. None requires new technology. They are extensions of the governance program you already have. That is the point — a well-designed governance program is extensible by design. You built the structure. These actions keep it current.

Action Item: 12-Month Governance Program Roadmap Template

Reference Appendix B for the complete template. Here is the quarter-by-quarter summary.

Q1 (now): Extend your AI inventory to cover agentic AI systems. Review insurance policies for AI exclusions and engage your broker. Establish your quarterly standards monitoring cadence.

Q2: Update your AI governance policies to address agentic AI. Conduct your first annual governance program review using the framework from Chapter 9. If you have EU exposure, begin preparing your EU AI Act evidence package.

Q3: August 2026 brings EU AI Act enforcement for high-risk AI systems. Ensure compliance if applicable. Review and update your risk classifications based on six months of operational data.

Q4: Conduct your annual governance program review. Update all policies to reflect the year's regulatory and standards changes. Plan next year's governance program based on lessons learned and the evolving landscape.

A Note on What Comes Next: Runtime Governance

Everything in this book has been about governance as a management discipline — inventories, policies, oversight structures, audit processes, documentation. These are essential. They are also, fundamentally, things that exist on paper and in organizational processes. A policy says "all AI outputs affecting customers must be reviewed by a human before delivery." But the policy does not enforce itself. A human must follow the process. And processes, as anyone who has worked in compliance knows, are only as reliable as the people following them.

There is a different approach emerging for agentic AI systems: runtime governance. The concept is straightforward — instead of writing a policy that says "this agent must not access customer financial data without authorization," you enforce that policy at the action boundary. Every action the agent attempts — every tool call, every data access, every external communication — is checked against policy before execution. Not by a human reviewer. By a governance engine that evaluates the action in real time and either permits it, blocks it, or escalates it for human review.

This is not policy on paper. It is policy enforced in code. And for organizations deploying agentic AI systems at scale, it is the difference between governance that depends on human compliance and governance that is architecturally enforced.

This book is not the place for a deep dive into runtime governance. The topic requires its own treatment — threat taxonomies for agentic AI, runtime enforcement architectures, incident response playbooks for agent-specific scenarios, and reference architectures for multi-agent governance systems. For that deep dive, including practical implementation guidance for securing agentic AI systems, see *Securing Agentic AI (2026 Edition)* by the same author.

Closing

You started this book with a governance gap. Maybe you had no AI governance program at all. Maybe you had something informal — a policy document that no one read, an inventory that was out of date, oversight that existed in theory but not in practice. You knew you needed to do better. You were not sure where to start.

If you have followed the program in Chapters 5 through 10, you have closed that gap. You have an AI inventory that accounts for every AI system in your organization. You have risk classifications that tell you which systems need the most governance attention. You have policies that define acceptable use, procurement requirements, and accountability. You have human oversight mechanisms calibrated to the risk level of each system. You have vendor assessment processes that evaluate AI-specific risks before you sign contracts. You have audit preparation procedures that produce the evidence auditors expect. And if you operate in a regulated sector, you have the sector-specific requirements layered on top.

The frameworks will evolve. NIST will publish new guidance. The EU AI Act will generate enforcement precedent. New standards will emerge for agentic AI, for multi-agent systems, for runtime governance. The threat landscape will shift. New AI capabilities will create new risks that no one has anticipated yet. The insurance market will continue to reprice AI risk. Auditors will reference standards that have not been published yet.

None of that changes the foundation. The discipline of governance — inventory, classify, policy, oversight, audit — is permanent. The specific controls and frameworks will update. The discipline does not. You now have that discipline. It is documented, it is operational, and it is extensible.

Use it.

Key Takeaways

- **Agentic AI is already in your environment, and your governance program needs to account for it.** AI agents that act autonomously — sending emails, placing orders, modifying data — introduce governance challenges around identity, authorization, cascading risk, and accountability that traditional AI governance does not address. Extend your AI inventory now to cover agentic systems before NIST and sector regulators formalize requirements.

- **The AI governance standards ecosystem crystallized between November 2025 and March 2026.** OWASP, MITRE, NIST, OpenID, CSA, and CoSAI all published significant frameworks in a five-month window. These standards will be referenced by auditors, regulators, and insurers within twelve months. Establish a quarterly monitoring cadence so you are adapting to new standards on your schedule, not scrambling when an auditor asks about them.

- **AI insurance is following the cyber insurance trajectory at compressed speed.** Existing policies are adding AI exclusions. New AI-specific products require governance documentation as an underwriting prerequisite. Review your current coverage for AI exclusions now and engage your broker with your governance documentation in hand — it directly impacts your coverage terms and premiums.

- **A well-designed governance program is inherently extensible.** The three actions in this chapter — extending your inventory, reviewing your insurance, establishing standards monitoring — do not require new programs or new budgets. They are natural extensions of the governance framework you built in Chapters 5 through 10. That extensibility is the payoff of building the program right the first time.

- **The discipline of governance is permanent.** Frameworks will evolve. Threats will evolve. Regulations will evolve. But the core practice — inventory, classify, policy, oversight, audit — does not change. You now have that practice in place. Keep it current, keep it documented, and it will serve you through whatever comes next.

Part VI: Reference

"Good judgment comes from experience, and experience comes from bad judgment."

— Rita Mae Brown (attributed)

Appendix A: Template AI Policies

The templates in this appendix are referenced throughout the book. They are designed to be adapted, not adopted verbatim. Every organization is different — your industry, jurisdiction, size, risk appetite, and existing governance infrastructure will all shape what these documents look like in practice.

Each template includes instructions in italics where you need to customize. Fill in the bracketed fields, delete sections that do not apply, and add sections for requirements specific to your context. Then route the document through whatever approval process your organization uses for policy documents.

These templates reflect the regulatory landscape as of early 2026. Review them against current requirements before adoption.

A.1: AI Acceptable Use Policy Template

This template implements the policy structure described in Chapter 7. Customize all bracketed fields and italicized instructions before adoption.

[ORGANIZATION NAME] AI Acceptable Use Policy

Document ID: *[e.g., POL-AI-001]* **Version:** *[e.g., 1.0]* **Effective Date:** *[Date]* **Last Reviewed:** *[Date]* **Policy Owner:** *[Title/Department]* **Approved By:** *[Name, Title]*

---

1. Purpose and Scope

This policy establishes the rules governing the use of artificial intelligence systems by all employees, contractors, and third parties acting on behalf of [ORGANIZATION NAME]. It applies to every AI tool, service, model, and AI-enabled feature used in connection with organizational business, whether provided by the organization, a third-party vendor, or accessed independently by personnel.

This policy applies regardless of whether the AI system is accessed through a corporate device, a personal device, a web browser, a mobile application, an API, or any other interface.

Scope includes: - AI tools provided or approved by [ORGANIZATION NAME] - AI features embedded in approved SaaS platforms (e.g., Microsoft Copilot, Salesforce Einstein) - External AI services accessed for work purposes (e.g., ChatGPT, Claude, Gemini) - Internally developed AI models and systems - AI agents, plugins, and integrations connected to organizational data

Scope excludes: - *[Define any exclusions, e.g., personal use of AI tools on personal devices for non-work purposes]*

2. Definitions

Term	Definition
AI System	A machine-based system that, for explicit or implicit objectives, infers from the input it receives how to generate outputs such as predictions, content, recommendations, or decisions that can influence physical or virtual environments. This includes both traditional machine learning systems and generative AI.
Generative AI	AI systems that generate text, images, audio, video, code, or other content in response to prompts or instructions. Includes large language models (LLMs), image generators, and multimodal models.
Agentic AI	AI systems capable of autonomous action, including planning multi-step tasks, using tools, interacting with external systems, and operating with limited or no human intervention for extended sequences of actions.
AI Deployer	An entity that uses an AI system under its authority, except where the AI system is used in the course of a personal non-professional activity. Under the EU AI Act, deployers bear specific compliance obligations. [ORGANIZATION NAME] is a deployer for all third-party AI systems it uses.

Term	Definition
AI User	Any employee, contractor, or authorized third party who interacts with an AI system in the course of performing work for [ORGANIZATION NAME].
AI Provider	The entity that develops or places an AI system on the market. Also referred to as a vendor or supplier in this policy.
Prompt	Any input provided to an AI system, including text queries, uploaded documents, images, data files, or configuration instructions.

3. Approved AI Tools

Maintain a current list of approved tools as a living document. Update it whenever tools are added, removed, or have their approved use cases modified. Publish the current version on your intranet or governance portal so employees can check before using a tool.

For each approved tool, record:

- **Tool Name**
- **Vendor**
- **Approved Use Cases**
- **Data Classification Allowed** (Public / Internal / Confidential / Restricted)
- **Approval Date**

Common approved-tool entries look like:

- *Microsoft Copilot* (Microsoft) — document drafting, email summarization, data analysis within M365 — Public, Internal, Confidential (within tenant) — *[approval date]*
- *GitHub Copilot Enterprise* (GitHub/Microsoft) — code assistance, code review, documentation generation — Public, Internal (source code per classification) — *[approval date]*
- *ChatGPT Enterprise* (OpenAI) — research, brainstorming, first-draft content generation — Public, Internal — *[approval date]*

Tools not on this list are not approved for use with organizational data.

Requesting a new tool: To request approval for a new AI tool, submit a request through *[process/system name]* to *[approving body]*. Include the vendor name, intended use case, data types involved, and any vendor documentation on data handling. Allow *[X]* business days for review.

4. Prohibited Uses

The following uses of AI systems are prohibited regardless of the tool used:

1. **Submitting personally identifiable information (PII) or protected health information (PHI) to external AI systems** unless the system is specifically approved for that data classification and a Data Processing Agreement (DPA) is in place.
2. **Using AI for final decisions in regulated domains** without qualified human review and approval. This includes decisions related to credit, insurance, employment, housing, healthcare, benefits eligibility, and law enforcement.
3. **Deploying AI-generated code to production** without the code passing standard code review processes, including security review where applicable.
4. **Using AI to create content attributed to specific individuals** without their knowledge and explicit consent. This includes generating text, images, audio, or video that is presented as if created by or depicting a specific person.
5. **Circumventing security controls using AI**, including using AI to bypass access controls, defeat monitoring systems, generate malicious code, exploit vulnerabilities, or evade data loss prevention measures.
6. **Using AI to generate or disseminate misinformation**, fabricate evidence, create deceptive communications, or produce fraudulent documents.
7. **Submitting trade secrets, proprietary algorithms, unpublished financial data, or material non-public information** to any external AI system.

8. **Using AI to monitor, profile, or score employees** without explicit authorization from *[HR/Legal/Ethics function]* and notification to affected personnel where required by law.

9. **Using non-approved AI tools** with any organizational data classified as Internal, Confidential, or Restricted.

10. *[Add organization-specific prohibitions based on your industry, regulatory environment, and risk appetite.]*

5. Data Classification Requirements

Before submitting any data to an AI system, determine the data classification and verify that the tool is approved for that classification level.

Public. Any approved AI tool. No requirements beyond standard use guidelines.

Internal. Enterprise AI tools only — tools deployed within organizational infrastructure or with enterprise agreements that contractually prohibit data use for training. Verify enterprise agreement terms. Do not use consumer-tier versions of AI tools.

Confidential. Approved enterprise AI tools with Data Loss Prevention (DLP) controls active. DLP must be configured and operational. A Data Processing Agreement must be in place. Log all submissions for audit purposes.

Restricted. No external AI processing permitted. AI processing of Restricted data may only occur on systems fully controlled by [ORGANIZATION NAME], with no external data transmission. Approval from *[CISO/DPO/appropriate authority]* required for any exception.

If you are unsure of a data element's classification, treat it as Confidential until you confirm. When in doubt, do not submit it to an external AI system.

6. Output Review Requirements

All AI-generated outputs carry risk of inaccuracy, bias, intellectual property infringement, and other defects. The following review requirements apply:

- **External-facing content:** All AI-generated or AI-assisted content intended for customers, partners, regulators, the public, or any external audience must be reviewed and approved by a qualified person before distribution. The reviewer must have subject-matter expertise relevant to the content.

- **Code:** AI-generated code must pass the same code review process as human-written code. This includes peer review, automated testing, static analysis, and security scanning as applicable to the code's deployment context. AI-generated code must not be committed to repositories without attribution *[per your engineering standards]*.

- **Regulated contexts:** AI outputs used in regulated decision-making (financial, healthcare, legal, employment, safety-critical) must be independently verified against authoritative sources by a qualified professional. The verification must be documented.

- **Data analysis:** AI-generated analyses, summaries, or statistical outputs used for business decisions must be validated against source data. Do not rely on AI-generated statistics without verification.

- **Legal and compliance content:** AI must not be used as the sole source for legal advice, regulatory interpretation, or compliance guidance. All such outputs require review by qualified legal or compliance personnel.

7. Disclosure Requirements

[ORGANIZATION NAME] is committed to transparency in its use of AI. The following disclosure requirements apply:

- **Customer-facing interactions:** Disclose AI involvement when AI is used to generate substantive content delivered to customers, when customers interact directly with an AI system (e.g., chatbots), or when AI plays a material role in decisions affecting customers. *[Customize the specific disclosure mechanism and language.]*

- **Partner and vendor communications:** Disclose AI use when AI-generated content forms part of contractual deliverables, proposals, or formal communications, unless the partner's agreement explicitly permits AI use without disclosure.

- **Regulatory filings:** Follow all applicable regulatory requirements for AI disclosure. When in doubt, disclose. *[Reference specific regulatory requirements for your industry.]*
- **Internal communications:** Clearly label AI-generated content shared internally when the content could be mistaken for original expert analysis or when the accuracy of the content is material to decisions being made.

8. Incident Reporting

Report any of the following immediately through *[reporting channel – e.g., email, ticketing system, hotline]*:

- **Harmful or incorrect output:** AI system produces output that is materially incorrect, biased, offensive, or potentially harmful, particularly if the output was or could be distributed externally.
- **Unauthorized AI tool use:** Discovery that an employee or contractor is using a non-approved AI tool with organizational data.
- **Suspected data exposure:** Any instance where Confidential or Restricted data may have been submitted to an unauthorized AI system, or where an AI system may have exposed organizational data.
- **Unexpected AI behavior:** AI systems acting outside their expected parameters, producing anomalous outputs, or exhibiting behavior suggesting compromise (e.g., prompt injection).
- **Vendor incidents:** Notification from an AI vendor of a security breach, data incident, or material change to their service that affects data handling.

Reports should be submitted to *[incident response team/email/system]* within *[X hours]* of discovery. Do not attempt to investigate or remediate independently. Preserve all evidence, including prompts, outputs, screenshots, and timestamps.

9. Consequences of Violation

Violations of this policy will be addressed through progressive discipline consistent with [ORGANIZATION NAME]'s existing disciplinary framework:

1. **First violation (minor):** Verbal warning and mandatory completion of AI Acceptable Use training within *[X]* business days.

2. **Repeated or moderate violation:** Written warning, mandatory retraining, and temporary restriction of AI tool access pending review.
3. **Serious violation** (e.g., submitting Restricted data to external AI, circumventing security controls): Formal disciplinary action up to and including termination of employment or contract, consistent with *[HR policy reference]*.
4. **Violations involving legal or regulatory breach:** Referred to *[Legal/Compliance]* for additional action as required.

Intentional violations, attempts to conceal violations, and violations that result in data breaches or regulatory action will be treated as serious regardless of whether they are a first offense.

10. Review Schedule

This policy will be reviewed:

- **At minimum annually**, on or before *[month/date]* each year.
- **Within 30 days** of any of the following triggers:
  - Material change in applicable AI regulation (e.g., new EU AI Act obligations taking effect)
  - Significant AI-related incident involving [ORGANIZATION NAME]
  - Addition of a new AI system processing Confidential or Restricted data
  - Material change in organizational AI strategy or risk appetite
  - Change in the regulatory environment affecting AI disclosure, risk management, or data handling requirements

The policy owner is responsible for initiating reviews and routing updated versions through the approval process.

11. Acknowledgment

I have read and understood the [ORGANIZATION NAME] AI Acceptable Use Policy. I agree to comply with all requirements set forth in this policy. I understand the consequences of non-compliance.

Name:	______________________________

Title:	______________________
Department:	______________________
Signature:	______________________
Date:	______________________

A.2: AI Risk Assessment Template

Use this template to document the risk profile of each AI system your organization uses or deploys. Complete one row per AI system. Review and update at least annually, or when material changes occur to the system, its data inputs, or the regulatory environment. The NIST Trustworthiness characteristics are described in Chapter 4. The EU AI Act risk tiers are described in Chapter 2.

NIST Trustworthiness Rating Key

Rate each characteristic as **H** (High confidence/low concern), **M** (Moderate confidence/some concerns), or **L** (Low confidence/significant concerns):

1. **Valid & Reliable** — Accuracy, consistency, robustness of outputs
2. **Safe** — Freedom from conditions that can cause harm
3. **Secure & Resilient** — Resistance to attack, ability to recover
4. **Accountable & Transparent** — Explainability, auditability
5. **Explainable & Interpretable** — Can users understand why it produced an output?
6. **Privacy-Enhanced** — Data minimization, consent, protection
7. **Fair (Bias Managed)** — Equitable treatment across demographics

Risk Score Calculation

Assign numeric values: H=3, M=2, L=1. Sum the seven NIST characteristics (max 21). Weight by EU AI Act tier: Minimal risk ×1, Limited risk ×1.5, High risk ×2, Unacceptable = do not deploy. The resulting score guides prioritization but does not replace judgment.

Assessment Register

Document each AI system in your inventory using the card format below. Three example entries follow.

System #1: Customer Support Chatbot

- **Vendor:** Vendor X
- **Model Type:** LLM (GPT-4o)
- **Data Inputs:** Customer inquiries, account data (name, email, order history)
- **Data Outputs:** Text responses, ticket summaries, escalation flags
- **Users:** Support team (25 users), customers (~10K/month)
- **EU AI Act Risk Tier:** Limited
- **NIST Trustworthiness Scores:** V&R: M | Safety: H | S&R: M | A&T: M | E&I: L | Privacy: M | Fairness: H
- **Risk Score:** 13
- **Owner:** VP Customer Ops
- **Last Review:** 2026-01-15

System #2: Resume Screening Tool

- **Vendor:** Vendor Y
- **Model Type:** Classification model + NLP
- **Data Inputs:** Resumes, job descriptions, candidate PII (name, education, experience)
- **Data Outputs:** Ranked candidate lists, match scores, rejection recommendations
- **Users:** HR team (8 users)
- **EU AI Act Risk Tier:** High
- **NIST Trustworthiness Scores:** V&R: M | Safety: M | S&R: M | A&T: L | E&I: L | Privacy: L | Fairness: L
- **Risk Score:** 20

- **Owner:** CHRO
- **Last Review:** 2026-02-01

System #3: Code Assistant

- **Vendor:** GitHub
- **Model Type:** LLM (Copilot)
- **Data Inputs:** Source code, comments, documentation
- **Data Outputs:** Code suggestions, test generation, documentation drafts
- **Users:** Engineering team (40 users)
- **EU AI Act Risk Tier:** Minimal
- **NIST Trustworthiness Scores:** V&R: M | Safety: H | S&R: M | A&T: H | E&I: M | Privacy: H | Fairness: H
- **Risk Score:** 18
- **Owner:** VP Engineering
- **Last Review:** 2026-01-30

Add entries as your AI inventory grows. This register should be maintained as a living document, ideally in a shared spreadsheet or governance tool rather than a static document.

A.3: AI Vendor Assessment Scorecard

This is the 10-question scorecard introduced in Chapter 8. Use it to evaluate any AI vendor before procurement and at each contract renewal. Each question is scored 1 through 5 using the rubric below.

Vendor Name: ______________________________ **Assessment Date:** ______________________________ **Assessor(s):** ______________________________ **Product/Service Evaluated:** ______________________________

Scorecard

Work through each question below. Score it 1 to 5 using the rubric that follows, and capture supporting evidence or notes in the space provided.

1. Does the vendor clearly document what AI models power their product, including model names, versions, and providers?

Score (1-5): ______

Evidence / Notes:

____

____

____

2. Does the vendor's data processing agreement explicitly address AI-specific data handling, including whether customer data is used for model training?

Score (1-5): ______

Evidence / Notes:

____

____

____

3. Does the vendor provide transparency into how the AI system makes decisions or generates outputs, including known limitations and failure modes?

Score (1-5): ______

Evidence / Notes:

____

____

____

____

____

4. Does the vendor conduct and share results of bias testing, fairness audits, or impact assessments relevant to the product's use case?

Score (1-5): ______

Evidence / Notes:

____

____

____

____

____

____

5. Does the vendor have documented security controls for AI-specific threats (prompt injection, data poisoning, model extraction, adversarial attacks)?

Score (1-5): ______

Evidence / Notes:

____

____

____

____

____

____

6. Does the vendor provide contractual commitments on data residency, data retention, data deletion, and sub-processor transparency?

Score (1-5): ______

Evidence / Notes:

____

____

____

______

____

______

7. Does the vendor notify customers of material changes to AI models, training data, or system behavior before those changes take effect?

Score (1-5): ______

Evidence / Notes:

____

______

____

______

____

______

8. Does the vendor maintain relevant certifications or compliance attestations (SOC 2 Type II, ISO 27001, ISO 42001, GDPR compliance documentation)?

Score (1-5): ______

Evidence / Notes:

____

______

____

______

____

______

9. Does the vendor provide an AI Bill of Materials (AI-BOM) or equivalent supply chain documentation identifying model provenance, training data sources, and third-party components?

Score (1-5): ______

Evidence / Notes:

____

______

____

____

____

____

10. Does the vendor have a documented incident response process for AI-specific incidents, including notification timelines and customer communication procedures?

Score (1-5): _______

Evidence / Notes:

____

____

____

____

____

____

Scoring Rubric

Question	Score: 1 (Poor)	Score: 3 (Adequate)	Score: 5 (Excellent)
1. Model transparency	No documentation of AI models used. Vendor describes capability as "proprietary AI" with no specifics.	Names the model provider and general model type but does not specify versions or provide update notification.	Full documentation of model names, versions, providers, and architecture. Publishes model cards or equivalent. Notifies customers of model changes.
2. Data processing for AI	Standard DPA with no AI-specific terms. Unclear whether data is used for training.	DPA addresses AI data handling. Opt-out from training available but not default. Retention terms specified.	AI-specific DPA addendum. Customer data excluded from training by default. Clear retention, deletion, and sub-processor terms. Data flow diagrams provided.

Question	Score: 1 (Poor)	Score: 3 (Adequate)	Score: 5 (Excellent)
3. Decision transparency	Black-box system with no explanation of outputs. No documentation of limitations.	General documentation of how the system works. Known limitations listed but not comprehensive. Some explainability features.	Detailed system documentation. Explainability features built in. Comprehensive limitation documentation. Confidence scores provided with outputs.
4. Bias and fairness	No bias testing conducted or shared. No fairness documentation.	Bias testing conducted but results not shared with customers. General fairness statement published.	Regular bias audits conducted by independent third parties. Results shared with customers. Fairness metrics published. Remediation process documented.
5. AI security controls	No AI-specific security measures documented. Relies only on standard application security.	Some AI-specific controls documented (e.g., input validation, output filtering). No evidence of adversarial testing.	Comprehensive AI security program including red-teaming, prompt injection defenses, output guardrails, and adversarial testing. Results shared. Bug bounty covers AI-specific vulnerabilities.
6. Data commitments	No contractual data residency, retention, or deletion commitments. Sub-processors undisclosed.	Contractual commitments on data residency and retention. Sub-processor list available on request. Deletion available but not automated.	Contractual data residency guarantees with specific regions. Automated data deletion. Sub-processor list published with change notifications. Data sovereignty options available.

Question	Score: 1 (Poor)	Score: 3 (Adequate)	Score: 5 (Excellent)
7. Change notification	No notification of model or system changes. Customers discover changes after the fact.	Notification of major changes after they occur. Changelog maintained but not proactively communicated.	Advance notification of material changes with minimum notice period. Customer opt-in for changes where feasible. Rollback options available. Changelog proactively communicated.
8. Certifications	No relevant security or AI certifications. No compliance documentation available.	SOC 2 Type II or ISO 27001 certified. GDPR compliance documented. No AI-specific certifications.	SOC 2 Type II and ISO 27001 certified. ISO 42001 certified or in progress. GDPR and applicable AI regulation compliance documented. Third-party audit reports available.
9. AI-BOM / supply chain	No supply chain documentation. Model provenance unknown.	Partial documentation of model provenance. Training data sources described at high level. Third-party components listed.	Full AI-BOM provided. Model provenance documented with training data descriptions. Third-party components listed with versions. Dependency update process documented.
10. Incident response	No AI-specific incident response process. No defined notification timeline.	AI incidents covered under general incident response. Notification within 72 hours. Post-incident reports available on request.	Dedicated AI incident response process. Notification within 24 hours. Proactive communication. Post-incident reports provided automatically. Customer-specific impact assessments included.

Risk Tier Thresholds

Total Score	Risk Tier	Recommendation

Total Score	Risk Tier	Recommendation
40 – 50	Low Risk	Proceed with standard contract terms and monitoring.
25 – 39	Medium Risk	Proceed with additional controls: enhanced monitoring, contractual protections for identified gaps, compensating controls where vendor capability is weak. Document accepted gaps and remediation timeline.
Below 25	High Risk	Do not proceed without remediation. Require vendor to address critical gaps before contract execution. If vendor cannot remediate, seek alternatives. Document the decision and rationale if proceeding despite high risk (executive sign-off required).

Assessment Summary

Overall Score:	_______ / 50
Risk Tier:	________________________________ ___
Key Strengths:	________________________________ ___
Key Gaps:	________________________________ ___
Recommended Controls:	________________________________ ___
Recommendation:	Approve / Approve with Conditions / Do Not Approve
Approver Signature:	________________________________ ___
Approval Date:	________________________________ ___

A.4: AI Incident Response Plan Template

Customize this template for your organization. Keep it to a single printed page (front and back) so it can be posted, laminated, and referenced quickly during an incident. Detailed runbooks can supplement this template but should not replace it as the first-response reference.

[ORGANIZATION NAME] — AI Incident Response Plan

Document ID: *[e.g., IRP-AI-001]* **Version:** *[e.g., 1.0]* **Effective Date:** *[Date]* **Last Tested:** *[Date of last tabletop exercise or drill]*

Incident Lead

Role	Primary	Backup
Incident Commander	*[Name, Title, Phone, Email]*	*[Name, Title, Phone, Email]*
Technical Lead	*[Name, Title, Phone, Email]*	*[Name, Title, Phone, Email]*
Communications Lead	*[Name, Title, Phone, Email]*	*[Name, Title, Phone, Email]*

Incident Classification

Prompt Injection AI system manipulated through adversarial input to produce unintended behavior. *Examples:* jailbreaking; indirect prompt injection via ingested documents; instruction override.

Data Exposure Organizational data exposed through or by an AI system. *Examples:* training data leakage; PII in AI outputs; data sent to an unauthorized AI tool.

Harmful Output AI produces output that causes or could cause harm. *Examples:* biased decisions; dangerous advice; defamatory content; hallucinated facts acted upon.

Unauthorized AI Use AI tools used without approval or outside approved parameters. *Examples:* shadow AI; unapproved tools processing organizational data; scope creep beyond approved use cases.

Vendor Incident AI vendor reports or experiences a security or operational incident. *Examples:* vendor data breach; model compromise; service degradation affecting AI reliability.

Quick reference:

Type	Category
Prompt Injection	Adversarial input
Data Exposure	Confidentiality
Harmful Output	Output quality & safety
Unauthorized AI Use	Policy violation
Vendor Incident	Third-party risk

Severity Levels

Severity 1 — Critical Confirmed data breach, active harm to individuals, regulatory reporting triggered, or AI system actively producing dangerous outputs. *Response time: immediate (within 1 hour). Examples:* PII/PHI breach via AI; AI system making harmful autonomous decisions; confirmed prompt injection exposing sensitive data at scale.

Severity 2 — High Significant risk of harm or data exposure, AI system producing materially incorrect outputs in high-stakes context, or regulatory compliance at risk. *Response time: within 4 hours. Examples:* biased hiring recommendations discovered; confidential data submitted to unauthorized AI; AI-generated medical, legal, or financial advice distributed without review.

Severity 3 — Medium AI system malfunction or policy violation without confirmed data exposure or harm, but with potential for escalation. *Response time: within 24 hours. Examples:* AI tool producing low-quality outputs affecting business decisions; employee using unapproved AI tool with Internal data; vendor notification of model change affecting outputs.

Severity 4 — Low Minor policy deviation, AI curiosity or experimentation without data risk, or vendor advisory with no immediate impact. *Response time:*

within 72 hours. Examples: employee tested a free AI tool with non-sensitive data; AI-generated content published internally with minor errors; vendor advisory about upcoming changes.

Quick reference:

Level	Response Time
Severity 1 — Critical	Immediate (within 1 hour)
Severity 2 — High	Within 4 hours
Severity 3 — Medium	Within 24 hours
Severity 4 — Low	Within 72 hours

Immediate Actions Checklist

When an AI incident is reported, the Incident Commander (or first responder) should run through the following:

- ☐ **Assess and classify** — Determine incident type and severity using the tables above.
- ☐ **Disable the system** — If the AI system is actively producing harmful outputs or leaking data, disable it immediately. For SaaS tools: revoke API keys, disable user access, or contact vendor for emergency shutdown.
- ☐ **Preserve evidence** — Capture and save: all prompts and inputs, all outputs and responses, system logs and timestamps, screenshots, user session data, and any communications about the incident. Do not delete, modify, or re-run prompts to "test" the issue.
- ☐ **Contain the impact** — Identify and quarantine affected data. Revoke access for compromised accounts. Disable downstream systems consuming affected AI outputs.
- ☐ **Activate the response team** — Notify the Incident Commander, Technical Lead, and Communications Lead per the roster above.
- ☐ **Begin notification cascade** — Use the notification matrix below to determine who else to notify based on severity level.
- ☐ **Open incident log** — Begin documenting all actions, decisions, and communications with timestamps.

Notification Matrix

For each severity level, notify per the timelines below. Conditions in parentheses (personal data involved, vendor system) apply where stated.

Sev 1 (Critical)

- *Immediate:* Incident Response Team, CISO/Security, Legal/General Counsel, DPO/Privacy Office (if personal data involved), AI Vendor (if vendor system)
- *Within 2 hrs:* CEO / Executive Leadership
- *Within 24 hrs:* Board / Audit Committee, Cyber Insurance Carrier
- *Per regulatory timeline:* Affected Customers/Users
- *Per statutory deadline:* Regulators

Sev 2 (High)

- *Within 4 hrs:* Incident Response Team, CISO/Security, Legal/General Counsel, DPO/Privacy Office (if personal data involved), AI Vendor (if vendor system)
- *Within 8 hrs:* CEO / Executive Leadership
- *As needed:* Board / Audit Committee, Cyber Insurance Carrier
- *Per regulatory timeline:* Affected Customers/Users
- *Per statutory deadline:* Regulators

Sev 3 (Medium)

- *Within 24 hrs:* Incident Response Team, CISO/Security
- *As needed:* Legal/General Counsel, DPO/Privacy Office, AI Vendor, Affected Customers/Users
- *Weekly report:* CEO / Executive Leadership
- *Not required:* Board/Audit Committee, Regulators, Cyber Insurance Carrier

Sev 4 (Low)

- *Next business day:* Incident Response Team
- *Weekly report:* CISO/Security

- *Not required:* All others

Customize notification timelines to match your regulatory obligations. GDPR requires supervisory authority notification within 72 hours of becoming aware of a personal data breach. The EU AI Act requires serious incident reporting to market surveillance authorities. US state breach notification laws vary.

Post-Incident Review Structure

Complete within [X] business days of incident closure. Circulate to all stakeholders identified in the notification matrix.

A post-incident review document should capture the following:

- **Incident ID** — assigned tracking number
- **Incident Date/Time** — when the incident occurred or was discovered
- **Incident Type** — from the classification table above
- **Severity Level** — 1 to 4
- **AI System Involved** — name, vendor, model
- **What Happened** — factual description of the incident: what occurred, what was affected, what data was involved
- **Root Cause** — technical root cause, human factors, process gaps, and contributing conditions
- **Impact** — number of affected individuals, data types exposed, business impact, regulatory implications, financial cost
- **Response Timeline** — chronological list of response actions with timestamps
- **What Worked** — aspects of the response that were effective
- **What We Will Change** — specific, actionable improvements (policy, controls, training, vendor requirements)
- **Action Items** — each with an owner, due date, and tracking mechanism
- **Review Participants** — names and titles of everyone involved in the review
- **Review Date**
- **Next Review** — date for follow-up to verify action items are complete

Use this structure as the framework for a post-incident review document kept in your incident-management system or document repository.

Appendix B: Compliance Checklists

These checklists help you track compliance with the three frameworks that matter most for practitioners: the EU AI Act, the NIST AI RMF, and ISO 42001. They are current as of early 2026. Regulatory requirements evolve — verify against the latest published guidance before relying on these checklists for compliance decisions.

Treat these as tracking tools, not legal advice. They identify what you need to address, not how to address it. Chapters 2, 3, 5, and 9 provide the operational guidance.

B.1: EU AI Act Compliance Checklist

Organized by compliance timeline. Mark each item's status, document your evidence, and assign an owner. Not all items apply to all organizations — mark items as "N/A" with a justification if they do not apply to your use case.

For each requirement below, mark status (Not Started / In Progress / Complete / N/A), record where supporting evidence lives, and assign an owner.

Phase 1: Already Required (Since February 2, 2025)

1.1 — Prohibited practices review *(Art. 5)* Conduct a prohibited practices review: confirm no AI systems are used for social scoring, real-time biometric identification in public spaces (unless exempted), manipulation of vulnerable groups, or other prohibited practices under Article 5. *Status:* ______________________ *Owner:* ______________________
Evidence Location: ____

1.2 — AI literacy program *(Art. 4)* Establish an AI literacy program ensuring all personnel involved in AI operation and oversight have sufficient understanding of AI systems relevant to their roles. *Status:* ______________________ *Owner:* ______________________

Evidence Location:

____

1.3 — AI literacy documentation *(Art. 4)* Document the AI literacy training program including content, delivery method, attendance records, and refresh schedule. *Status:* ______________________ *Owner:* ______________________ *Evidence Location:*

____

Phase 2: Required August 2, 2025 — General-Purpose AI (GPAI) Obligations

These apply if you develop or provide general-purpose AI models. Most practitioners are deployers, not providers, and these will not apply. Mark N/A if you do not develop or provide GPAI models.

2.1 — GPAI technical documentation *(Art. 53)* Prepare and maintain technical documentation for GPAI models, including training methodology, data sources, and evaluation results. *Status:* ______________________ *Owner:* ______________________ *Evidence Location:*

____

2.2 — Copyright compliance policy *(Art. 53)* Establish a policy for compliance with EU copyright law, including identification of content used in training and compliance with text and data mining opt-out requests. *Status:* ______________________ *Owner:* ______________________
Evidence Location:

____

2.3 — Training data summary *(Art. 53)* Publish a sufficiently detailed summary of training data content. *Status:* ______________________
Owner: ______________________ *Evidence Location:*

____

2.4 — Systemic risk obligations *(Art. 55)* For GPAI models with systemic risk: conduct and document model evaluations including adversarial testing, assess and mitigate systemic risks, report serious incidents, and ensure adequate cybersecurity protections. *Status:* ______________________ *Owner:* ______________________ *Evidence Location:*

____

Phase 3: Required August 2, 2026 — High-Risk Systems and Transparency

3.1 — Annex III classification *(Art. 6)* Classify all AI systems against Annex III categories (biometrics, critical infrastructure, education, employment, essential services, law enforcement, migration, justice). Document classification rationale. *Status:* ________________________ *Owner:* ________________________ *Evidence Location:* ____

3.2 — Risk management system *(Art. 9)* For each high-risk system: implement a risk management system that is iterative, continuously updated, and documented throughout the system lifecycle. *Status:* ________________________ *Owner:* ________________________ *Evidence Location:* ____

3.3 — Data governance *(Art. 10)* For each high-risk system: ensure data governance — training, validation, and testing datasets must be relevant, sufficiently representative, and free of errors to the extent possible. *Status:* ________________________ *Owner:* ________________________ *Evidence Location:* ____

3.4 — Technical documentation *(Art. 11)* For each high-risk system: maintain technical documentation sufficient for authorities to assess compliance. *Status:* ________________________ *Owner:* ________________________ *Evidence Location:* ____

3.5 — Automatic logging *(Art. 12)* For each high-risk system: implement automatic logging of system activity to enable traceability during operation. *Status:* ________________________ *Owner:* ________________________ *Evidence Location:* ____

3.6 — Transparency to deployers *(Art. 13)* For each high-risk system: ensure transparency — provide clear instructions for use to deployers, including system purpose, limitations, and human oversight measures. *Status:* ________________________ *Owner:* ________________________

Evidence Location:

____

3.7 — Human oversight *(Art. 14)* For each high-risk system: design for effective human oversight, allowing human operators to understand capabilities and limitations, monitor operation, and intervene or override. *Status:* ______________________ *Owner:* ______________________ *Evidence Location:*

____

3.8 — Accuracy, robustness, cybersecurity *(Art. 15)* For each high-risk system: achieve appropriate levels of accuracy, robustness, and cybersecurity throughout the lifecycle. *Status:* ______________________ *Owner:* ______________________ *Evidence Location:*

____

3.9 — Quality management system *(Art. 17)* Implement a quality management system covering all high-risk AI system requirements. *Status:* ______________________ *Owner:* ______________________ *Evidence Location:*

____

3.10 — Deployer obligations *(Art. 26)* As a deployer: implement appropriate technical and organizational measures to ensure use in accordance with instructions, assign human oversight to competent individuals, and ensure input data is relevant. *Status:* ______________________ *Owner:* ______________________ *Evidence Location:*

____

3.11 — Fundamental rights impact assessment *(Art. 27)* As a deployer: conduct a fundamental rights impact assessment (FRIA) before deploying high-risk AI systems. *Status:* ______________________ *Owner:* ______________________ *Evidence Location:*

____

3.12 — AI interaction disclosure *(Art. 50(1))* Transparency obligations: ensure individuals are informed when they interact with an AI system (unless obvious from context). *Status:* ______________________ *Owner:* ______________________ *Evidence Location:*

____

3.13 — Synthetic content labeling *(Art. 50(2))* Transparency obligations: label AI-generated synthetic content (audio, image, video, text) in a machine-readable format. *Status:* ________________________ *Owner:* ________________________ *Evidence Location:* ____

3.14 — AI-generated text disclosure *(Art. 50(4))* Transparency obligations: disclose when text is generated by AI and published to inform the public on matters of public interest, unless human-reviewed and editorially controlled. *Status:* ________________________ *Owner:* ________________________ *Evidence Location:* ____

3.15 — EU database registration *(Art. 49)* Register high-risk AI systems in the EU database before placing on market or putting into service. *Status:* ________________________ *Owner:* ________________________ *Evidence Location:* ____

3.16 — Regulatory sandbox readiness *(Art. 57-62)* Assess readiness for regulatory sandbox participation if available in your jurisdiction. *Status:* ________________________ *Owner:* ________________________ *Evidence Location:* ____

Phase 4: Required August 2, 2027 — Legacy High-Risk Systems (Annex I)

4.1 — Annex I safety component identification *(Art. 6(1))* Identify any AI systems that are safety components of products covered by Annex I EU harmonization legislation (e.g., machinery, medical devices, toys, radio equipment, civil aviation, vehicles). *Status:* ________________________ *Owner:* ________________________ *Evidence Location:* ____

4.2 — Legacy system compliance *(Art. 111)* Ensure all Annex I high-risk AI systems that were placed on the market or put into service before August 2, 2026 comply with the full requirements by this date, if they are significantly modified. *Status:* ________________________ *Owner:* ________________________ *Evidence Location:* ____

4.3 — Conformity assessment *(Art. 43)* Confirm conformity assessment procedures are complete for all Annex I high-risk AI systems. *Status:* _________________________ *Owner:* __________________________
Evidence Location: ____

B.2: NIST AI RMF Implementation Checklist

Organized by function and category per NIST AI RMF 1.0 and the Playbook (January 2023, updated 2024). Track your implementation status for each category. The Key Actions listed are representative, not exhaustive — consult the Playbook for the full action set.

For each category below, work through the key actions, mark status (Not Started / In Progress / Complete), record evidence, and assign an owner.

GOVERN Function — Policies, Processes, Procedures, and Practices

GOVERN 1 — Policies, processes, and procedures Establish AI governance policies; define roles and responsibilities for AI risk management; align AI policies with organizational risk tolerance. *Status:* _________________________ *Owner:* __________________________
Evidence: ____

GOVERN 2 — Accountability structures Assign accountability for AI systems to specific individuals; document reporting lines and escalation paths; establish oversight mechanisms for AI risk decisions. *Status:* _________________________ *Owner:* __________________________
Evidence: ____

GOVERN 3 — Workforce diversity and AI expertise Assess AI risk management competencies across the workforce; provide AI risk training for relevant personnel; include diverse perspectives in AI risk governance. *Status:* _________________________ *Owner:* __________________________
Evidence: ____

GOVERN 4 — Organizational culture Foster a culture of responsible AI development and use; encourage reporting of AI risks and concerns without retaliation; integrate AI risk awareness into organizational values. *Status:* ______________________ *Owner:* ______________________
Evidence:
____

GOVERN 5 — Stakeholder engagement Identify and engage AI stakeholders (internal and external); establish feedback mechanisms for affected communities; document stakeholder input in governance decisions. *Status:* ______________________ *Owner:* ______________________
Evidence:
____

GOVERN 6 — Policies addressing third-party AI Establish vendor assessment processes for AI suppliers; define requirements for third-party AI risk documentation; monitor third-party AI risks on an ongoing basis. *Status:* ______________________ *Owner:* ______________________
Evidence:
____

MAP Function — Contextualize and Identify Risks

MAP 1 — Intended purpose and context Document the intended purpose and operating context of each AI system; identify and document assumptions about deployment context; assess gap between intended use and actual use. *Status:* ______________________ *Owner:* ______________________
Evidence:
____

MAP 2 — AI system categorization Classify AI systems by risk level and impact; identify regulatory requirements applicable to each system; map systems to organizational risk categories. *Status:* ______________________ *Owner:* ______________________ *Evidence:*
____

MAP 3 — Benefits and costs Document expected benefits and potential negative impacts; identify populations and communities affected by AI systems; assess distributional effects across stakeholder groups. *Status:* ______________________ *Owner:* ______________________

Evidence:

___

MAP 4 — Risks and impacts Identify risks specific to each AI system's context; assess likelihood and severity of identified risks; evaluate risks to individuals, groups, communities, organizations, and ecosystems. *Status:* ___ *Owner:* ___
Evidence:

___

MAP 5 — AI impacts on affected communities Engage with communities potentially impacted by AI systems; assess impacts on equity and access; document community input and how it influenced design and deployment.
Status: ___ *Owner:* ___
Evidence:

___

MEASURE Function — Assess, Analyze, and Track Risks

MEASURE 1 — Metrics and methods Define metrics for AI trustworthiness characteristics; select measurement methods appropriate to system context; establish baselines and thresholds for acceptable performance. *Status:* ___ *Owner:* ___
Evidence:

___

MEASURE 2 — AI systems are evaluated Conduct evaluations for validity, reliability, and robustness; conduct evaluations for bias and fairness; test AI systems for security vulnerabilities and adversarial resilience. *Status:* ___ *Owner:* ___
Evidence:

___

MEASURE 3 — Mechanisms for tracking risks Implement monitoring for AI system performance over time; track identified risks and mitigation effectiveness; establish triggers for reassessment based on performance changes.
Status: ___ *Owner:* ___
Evidence:

___

MEASURE 4 — Feedback from affected communities Collect and analyze feedback from AI system users and affected parties; integrate feedback into risk measurement and mitigation; report measurement findings to governance structures. *Status:* ________________________ *Owner:* ________________________ *Evidence:* ____

MANAGE Function — Respond to and Recover from Risks

MANAGE 1 — Risk response Prioritize AI risks based on assessment results; select and implement risk treatment options (mitigate, transfer, accept, avoid); document risk response decisions and rationale. *Status:* ________________________ *Owner:* ________________________ *Evidence:* ____

MANAGE 2 — Risk management planned and implemented Develop risk management plans for each high-priority AI system; implement controls and mitigations per plan; allocate resources for ongoing risk management. *Status:* ________________________ *Owner:* ________________________ *Evidence:* ____

MANAGE 3 — Risk management monitored Monitor effectiveness of risk management controls; conduct periodic reviews of risk management plans; update risk treatments when monitoring reveals gaps. *Status:* ________________________ *Owner:* ________________________ *Evidence:* ____

MANAGE 4 — Incidents and errors Establish incident response procedures for AI systems; document incidents, near-misses, and errors; conduct root cause analysis and implement corrective actions. *Status:* ________________________ *Owner:* ________________________ *Evidence:* ____

B.3: ISO 42001 Gap Assessment Checklist

This checklist covers the main requirements of ISO/IEC 42001:2023, the AI management system standard. Use it to assess your current state against the standard's requirements and identify gaps requiring action. If you are already certified to ISO 27001, many controls in Clauses 4-10 will be familiar — focus on Annex A for AI-specific requirements.

For each clause or control below, describe current state, identify any gap, note the action required, set a priority (H/M/L), and assign an owner.

Main Clauses

Clause 4.1 — Understanding the organization and its context Determine external and internal issues relevant to AI management. *Current State:* ____ *Gap:* ____ ____ *Action Required:* ____ *Priority (H/M/L):* ______ *Owner:* ____________________

Clause 4.2 — Needs and expectations of interested parties Identify stakeholders and their requirements related to AI. *Current State:* ____ *Gap:* ____ ____ *Action Required:* ____ *Priority (H/M/L):* ______ *Owner:* ____________________

Clause 4.3 — Determining the scope of the AIMS Define boundaries and applicability of the AI management system. *Current State:* ____ *Gap:* ____ ____ *Action Required:* ____ *Priority (H/M/L):* ______ *Owner:* ____________________

Clause 4.4 — AI management system Establish, implement, maintain, and continually improve the AIMS. *Current State:*

____ *Gap:*

____

_____ *Action Required:*

____ *Priority (H/M/L):* _______ *Owner:* ____________________

Clause 5.1 — Leadership and commitment Top management demonstrates commitment to the AIMS. *Current State:*

____ *Gap:*

____

_____ *Action Required:*

____ *Priority (H/M/L):* _______ *Owner:* ____________________

Clause 5.2 — AI policy Establish an AI policy appropriate to the organization's purpose. *Current State:*

____ *Gap:*

____

_____ *Action Required:*

____ *Priority (H/M/L):* _______ *Owner:* ____________________

Clause 5.3 — Organizational roles, responsibilities, and authorities Assign and communicate AIMS roles. *Current State:*

____ *Gap:*

____

_____ *Action Required:*

____ *Priority (H/M/L):* _______ *Owner:* ____________________

Clause 6.1 — Actions to address risks and opportunities Plan actions to address AI-specific risks and opportunities. *Current State:*

____ *Gap:*

____

_____ *Action Required:*

____ *Priority (H/M/L):* _______ *Owner:* ____________________

Clause 6.2 — AI objectives and planning to achieve them Establish measurable AI objectives at relevant functions and levels. *Current State:*
____ *Gap:*
____
_____ *Action Required:*
____ *Priority (H/M/L):* _______ *Owner:* ____________________

Clause 7.1 — Resources Determine and provide resources needed for the AIMS. *Current State:*
____ *Gap:*
____
_____ *Action Required:*
____ *Priority (H/M/L):* _______ *Owner:* ____________________

Clause 7.2 — Competence Ensure personnel have necessary AI-related competence. *Current State:*
____ *Gap:*
____
_____ *Action Required:*
____ *Priority (H/M/L):* _______ *Owner:* ____________________

Clause 7.3 — Awareness Ensure personnel are aware of the AI policy, their contribution, and implications of non-conformity. *Current State:*
____ *Gap:*
____
_____ *Action Required:*
____ *Priority (H/M/L):* _______ *Owner:* ____________________

Clause 7.4 — Communication Determine internal and external communication needs for the AIMS. *Current State:*
____ *Gap:*
____
_____ *Action Required:*
____ *Priority (H/M/L):* _______ *Owner:* ____________________

Clause 7.5 — Documented information Maintain documented information required by the AIMS. *Current State:*
____ *Gap:*
____
_____ *Action Required:*
____ *Priority (H/M/L):* _______ *Owner:* ____________________

Clause 8.1 — Operational planning and control Plan, implement, and control processes to meet AIMS requirements. *Current State:*
____ *Gap:*
____
_____ *Action Required:*
____ *Priority (H/M/L):* _______ *Owner:* ____________________

Clause 8.2 — AI risk assessment Conduct AI risk assessments at planned intervals or when significant changes occur. *Current State:*
____ *Gap:*
____
_____ *Action Required:*
____ *Priority (H/M/L):* _______ *Owner:* ____________________

Clause 8.3 — AI risk treatment Implement AI risk treatment plans. *Current State:* ____
Gap:
____
_____ *Action Required:*
____ *Priority (H/M/L):* _______ *Owner:* ____________________

Clause 8.4 — AI system impact assessment Assess the potential impacts of AI systems on individuals, groups, and societies. *Current State:*
____ *Gap:*
____
_____ *Action Required:*
____ *Priority (H/M/L):* _______ *Owner:* ____________________

Clause 9.1 — Monitoring, measurement, analysis, and evaluation Determine what needs to be monitored and measured for AI. *Current State:*
____ *Gap:*
____
_____ *Action Required:*
____ *Priority (H/M/L):* _______ *Owner:* ____________________

Clause 9.2 — Internal audit Conduct internal audits at planned intervals to verify AIMS conformance. *Current State:*
____ *Gap:*
____
_____ *Action Required:*
____ *Priority (H/M/L):* _______ *Owner:* ____________________

Clause 9.3 — Management review Top management reviews the AIMS at planned intervals. *Current State:*
____ *Gap:*
____
_____ *Action Required:*
____ *Priority (H/M/L):* _______ *Owner:* ____________________

Clause 10.1 — Continual improvement Continually improve the suitability, adequacy, and effectiveness of the AIMS. *Current State:*
____ *Gap:*
____
_____ *Action Required:*
____ *Priority (H/M/L):* _______ *Owner:* ____________________

Clause 10.2 — Nonconformity and corrective action React to nonconformities and take corrective action. *Current State:*
____ *Gap:*
____
_____ *Action Required:*
____ *Priority (H/M/L):* _______ *Owner:* ____________________

Control A.2 — AI policies Policies addressing responsible development and use of AI. *Current State:*
____ *Gap:*
____

_____ *Action Required:*
____ *Priority*
(H/M/L): ______ *Owner:* ____________________

Control A.3 — Internal organization Defined roles for AI governance, including oversight of AI systems. *Current State:*
____ *Gap:*
____

_____ *Action Required:*
____ *Priority*
(H/M/L): ______ *Owner:* ____________________

Control A.4 — Resources for AI systems Allocation of human, technical, and financial resources for AI management. *Current State:*
____ *Gap:*
____

_____ *Action Required:*
____ *Priority*
(H/M/L): ______ *Owner:* ____________________

Control A.5 — Assessing impacts of AI systems Process for impact assessment throughout the AI lifecycle. *Current State:*
____ *Gap:*
____

_____ *Action Required:*
____ *Priority*
(H/M/L): ______ *Owner:* ____________________

Control A.6 — AI system lifecycle Management of AI systems through their lifecycle including design, development, deployment, operation, and decommissioning. *Current State:*
____ *Gap:*
____

____ *Action Required:*
____ *Priority (H/M/L):* ______ *Owner:* ____________________

Control A.7 — Data for AI systems Data quality, data management, data provenance, and data governance for AI. *Current State:*
____ *Gap:*
____
____ *Action Required:*
____ *Priority (H/M/L):* ______ *Owner:* ____________________

Control A.8 — Information for interested parties Transparency and communication about AI systems to relevant stakeholders. *Current State:*
____ *Gap:*
____
____ *Action Required:*
____ *Priority (H/M/L):* ______ *Owner:* ____________________

Control A.9 — Use of AI systems Processes ensuring appropriate use, including human oversight and monitoring. *Current State:*
____ *Gap:*
____
____ *Action Required:*
____ *Priority (H/M/L):* ______ *Owner:* ____________________

Control A.10 — Third-party and customer relationships Managing AI risks in the supply chain and customer relationships. *Current State:*
____ *Gap:*
____
____ *Action Required:*
____ *Priority (H/M/L):* ______ *Owner:* ____________________

Appendix C: Framework Comparison Matrix

This matrix compares the five major AI governance frameworks discussed in Chapters 2 and 3. Use it to identify which frameworks are relevant to your organization and how they differ across key dimensions.

The comparison below covers ten dimensions across all five frameworks. Each dimension is presented with all five frameworks side by side for easy reference.

Scope

- **EU AI Act:** AI systems placed on the EU market or affecting people in the EU. Covers providers, deployers, importers, and distributors.
- **NIST AI RMF 1.0:** All AI systems across all sectors. Designed for US organizations but applicable globally.
- **ISO/IEC 42001:2023:** Any organization developing, providing, or using AI systems. Industry-agnostic.
- **Council of Europe Convention:** AI activities within the jurisdiction of parties to the Convention. Covers public sector; private sector covered indirectly through domestic frameworks.
- **Singapore MGF:** AI systems deployed in Singapore. Voluntary guidance for all sectors, with sector-specific additions for finance and healthcare.

Mandatory / Voluntary

- **EU AI Act:** Mandatory (regulation with direct legal effect in all EU member states).
- **NIST AI RMF 1.0:** Voluntary (framework, not regulation; may become de facto required through federal procurement and sector guidance).
- **ISO/IEC 42001:2023:** Voluntary (certifiable standard; mandatory only if required by contract, customer, or sector regulation).
- **Council of Europe Convention:** Binding on signatory states (treaty obligation); states implement through domestic law.

- **Singapore MGF:** Voluntary (guidance, not regulation; de facto expected in regulated sectors like finance).

Risk-Based Approach

- **EU AI Act:** Yes. Four tiers: Unacceptable (prohibited), High Risk (heavy requirements), Limited Risk (transparency obligations), Minimal Risk (no specific obligations).
- **NIST AI RMF 1.0:** Yes. Risk is central but the framework does not prescribe tiers. Organizations define their own risk tolerance and assessment methodology.
- **ISO/IEC 42001:2023:** Yes. Requires AI risk assessment and treatment but does not prescribe specific tiers. Organizations define risk criteria within their AIMS.
- **Council of Europe Convention:** Yes. Risk-based and proportionate approach. Signatory states must ensure risks are assessed, but specific methodology is left to domestic implementation.
- **Singapore MGF:** Yes. Two-tier approach: general obligations for all AI, plus additional requirements for higher-risk systems. Organizations self-assess risk level.

Key Requirements

- **EU AI Act:** Prohibited practices ban; risk classification; conformity assessments for high-risk systems; transparency obligations; human oversight; technical documentation; post-market monitoring; incident reporting; registration in EU database.
- **NIST AI RMF 1.0:** Governance structures; risk mapping; risk measurement; risk management; stakeholder engagement; documentation; continuous monitoring. Four functions: GOVERN, MAP, MEASURE, MANAGE.
- **ISO/IEC 42001:2023:** AI management system (AIMS); AI policy; risk assessment and treatment; impact assessment; lifecycle management; data governance; transparency; third-party management; continual improvement. PDCA cycle.
- **Council of Europe Convention:** Human rights protection; transparency; accountability; non-discrimination; safety and security;

human oversight; privacy protection; democratic oversight. States must ensure remedies for AI-caused harm.

- **Singapore MGF:** Explainability; transparency; fairness; human-centricity; accountability structures; data governance; stakeholder communication; internal governance. FEAT principles for financial sector.

Enforcement Mechanism

- **EU AI Act:** National market surveillance authorities. Fines up to 35M EUR or 7% of global annual turnover. AI Office in Brussels coordinates enforcement for GPAI models.
- **NIST AI RMF 1.0:** No direct enforcement. May be referenced in sector-specific guidance, procurement requirements, or litigation standards of care. NIST does not enforce.
- **ISO/IEC 42001:2023:** Certification bodies accredited under national accreditation systems (e.g., UKAS, ANAB). Certification is voluntary but contractually enforceable once obtained.
- **Council of Europe Convention:** Treaty monitoring mechanism (Conference of the Parties). Domestic enforcement through national legislation implementing the Convention.
- **Singapore MGF:** No direct enforcement. Infocomm Media Development Authority (IMDA) publishes guidance. Financial sector compliance monitored by Monetary Authority of Singapore (MAS).

SMB Provisions

- **EU AI Act:** Reduced documentation requirements for SMEs. Regulatory sandboxes mandated for member states. Priority sandbox access for SMEs. Fee reductions for conformity assessment.
- **NIST AI RMF 1.0:** Designed to be scalable. Playbook provides tiered implementation guidance. No cost barriers (free, publicly available).
- **ISO/IEC 42001:2023:** Certification cost may be prohibitive for small organizations (~$20K-100K+ depending on scope). Standard purchase required (~$200). No SMB-specific provisions in the standard itself.
- **Council of Europe Convention:** No specific SMB provisions in the Convention. Implementation depends on domestic legislation.

- **Singapore MGF:** Designed with SMBs in mind. AI Verify toolkit is free and open source. Implementation guides available at no cost. Proportionate approach encouraged.

Agentic AI Coverage

- **EU AI Act:** Limited. The Act was finalized before agentic AI became widespread. GPAI provisions may apply to foundation models powering agents. European Commission expected to issue guidance. Deployer obligations apply to agentic system deployment.
- **NIST AI RMF 1.0:** General AI RMF applicable but no agent-specific guidance as of early 2026. Expected updates may address autonomous systems and multi-agent scenarios.
- **ISO/IEC 42001:2023:** Not specifically addressed. Lifecycle management and risk assessment clauses are general enough to apply. Organizations must interpret for agentic contexts.
- **Council of Europe Convention:** General principles (human oversight, accountability) apply but no agent-specific provisions.
- **Singapore MGF:** Not specifically addressed in the current framework. Sector-specific guidance for finance may evolve to cover autonomous agents.

Certification Available

- **EU AI Act:** Conformity assessment required for high-risk systems (self-assessment or third-party depending on category). Not a "certification" in the ISO sense.
- **NIST AI RMF 1.0:** No certification. Self-assessment tools available (NIST AI RMF Playbook, AI RMF Crosswalk).
- **ISO/IEC 42001:2023:** Yes. Third-party certification by accredited certification bodies. Certificates typically valid for 3 years with annual surveillance audits.
- **Council of Europe Convention:** No certification. Treaty compliance monitored at the state level.
- **Singapore MGF:** AI Verify testing framework available for self-assessment. No formal certification program, but AI Verify results can be shared with stakeholders.

Primary Jurisdiction

- **EU AI Act:** European Union (27 member states + EEA). Extraterritorial effect on non-EU organizations placing AI on the EU market or affecting EU individuals.
- **NIST AI RMF 1.0:** United States. Global influence through adoption by multinational companies and reference in international guidance.
- **ISO/IEC 42001:2023:** Global (ISO standard). Applicable in any jurisdiction. Recognized internationally.
- **Council of Europe Convention:** Council of Europe member states (46 countries). Open for accession by non-member states (US, Canada, Japan, and others participated in negotiations).
- **Singapore MGF:** Singapore. Regional influence across ASEAN. Referenced by organizations operating in Asia-Pacific.

Entry Point for Practitioners

- **EU AI Act:** Start with Article 5 (prohibited practices) and Article 6 + Annex III (risk classification). Classify your systems. Then address applicable obligations based on your role (deployer vs. provider).
- **NIST AI RMF 1.0:** Start with the GOVERN function. Establish governance structures, then MAP your AI systems, MEASURE risks, and MANAGE responses. Use the Playbook for detailed guidance on each category.
- **ISO/IEC 42001:2023:** Start with Clause 4 (context) and Clause 5 (leadership). Secure management commitment and define scope. Then gap-assess against Annex A controls.
- **Council of Europe Convention:** Review the Convention text (short — about 20 pages). Assess which provisions your domestic legislation implements. Align with domestic requirements.
- **Singapore MGF:** Start with the FEAT Assessment Methodology Guide if in financial services. Otherwise start with the Model Framework Second Edition and self-assess using AI Verify.

Appendix D: Decision Trees

These decision trees help you navigate common governance questions raised throughout the book. Follow the branches from the starting question to reach a recommended action. Many decisions require nuance beyond a binary yes/no — treat these trees as starting points for analysis, not substitutes for qualified advice.

D.1: "Which Framework Applies to Me?"

Start here: Does your organization develop, deploy, or use AI systems?

- **No** → You do not need an AI governance framework at this time. Revisit this question annually — your organization may adopt AI through vendor products without realizing it. Consider a shadow AI audit (Chapter 8).
- **Yes** → Continue below.

Question 1: Does your organization sell to, serve, or employ people in the European Union, or do you place AI systems on the EU market?

- **Yes → The EU AI Act applies to you.** Begin with Appendix B.1. Continue to Question 2 to determine if additional frameworks apply.
- **No** → Continue to Question 2.

Question 2: Is your organization a US federal agency, a US federal contractor, or does your organization supply AI systems to the US federal government?

- **Yes → NIST AI RMF is strongly recommended** and may be effectively required through procurement policy (OMB M-24-10, EO 14110 successors). Begin with Appendix B.2. Continue to Question 3.
- **No** → Continue to Question 3.

Question 3: Do your customers, partners, or industry regulators require or expect a certified AI management system?

- **Yes → ISO 42001 certification should be pursued.** Begin with Appendix B.3. This is especially true if you already hold ISO 27001 — the management system structure is shared, and incremental effort is manageable. Continue to Question 4.

- **No** → Continue to Question 4.

Question 4: Do you operate in Singapore or serve customers in ASEAN markets, particularly in financial services?

- **Yes → Singapore's Model AI Governance Framework applies.** Consider using AI Verify for self-assessment. Continue to Question 5.
- **No** → Continue to Question 5.

Question 5: Does your organization operate in a Council of Europe member state (46 countries including all EU members plus the UK, Turkey, and others)?

- **Yes → The Council of Europe Framework Convention on AI may apply** once ratified and implemented domestically in your jurisdiction. Monitor domestic legislation. Continue to the recommendation.
- **No** → Continue to the recommendation.

Recommendation based on your answers:

- **No frameworks triggered** → Use NIST AI RMF as your voluntary baseline. It is free, well-documented, and widely recognized. It also maps cleanly to most regulatory requirements if your situation changes. Start with Chapter 5's governance charter and Appendix B.2.
- **One framework triggered** → Implement that framework. Use NIST AI RMF as a complementary implementation guide — its Playbook provides practical actions that support compliance with any regulatory framework.
- **Multiple frameworks triggered** → Start with ISO 42001 as your management system foundation. It provides the structural backbone. Then layer EU AI Act requirements on top (they are the most prescriptive). Map NIST AI RMF categories to your ISO 42001 controls for coverage validation. See the comparison matrix in Appendix C.

D.2: "Is My AI System High-Risk Under the EU AI Act?"

Start here: Is the AI system used as a safety component of a product covered by EU harmonization legislation listed in Annex I (e.g., machinery, medical devices, toys, lifts, pressure equipment, radio equipment, civil aviation, motor vehicles, rail systems)?

- **Yes** → Does the AI system itself require a third-party conformity assessment under that Annex I legislation?
  - **Yes → The AI system is high-risk** under Article 6(1). Full high-risk requirements apply.
  - **No** → The AI system is **not classified as high-risk** solely under Article 6(1), but check Annex III below.
- **No** → Continue to Annex III assessment.

Annex III Assessment: Is the AI system used in any of the following areas?

1. Biometrics (remote biometric identification, emotion recognition, biometric categorization)
2. Critical infrastructure (safety components of road traffic, water/gas/heating/electricity supply, digital infrastructure)
3. Education and vocational training (determining access, admission, assignment, or assessment)
4. Employment (recruitment, selection, job advertising, evaluation, promotion, termination decisions)
5. Access to essential private and public services (credit scoring, insurance risk assessment, emergency services dispatch)
6. Law enforcement (individual risk assessment, polygraphs, evidence reliability assessment, crime prediction)
7. Migration, asylum, and border control (polygraphs, application assessment, identification)
8. Administration of justice and democratic processes (legal research, legal interpretation application)

- **No to all → The AI system is not high-risk** under Annex III. It is classified as Limited Risk (if it involves AI-human interaction, emotion recognition, biometric categorization, or generates deepfakes —

transparency obligations under Article 50 apply) or Minimal Risk (no specific obligations beyond the general requirements).

- **Yes to one or more** → Continue to the exception assessment.

Exception Assessment (Article 6(3)): Even if the system falls under an Annex III area, it is **not** classified as high-risk if it meets **all** of the following conditions:

- **Condition 1: Narrow procedural task.** The AI system performs a narrow procedural task — does the system perform a narrowly defined task such as converting unstructured data to structured data, classifying documents into categories, or detecting duplicates?
  - **Yes** → Continue to Condition 2.
  - **No → The system is high-risk.** The exception does not apply.
- **Condition 2: Improvement of human activity.** Is the AI system intended to improve the result of a previously completed human activity — does it review, enhance, or refine a human's prior work rather than replacing the human decision entirely?
  - **Yes** → Continue to Condition 3.
  - **No → The system is high-risk.** The exception does not apply.
- **Condition 3: No profiling.** Does the system refrain from profiling natural persons (i.e., it does not evaluate personal aspects to analyze or predict behavior, preferences, economic situation, health, interests, reliability, location, or movements)?
  - **Yes** → Continue to Condition 4.
  - **No → The system is high-risk.** The exception does not apply.
- **Condition 4: No material influence on decision-making.** Does the AI system only perform a preparatory task with no material influence on the decision that follows — meaning a human decision-maker can readily disregard the AI output with no meaningful penalty or pressure?
  - **Yes, all four conditions are met → The system is not high-risk** despite falling under an Annex III area. However, you must document why the exception applies. The European Commission may update the list of exceptions — monitor for changes.

- **No → The system is high-risk.** Full high-risk requirements under Articles 8-15 (providers) and Article 26 (deployers) apply. Proceed to Appendix B.1, Phase 3.

D.3: "Do I Need ISO 42001 Certification?"

Start here: Do any of your customers, partners, or procurement bodies currently require or explicitly request ISO 42001 certification?

- **Yes → Pursue certification.** The business case is straightforward — you need it to maintain or win business. Proceed to budget and timeline planning below.
- **No** → Continue to Question 1.

Question 1: Have regulators in your jurisdiction indicated that ISO 42001 (or equivalent AI management system certification) will become mandatory or expected for your sector?

- **Yes → Plan for certification proactively.** Getting ahead of regulatory requirements is significantly less expensive than reactive compliance. Proceed to budget and timeline planning below.
- **No, or unclear** → Continue to Question 2.

Question 2: Do your competitors hold or advertise ISO 42001 certification?

- **Yes → Certification provides competitive advantage.** If your market is beginning to treat ISO 42001 as a trust signal, early certification differentiates you. Proceed to Question 3 to assess readiness.
- **No** → Continue to Question 3.

Question 3: Does your organization currently hold ISO 27001 (information security management) certification?

- **Yes → The incremental effort for ISO 42001 is manageable.** ISO 42001 uses the same Harmonized Structure (Clauses 4-10) as ISO 27001. Your existing management system, internal audit program, document control, and management review processes transfer directly. You primarily need to add the AI-specific Annex A controls. Estimated incremental effort: 3-6 months. Continue to budget assessment below.

- **No** → Continue to Question 4.

Question 4: Do you have the budget and organizational capacity for certification?

Estimate the following costs: - Standard purchase: ~$200 (ISO/IEC 42001:2023) - Gap assessment and remediation: ~$15K-$50K (consultant engagement, varies by scope) - Certification audit (Stage 1 + Stage 2): ~$15K-$50K (varies by certification body and scope) - Annual surveillance audits: ~$8K-$20K per year - Internal resource allocation: 0.5-1.0 FTE for 6-12 months during implementation - Ongoing maintenance: 0.25-0.5 FTE

- **Yes, budget and capacity are available → Pursue certification.** Even without an immediate customer or regulatory requirement, ISO 42001 provides a structured approach to AI governance that prevents future rework. Begin with the gap assessment in Appendix B.3.
- **No, or not at this time → Implement ISO 42001 principles without pursuing formal certification.** Use the standard as a guide for your AI management system. Complete the gap assessment in Appendix B.3 to identify priorities. Pursue certification when budget allows or when external pressure requires it. In the interim, NIST AI RMF provides a free, publicly available framework that covers much of the same ground (see Appendix C for mapping).

Budget and Timeline Planning:

- **With ISO 27001 already in place:** 3-6 months to certification. Focus on Annex A gap analysis and AI-specific controls. Budget: $30K-$80K total (first year including audit).
- **Without ISO 27001:** 9-18 months to certification. You are building the full management system. Consider pursuing ISO 27001 and ISO 42001 in parallel — the shared clauses mean significant overlap. Budget: $60K-$150K total (first year including audit).
- **Minimum viable approach:** Engage a consultant for a gap assessment (~$10K-$20K), build an implementation roadmap, and phase the work over 12-18 months. This delays certification but manages cash flow for smaller organizations.

Appendix E: Glossary

The definitions below are written for governance practitioners, not computer scientists. Where a term has a specific legal or regulatory meaning under the EU AI Act or another framework, that meaning is noted. Entries are alphabetical.

Agentic AI. An AI system that can take autonomous actions in the real world – sending emails, executing code, calling APIs, modifying databases – without requiring human approval for each individual action. Agentic AI introduces governance challenges that traditional advisory AI does not, including action authorization, cascading risk, and accountability gaps.

AI agent. A specific instance of agentic AI deployed to perform tasks on behalf of a user or organization. An AI agent typically has access to tools (APIs, databases, file systems) and can chain multiple actions together to accomplish goals. The term is used broadly across the industry; there is no single agreed-upon technical definition.

AI literacy. Under Article 4 of the EU AI Act, providers and deployers must ensure that staff involved in the operation and use of AI systems have a sufficient level of AI literacy, taking into account their technical knowledge, experience, education, and the context of use. This is not a suggestion – it is a legal obligation with enforcement deadlines.

AI system. Under the EU AI Act (Article 3(1)), a machine-based system designed to operate with varying levels of autonomy, that may exhibit adaptiveness after deployment, and that, for explicit or implicit objectives, infers from the input it receives how to generate outputs such as predictions, content, recommendations, or decisions that can influence physical or virtual environments. The definition is deliberately broad and technology-neutral.

Algorithm. A set of rules or instructions that a computer follows to solve a problem or perform a task. In the governance context, an algorithm is relevant when it makes or influences decisions that affect people – hiring, lending, content moderation, risk scoring. Not all algorithms involve AI, but all AI systems rely on algorithms.

Artificial intelligence. The broad field of computer science concerned with building systems that can perform tasks typically requiring human intelligence. For governance purposes, the specific technical approach matters less than the system's capabilities, autonomy level, and impact on people and organizations.

Bias (algorithmic). Systematic and repeatable errors in an AI system's outputs that create unfair outcomes for particular groups. Algorithmic bias can originate from training data that reflects historical discrimination, from design choices that favor certain populations, or from deployment contexts that were not anticipated during development. The EU AI Act requires bias testing for high-risk systems.

Big data. Datasets too large, fast-moving, or complex to process with traditional tools. In AI governance, big data matters because the training data behind AI systems is often so large that no human has reviewed all of it, creating risks around data quality, bias, consent, and regulatory compliance that governance programs must address.

CE marking. The conformity marking required for products sold in the European Economic Area. Under the EU AI Act, high-risk AI systems will require CE marking to demonstrate compliance with the regulation's requirements. This brings AI systems into the same conformity assessment regime as medical devices, machinery, and other regulated products.

Confabulation. See *Hallucination*.

Conformity assessment. The process of evaluating whether an AI system meets the requirements of a regulation or standard. Under the EU AI Act, high-risk AI systems must undergo conformity assessment before being placed on the market. For most high-risk categories, providers can self-assess; for biometric identification systems, third-party assessment by a notified body is required.

Constitutional AI. A technique developed by Anthropic for training AI models to be helpful and harmless by having the AI evaluate its own outputs against a set of principles (a "constitution") during training. Constitutional AI operates at the model layer during training; it is complementary to, not a substitute for, runtime governance enforcement at deployment.

CVSS (Common Vulnerability Scoring System). A standardized framework for rating the severity of security vulnerabilities on a scale from 0 to 10. CVSS scores help organizations prioritize remediation. For AI-specific vulnerabilities, OWASP has developed the AIVSS (AI Vulnerability Scoring System) as an extension adapted to agentic AI risk factors.

Data governance. The set of policies, processes, and standards that ensure data is managed consistently, securely, and in compliance with applicable regulations throughout its lifecycle. In AI governance, data governance is foundational – an AI system is only as trustworthy as the data it was trained on and the data it operates on at runtime.

Data poisoning. An attack in which an adversary deliberately corrupts the training data used to build an AI model, causing the model to learn incorrect patterns or behaviors. Data poisoning is particularly dangerous because it is difficult to detect after the fact and can produce targeted, predictable failures that an attacker can exploit.

Deepfake. Synthetic media – typically video, audio, or images – generated by AI to convincingly depict events that did not occur or statements that were never made. Deepfakes are relevant to governance because they can be used for fraud, manipulation, and reputational damage. The EU AI Act requires labeling of AI-generated content.

Deployer (EU AI Act). Under Article 3(4), any natural or legal person, public authority, agency, or other body using an AI system under its authority, except where the AI system is used in the course of a personal, non-professional activity. Deployers have distinct obligations under the EU AI Act, including conducting fundamental rights impact assessments for high-risk systems and ensuring human oversight.

DID (Decentralized Identifier). A globally unique identifier defined by the W3C that does not require a centralized registration authority. DIDs enable AI agents and systems to establish verifiable, cryptographic identity without depending on any single identity provider. Relevant to federated AI governance architectures where agents from different organizations must establish trust.

EU AI Act. Regulation (EU) 2024/1689, the world's first comprehensive AI-specific legislation. The Act establishes a risk-based classification system (unacceptable, high, limited, minimal risk), sets requirements for high-risk AI systems, bans certain AI practiccs, and creates enforcement mechanisms with penalties up to 7% of global annual turnover. Full enforcement begins August 2026.

Excessive agency. Identified by OWASP as a top risk for LLM applications (LLM06), excessive agency occurs when an AI system is granted more permissions, autonomy, or tool access than it needs to perform its intended function. It is the AI equivalent of violating the principle of least privilege and is the root cause of many agentic AI incidents.

Explainability. The degree to which a human can understand how an AI system arrived at a particular output or decision. The EU AI Act requires that high-risk AI systems provide sufficient transparency for deployers to interpret outputs and use them appropriately. Explainability exists on a spectrum – a decision tree is fully explainable; a deep neural network may only be partially explainable through approximation techniques.

Fail-safe defaults. A security design principle from Saltzer and Schroeder (1975) stipulating that the default state of a system should be to deny access, and that permission must be explicitly granted. In AI governance, fail-safe defaults mean that an AI agent should be denied the ability to take actions unless those actions have been explicitly authorized. This is the opposite of how most AI agents are deployed today.

Foundation model. A large AI model trained on broad data at scale that can be adapted to a wide range of downstream tasks. GPT-4, Claude, Gemini, and Llama are foundation models. The EU AI Act regulates foundation models as general-purpose AI (GPAI) models, with additional obligations for models classified as presenting systemic risk.

FRIA (Fundamental Rights Impact Assessment). Required under Article 27 of the EU AI Act for deployers of high-risk AI systems that are public authorities or private entities providing public services. A FRIA evaluates the potential impact of an AI system on fundamental rights, including non-discrimination, privacy, human dignity, and access to justice. It must be completed before the system is put into use.

Generative AI. AI systems that create new content – text, images, audio, video, code – based on patterns learned from training data. Generative AI is the category that includes large language models, image generators, and code assistants. It is governed under the EU AI Act primarily through transparency obligations and, for GPAI models with systemic risk, through additional safety requirements.

Governance. The system of rules, practices, processes, and organizational structures through which an organization directs and controls its activities. AI governance specifically addresses how an organization manages the development, deployment, and use of AI systems to ensure they operate safely, ethically, legally, and in alignment with organizational values and risk tolerance.

GPAI (General-Purpose AI). Under the EU AI Act, an AI model that displays significant generality, is capable of competently performing a wide range of distinct tasks, and can be integrated into a variety of downstream systems or applications. GPAI models have specific obligations under Articles 51-56, including technical documentation, copyright compliance, and transparency requirements. GPAI models classified as posing systemic risk face additional obligations including adversarial testing and incident reporting.

Guardrails. Technical controls that constrain what an AI system can do or produce. Guardrails can operate at the model layer (content filters, output classifiers), at the application layer (input validation, output sanitization), or at the infrastructure layer (permission boundaries, action authorization, runtime enforcement). Effective governance uses guardrails at multiple layers simultaneously.

Hallucination (confabulation). The tendency of generative AI systems, particularly large language models, to produce outputs that are fluent and confident but factually incorrect or entirely fabricated. The term "hallucination" is widely used in the industry; some researchers prefer "confabulation" as more technically accurate. Hallucinations are a governance concern because they can lead to incorrect decisions, legal liability, and erosion of trust.

High-risk AI system. Under the EU AI Act (Article 6 and Annex III), an AI system used in specified domains – including biometric identification, critical infrastructure, education, employment, essential services, law enforcement, migration management, and administration of justice – that poses significant risks to health, safety, or fundamental rights. High-risk AI systems must meet extensive requirements for risk management, data governance, technical documentation, record-keeping, transparency, human oversight, accuracy, robustness, and cybersecurity.

Human-in-the-loop. A system design in which a human must review and approve an AI system's recommendation before it is acted upon. Human-in-the-loop is the strongest form of human oversight but is not feasible for all AI applications, particularly those operating at high speed or high volume. See also *Human oversight*.

Human oversight. The broader category of mechanisms that ensure humans maintain appropriate control over AI systems. Human oversight can include human-in-the-loop (approval before action), human-on-the-loop (monitoring with ability to intervene), and human-in-command (ability to override or shut down). The EU AI Act requires that high-risk AI systems be designed to allow effective human oversight.

Incident response. The organized approach to detecting, containing, analyzing, and recovering from security incidents or AI system failures. AI incident response extends traditional cybersecurity incident response with AI-specific considerations: model rollback, prompt injection containment, data poisoning detection, and communication with affected parties about AI-specific failure modes.

Interoperability. The ability of different AI systems, tools, and governance frameworks to work together and exchange information. Interoperability is increasingly important as organizations deploy AI systems from multiple vendors and must ensure consistent governance across all of them. Standards like the Model Context Protocol (MCP) and Agent-to-Agent (A2A) protocol aim to enable interoperability at the agent communication layer.

ISO 42001. ISO/IEC 42001:2023, the first international standard for AI management systems. ISO 42001 provides requirements for establishing, implementing, maintaining, and continually improving an AI management system within an organization. It follows the Annex SL management system structure familiar from ISO 27001 (information security) and ISO 9001 (quality), making it straightforward to integrate with existing management systems.

Jailbreaking. The practice of crafting inputs designed to bypass an AI system's safety measures and cause it to produce prohibited outputs or take unauthorized actions. Jailbreaking is conceptually similar to prompt injection but typically refers to attacks aimed at circumventing model-level safety training rather than exploiting application-level vulnerabilities. It is a persistent challenge because it exploits the fundamental tension between a model's helpfulness and its safety constraints.

Large Language Model (LLM). A type of foundation model trained on large amounts of text data that can understand and generate human language. LLMs are the technology behind chatbots like ChatGPT and Claude, code assistants like GitHub Copilot, and the reasoning engines powering many AI agents. LLMs are non-deterministic – they can produce different outputs for the same input – which has significant implications for governance, auditability, and reproducibility.

Least privilege. A security principle requiring that any entity (user, process, or AI agent) be granted only the minimum permissions necessary to perform its intended function. In AI governance, least privilege is critical because AI agents with excessive permissions can cause damage disproportionate to their intended purpose. See also *Excessive agency*.

Limited risk AI system. Under the EU AI Act, AI systems that do not qualify as high-risk or unacceptable but are subject to specific transparency obligations. This includes AI systems that interact with natural persons (chatbots), generate synthetic content (deepfakes), or are used for emotion recognition or biometric categorization. The primary obligation is to inform users that they are interacting with AI or viewing AI-generated content.

MCP (Model Context Protocol). An open protocol developed by Anthropic that standardizes how AI applications connect to external data sources and tools. MCP provides a uniform interface for AI agents to access files, databases, APIs, and other resources. From a governance perspective, MCP creates a standardized interception point where access controls and audit logging can be applied consistently.

MITRE ATLAS (Adversarial Threat Landscape for AI Systems). A knowledge base of adversarial tactics and techniques against AI systems, modeled after the MITRE ATT&CK framework used in cybersecurity. ATLAS catalogs real-world attacks on AI systems, including data poisoning, model evasion, and supply chain compromise. It is maintained by MITRE and is freely available.

Model Card. A standardized document that describes an AI model's intended use, performance characteristics, limitations, training data, evaluation results, and ethical considerations. Model cards were proposed by Mitchell et al. (2019) and have become an industry standard for model documentation. They are a key component of the transparency requirements under the EU AI Act for GPAI models.

Model risk management. The discipline of identifying, measuring, monitoring, and controlling the risks arising from the use of models in decision-making. Originally developed in the financial services sector (see SR 11-7/OCC 2011-12), model risk management principles are increasingly applied to AI systems across all sectors. It encompasses model validation, ongoing monitoring, and governance of the model lifecycle.

NIST AI RMF (AI Risk Management Framework). Published by the National Institute of Standards and Technology as NIST AI 100-1 in January 2023, the AI RMF provides a voluntary framework for managing AI risks throughout the AI system lifecycle. It is organized around four core functions: Govern, Map, Measure, and Manage. The accompanying Playbook and Generative AI Profile (AI 600-1) provide implementation guidance. The AI RMF is not legally binding but is widely adopted as a baseline for AI governance programs.

Non-determinism. The property of a system that can produce different outputs for identical inputs across different runs. Large language models are inherently non-deterministic due to sampling strategies, floating-point arithmetic, and temperature settings. Non-determinism creates governance challenges because it makes AI behavior difficult to predict, reproduce, and audit. Runtime enforcement provides deterministic guardrails around non-deterministic AI behavior.

Open Policy Agent (OPA). An open-source, general-purpose policy engine that decouples policy decision-making from policy enforcement. OPA evaluates policies written in its Rego language and returns authorization decisions. It is widely used in cloud-native environments for access control, API authorization, and infrastructure policy. OPA represents the PDP (Policy Decision Point) pattern that governance architectures increasingly apply to AI systems.

OWASP (Open Worldwide Application Security Project). A nonprofit foundation that produces freely available tools, standards, and guidance for application security. OWASP's Top 10 for Large Language Model Applications and Top 10 for Agentic AI Applications are essential references for AI security governance, cataloging the most critical risks specific to LLM and agentic AI deployments.

PDP (Policy Decision Point). In access control architecture, the component that evaluates access requests against policy and returns a decision (allow, deny, modify). In AI governance, the PDP concept extends to evaluating whether an AI agent's proposed action is authorized, compliant, and within defined risk boundaries. The PDP makes the decision; the PEP enforces it.

PEP (Policy Enforcement Point). The component that intercepts requests and enforces the decisions made by the PDP. In AI governance, PEPs are positioned at the boundaries where AI agents interact with infrastructure – API gateways, tool interfaces, database connections. The PEP ensures that only authorized, compliant actions are executed.

Prompt injection. An attack technique in which an adversary crafts input to an AI system that causes it to ignore its original instructions and follow the attacker's instructions instead. Prompt injection is the AI equivalent of SQL injection and is currently the most discussed vulnerability in LLM applications. It is listed as LLM01 in the OWASP Top 10 for LLM Applications.

Provider (EU AI Act). Under Article 3(3), any natural or legal person, public authority, agency, or other body that develops an AI system or a GPAI model, or that has an AI system or GPAI model developed, and places it on the market or puts it into service under its own name or trademark. Providers bear the primary compliance burden under the EU AI Act, including conformity assessment, technical documentation, and post-market monitoring.

RAG (Retrieval-Augmented Generation). A technique that combines a language model with an information retrieval system, allowing the model to access and reference external knowledge sources when generating responses. RAG reduces hallucination by grounding outputs in retrieved documents. From a governance perspective, RAG introduces data governance requirements for the retrieval corpus and creates new attack surfaces (e.g., poisoning retrieved documents).

Reference monitor. A security concept first articulated by James Anderson in 1972 describing a system component that mediates every access to protected resources. A reference monitor must be tamper-proof, always invoked (complete mediation), and small enough to be verified. The reference monitor concept is the theoretical foundation for runtime governance enforcement – a governance layer that mediates every AI agent action.

Risk management. The systematic process of identifying, analyzing, evaluating, and treating risks. In AI governance, risk management encompasses both the risks that AI systems pose to people and organizations (safety, bias, privacy, security) and the risks that organizations face from inadequate AI governance (regulatory penalties, reputational damage, operational failures, insurance exclusions).

Runtime enforcement. The practice of applying governance controls to an AI system at the moment it attempts to take an action, rather than relying solely on training-time alignment or pre-deployment testing. Runtime enforcement is deterministic – it produces the same governance decision for the same action regardless of the AI model's internal state. It is the architectural complement to model-layer safety measures.

Safety property. In formal security theory, a property that can be defined as "nothing bad ever happens" – no prohibited state is ever reached. Schneider (2000) proved that only safety properties are enforceable by runtime monitors. This is significant for AI governance because it means runtime enforcement can prevent prohibited actions (a safety property) but cannot guarantee that an AI system will eventually do something good (a liveness property).

Shadow AI. The use of AI tools and services by employees without the knowledge, approval, or oversight of their organization's IT or governance functions. Shadow AI is the AI equivalent of shadow IT and represents a significant governance risk because it means AI systems are processing organizational data, making decisions, and interacting with customers outside of any governance framework.

Supply chain (AI). The full chain of components, services, and organizations involved in building and deploying an AI system. An AI supply chain typically includes training data providers, model developers, fine-tuning services, hosting providers, API intermediaries, and application developers. Each link in the chain introduces potential risks – data quality issues, security vulnerabilities, licensing complications, and compliance gaps – that governance programs must assess and manage.

Supervisory authority. Under the EU AI Act, the national authority designated by each EU member state to oversee and enforce the regulation. Supervisory authorities have the power to conduct investigations, require corrective actions, and impose fines. At the EU level, the AI Office within the European Commission oversees GPAI model providers and coordinates enforcement across member states.

Tool poisoning. An attack in which an adversary compromises or manipulates the tools (APIs, databases, external services) that an AI agent has access to, causing the agent to receive malicious data or execute compromised operations. Tool poisoning is distinct from prompt injection in that it targets the agent's tool ecosystem rather than its language processing. It is particularly dangerous in agentic AI systems with broad tool access.

Transparency. The principle that AI systems should be understandable and their operation visible to relevant stakeholders. The EU AI Act imposes graduated transparency requirements: limited-risk systems must disclose that they are AI; high-risk systems must provide sufficient information for deployers to understand and use them appropriately; GPAI model providers must publish training data summaries and comply with copyright transparency obligations.

Trustworthiness (AI). The composite quality of an AI system that warrants confidence in its safe, secure, fair, and reliable operation. NIST identifies seven characteristics of trustworthy AI: valid and reliable, safe, secure and resilient, accountable and transparent, explainable and interpretable, privacy-enhanced, and fair with harmful bias managed. Trustworthiness is not a binary property – it exists on a continuum and must be continuously maintained.

Verifiable Credential. A tamper-evident credential whose authorship can be cryptographically verified. Defined by the W3C Verifiable Credentials Data Model, verifiable credentials enable AI agents and systems to present claims about their identity, capabilities, certifications, or compliance status in a way that can be independently verified without contacting the issuing authority.

Vulnerability scoring. The process of assigning a numerical severity rating to a security vulnerability to enable prioritization. For traditional IT vulnerabilities, CVSS is the standard. For AI-specific vulnerabilities, scoring must account for factors unique to AI systems – non-determinism, data dependency, model complexity, and the potential for cascading failures in agentic systems. OWASP's AIVSS adapts vulnerability scoring for agentic AI risks.

Zero trust architecture. A security model defined by NIST SP 800-207 based on the principle that no entity – whether inside or outside the network perimeter – should be automatically trusted. Every access request must be authenticated, authorized, and continuously validated. Zero trust is directly applicable to AI governance: AI agents should not be trusted by default, every action should be authorized, and trust should be continuously re-evaluated based on agent behavior.

Appendix F: Resource Directory

This directory collects the regulatory bodies, framework documents, governance tools, professional organizations, and incident databases most relevant to practitioners building and operating AI governance programs. URLs verified as of March 2026.

Regulatory Bodies and Contact Information

EU AI Office (DG CONNECT) The primary EU-level authority for AI governance, responsible for overseeing GPAI model providers, coordinating enforcement across member states, and publishing guidance on EU AI Act implementation. https://digital-strategy.ec.europa.eu/en/policies/ai-office

NIST Center for AI Standards and Innovation (CAISI) Formerly the AI Risk Management Framework team, CAISI leads US federal AI standards development, maintains the AI RMF, publishes the Generative AI Profile, and coordinates the AI Agent Standards Initiative launched in February 2026. https://airc.nist.gov

Spain AESIA (Agencia Espanola de Supervision de la Inteligencia Artificial) The first national AI supervisory authority established in the EU, operational since 2024. Spain's early establishment means AESIA will likely set precedents that other member state authorities follow. https://aesia.gob.es

Singapore IMDA (Infocomm Media Development Authority) Publisher of the Model AI Governance Framework and the Model Governance Framework for Agentic AI (January 2026). Singapore consistently leads on practical AI governance guidance and is twelve to eighteen months ahead of most other jurisdictions. https://www.imda.gov.sg

UK AI Safety Institute The UK government's dedicated AI safety research body, focused on evaluating frontier AI models and publishing safety assessments. While the UK has not enacted comprehensive AI legislation, the AI Safety Institute's technical work informs governance practice globally. https://www.aisi.gov.uk

US CISA (Cybersecurity and Infrastructure Security Agency) CISA addresses AI security as a subset of its broader cybersecurity mission, with particular focus on AI risks to critical infrastructure, AI-enabled cyber threats, and secure AI deployment guidance for government agencies. https://www.cisa.gov/ai

Framework Documents

EU AI Act (Regulation (EU) 2024/1689) – Full Text The complete regulation as published in the Official Journal of the European Union. This is the legally binding text. https://eur-lex.europa.eu/legal-content/EN/TXT/?uri=OJ:L_202401689

EU AI Act – Article-by-Article Guide A community-maintained, plain-language guide to every article of the EU AI Act, with cross-references and practical commentary. Essential for implementation work. https://artificialintelligenceact.eu

NIST AI Risk Management Framework (AI RMF 1.0) The voluntary US framework for managing AI risks, organized around four functions: Govern, Map, Measure, and Manage. Published January 2023. https://doi.org/10.6028/NIST.AI.100-1

NIST AI RMF Playbook Implementation guidance for each subcategory of the AI RMF, with suggested actions, references, and cross-walks to other frameworks. https://airc.nist.gov/AI_RMF_Playbook

NIST Generative AI Profile (AI 600-1) A companion to the AI RMF that maps generative AI-specific risks to the AI RMF framework, with additional risk actions for foundation models, fine-tuned models, and RAG-based systems. https://doi.org/10.6028/NIST.AI.600-1

ISO/IEC 42001:2023 – AI Management System The first international standard for establishing an AI management system. Follows the Annex SL structure familiar from ISO 27001 and ISO 9001. Available for purchase from ISO or national standards bodies. https://www.iso.org/standard/81230.html

Council of Europe Framework Convention on AI (CETS 225) The first legally binding international treaty on AI, adopted September 2024 in Vilnius. Covers human rights, democracy, and rule of law dimensions of AI governance.

Open for signature by Council of Europe members and non-member states. https://rm.coe.int/1680afae3c

Singapore Model Governance Framework for Agentic AI Published January 2026, this is the first national governance framework specifically addressing agentic AI systems. Covers agent monitoring, human override, decision boundaries, and multi-agent governance. https://www.imda.gov.sg

OWASP Top 10 for Large Language Model Applications The most widely referenced catalog of LLM-specific security risks, covering prompt injection, insecure output handling, training data poisoning, model denial of service, supply chain vulnerabilities, excessive agency, and more. https://owasp.org/www-project-top-10-for-large-language-model-applications/

OWASP Top 10 for Agentic AI Applications The companion to the LLM Top 10, focused specifically on risks unique to AI agents: excessive agency, tool poisoning, privilege escalation through tool chaining, insecure agent handoffs, and other agentic attack surfaces. https://owasp.org/www-project-agentic-ai-threats-and-mitigations/

NIST SP 800-207 – Zero Trust Architecture The canonical reference for zero trust architecture principles, directly applicable to AI governance. Every AI governance program should treat AI agents as zero-trust entities: never trust, always verify, continuously monitor. https://doi.org/10.6028/NIST.SP.800-207

AI Governance Tooling Directory

The AI governance tooling market is evolving rapidly. The entries below capture the landscape as of early 2026. Evaluate tools against your specific requirements – no single tool covers every governance need.

Credo AI An enterprise governance platform focused on policy management, risk assessment, and compliance mapping across multiple frameworks. A strong fit for organizations that need to operationalize governance policies and maintain traceability from policy to control to evidence. https://www.credo.ai

Holistic AI An enterprise governance and audit platform specializing in bias auditing, risk management, and regulatory compliance. Particularly well-suited for organizations preparing for EU AI Act conformity assessments. https://www.holisticai.com

ValidMind An enterprise model risk management platform built for financial services. Automates model documentation and supports regulatory compliance workflows familiar to banks and insurers operating under SR 11-7 and similar supervisory expectations. https://www.validmind.com

IBM watsonx.governance An enterprise governance platform providing end-to-end AI lifecycle governance, model monitoring, and drift detection. Integrated with watsonx.ai, making it a natural choice for organizations already invested in the IBM AI stack. https://www.ibm.com/watsonx

OneTrust A GRC platform with an AI governance module. The strongest fit for organizations already using OneTrust for privacy or broader GRC programs and looking to extend existing workflows to cover AI systems. https://www.onetrust.com

Arthur AI A mid-market and enterprise model monitoring platform covering production performance tracking, explainability, and hallucination detection. Well-suited to teams operating LLMs in production who need runtime observability beyond traditional ML metrics. https://www.arthur.ai

Fiddler AI A mid-market and enterprise platform for model monitoring and explainability, covering performance monitoring, bias detection, and drift analysis. A good fit where explainability is a first-class requirement alongside monitoring. https://www.fiddler.ai

LogicGate A mid-market and enterprise risk and compliance platform offering risk quantification, compliance workflow automation, and audit management. Useful for organizations integrating AI risk into a broader enterprise risk management program. https://www.logicgate.com

MLflow A free and open source experiment tracking and model registry. Covers model versioning, experiment tracking, deployment management, and metadata logging. The de facto baseline for teams building governance on open-source foundations. https://mlflow.org

Fairlearn A free and open source fairness assessment toolkit for algorithmic fairness assessment, bias mitigation, and disparity metrics across classification and regression tasks. A common choice for embedding fairness testing into ML pipelines. https://fairlearn.org

Microsoft Responsible AI Toolbox A free and open source responsible AI toolkit covering model debugging, error analysis, fairness assessment, and interpretability. Integrated with Azure ML and a strong fit for teams already on the Microsoft stack. https://responsibleaitoolbox.ai

AI Verify A free and open source AI governance testing framework developed by IMDA Singapore. Supports transparent AI governance testing against internationally recognized principles and is useful for organizations aligning with Singapore's model governance framework. https://aiverify.ai

Weights & Biases (W&B) An ML experiment platform with a free tier and enterprise offering. Covers experiment tracking, model versioning, dataset versioning, and collaborative ML development. Widely adopted across research and applied ML teams. https://wandb.ai

Arize AI An ML observability platform with a free tier and enterprise offering. Covers production ML observability, model monitoring, troubleshooting, and embedding drift detection. Particularly strong for LLM and embedding-based systems. https://arize.com

The table below summarizes the same tools for quick reference.

Tool	Type	Pricing Tier
Credo AI	Governance platform	Enterprise
Holistic AI	Governance & audit platform	Enterprise
ValidMind	Model risk management	Enterprise
IBM watsonx.governance	Governance platform	Enterprise
OneTrust	GRC platform (AI module)	Enterprise
Arthur AI	Model monitoring	Mid-market / Enterprise
Fiddler AI	Model monitoring & explainability	Mid-market / Enterprise

Tool	Type	Pricing Tier
LogicGate	Risk & compliance platform	Mid-market / Enterprise
MLflow	Experiment tracking & model registry	Free / Open Source
Fairlearn	Fairness assessment toolkit	Free / Open Source
Microsoft RAI Toolbox	Responsible AI toolkit	Free / Open Source
AI Verify	Governance testing framework	Free / Open Source
Weights & Biases	ML experiment platform	Free tier / Enterprise
Arize AI	ML observability	Free tier / Enterprise

Professional Organizations and Communities

IAPP (International Association of Privacy Professionals) The largest global privacy and data protection professional organization. IAPP has expanded its scope to include AI governance, offering the AIGP (Artificial Intelligence Governance Professional) certification, AI governance training, and a growing library of AI governance resources. https://iapp.org

ISACA A global professional association focused on IT governance, risk management, and cybersecurity. ISACA offers the CGEIT (Certified in the Governance of Enterprise IT) certification and has published AI governance guidance, audit programs, and risk frameworks relevant to practitioners integrating AI governance into existing IT governance structures. https://www.isaca.org

Cloud Security Alliance (CSA) CSA has established an AI Safety Initiative and published guidance on securing AI systems in cloud environments. Their AI-specific working groups address governance, security architecture, and compliance for cloud-hosted AI systems. https://cloudsecurityalliance.org

OWASP GenAI Project The OWASP community working group responsible for the Top 10 for LLM Applications, the Top 10 for Agentic AI Applications, and related guidance. The project maintains active working groups, hosts regular meetings, and accepts community contributions. https://owasp.org/www-project-top-10-for-large-language-model-applications/

CoSAI (Coalition for Secure AI) An OASIS open project launched by Google, Microsoft, Amazon, Anthropic, Intel, IBM, NVIDIA, and others focused on AI security research and best practices. CoSAI working groups address software supply chain security for AI, preparing defenders for a changing cybersecurity landscape, and AI risk governance. https://www.coalitionforsecureai.org

NIST AI RMF Community NIST maintains a mailing list and community forum for organizations implementing the AI RMF. This is a valuable resource for peer learning, implementation questions, and staying current on NIST AI standards development including the AI Agent Standards Initiative. https://airc.nist.gov

Incident Databases

These databases catalog real-world AI incidents and vulnerabilities. They are essential resources for risk assessment, governance program justification, and understanding the practical failure modes governance programs must address.

AI Incident Database (AIID) The most comprehensive public database of AI incidents, maintained by the Responsible AI Collaborative. AIID catalogs incidents where AI systems have caused or nearly caused harm, with structured data on the systems involved, the nature of the harm, and the affected parties. Invaluable for risk assessment and board-level communication about AI risks. https://incidentdatabase.ai

AIAAIC Repository A curated collection of AI, algorithmic, and automation incidents and controversies maintained by Charlie Pownall. AIAAIC focuses on the broader social and ethical dimensions of AI incidents, including bias, discrimination, surveillance, and manipulation. Useful for governance practitioners who need to communicate about AI risks beyond purely technical failures. https://aiaaic.org

AVID (AI Vulnerability Database) An open-source database focused specifically on AI security vulnerabilities and failure modes. AVID catalogs vulnerabilities using a structured taxonomy aligned with MITRE ATLAS and

OWASP classifications. Useful for security-focused governance practitioners and for conducting AI-specific vulnerability assessments. https://avidml.org

MIT AI Risk Repository A comprehensive, living database of AI risks maintained by researchers at MIT. The repository categorizes risks across multiple dimensions including cause, timing, domain, and severity. It is particularly useful for structured risk identification exercises during governance program design. https://airisk.mit.edu

MITRE ATLAS (Adversarial Threat Landscape for AI Systems) While primarily a threat knowledge base rather than an incident database, ATLAS catalogs real-world case studies of adversarial attacks on AI systems. Each case study maps attack techniques to the ATLAS matrix, providing governance practitioners with concrete examples of how AI systems are attacked in practice. https://atlas.mitre.org

Appendix G: Bibliography

The sources below are organized by category and collectively represent the research foundation for this book. URLs are provided where sources are available online. DOIs are included for academic papers where available.

1. Foundational Security Theory

Anderson, J.P. "Computer Security Technology Planning Study." ESD-TR-73-51, Vol. II. Deputy for Command and Management Systems, HQ Electronic Systems Division (AFSC), Hanscom Field, Bedford, MA. October 1972. https://csrc.nist.gov/files/pubs/conference/1998/10/08/proceedings-of-the-21st-nissc-1998/final/docs/early-cs-papers/ande72.pdf

Saltzer, J.H. and Schroeder, M.D. "The Protection of Information in Computer Systems." Proceedings of the IEEE, vol. 63, no. 9, pp. 1278-1308. September 1975. DOI: 10.1109/PROC.1975.9939.

Schneider, F.B. "Enforceable Security Policies." ACM Transactions on Information and System Security (TISSEC), vol. 3, no. 1, pp. 30-50. February 2000. DOI: 10.1145/353323.353382.

2. Runtime and Architectural Enforcement

Halle, S. and Villemaire, R. "Runtime Enforcement of Web Service Message Contracts with Data." IEEE Transactions on Services Computing, vol. 5, no. 2, pp. 192-206. April-June 2012. DOI: 10.1109/TSC.2011.10.

Rasthofer, S., Arzt, S., Lovat, E., and Bodden, E. "DroidForce: Enforcing Complex, Data-centric, System-wide Policies in Android." 2014 Ninth International Conference on Availability, Reliability and Security (ARES), Fribourg, Switzerland, pp. 40-49. 2014. DOI: 10.1109/ARES.2014.13.

Pearce, H., Pinisetty, S., Roop, P.S., Kuo, M.M.Y., and Ukil, A. "Smart I/O Modules for Mitigating Cyber-Physical Attacks on Industrial Control Systems." IEEE Transactions on Industrial Informatics, vol. 16, no. 7, pp. 4659-4669. July 2020. DOI: 10.1109/TII.2019.2945520.

Majumdar, S. et al. "ProSAS: Proactive Security Auditing System for Clouds." IEEE Transactions on Dependable and Secure Computing, vol. 19, no. 4, pp. 2517-2534. July-August 2022. DOI: 10.1109/TDSC.2021.3062204.

Baird, A., Panda, A., Pearce, H., Pinisetty, S., and Roop, P. "Scalable Security Enforcement for Cyber Physical Systems." IEEE Access, vol. 12, pp. 14385-14410. 2024. DOI: 10.1109/ACCESS.2024.3357714.

Arunachalam, K., Kayyidavazhiyil, A., and Santikellur, P. "POLYNIX: A Hybrid Policy Enforcement Framework for Zero-Trust Security in Virtualized Systems." 2026 IEEE 23rd Consumer Communications & Networking Conference (CCNC), Las Vegas, NV, USA. 2026. DOI: 10.1109/CCNC65079.2026.11366307.

3. AI Safety and Alignment

Christiano, P., Leike, J., Brown, T.B., Martic, M., Legg, S., and Amodei, D. "Deep Reinforcement Learning from Human Preferences." Advances in Neural Information Processing Systems (NeurIPS). 2017. https://arxiv.org/abs/1706.03741

Bai, Y. et al. "Constitutional AI: Harmlessness from AI Feedback." arXiv:2212.08073. 2022. https://arxiv.org/abs/2212.08073

Agbemabiese, W.T. "Toward Constitutional Autonomy in AI Systems: A Theoretical Framework for Aligned Agentic Intelligence." IEEE Access, vol. 14, pp. 11385-11402. 2026. DOI: 10.1109/ACCESS.2026.3654907.

4. Standards and Frameworks

European Parliament and Council of the European Union. "Regulation (EU) 2024/1689 – Artificial Intelligence Act." Official Journal of the European Union, vol. 67, series OJ L. July 2024. https://eur-lex.europa.eu/legal-content/EN/TXT/?uri=OJ:L_202401689

National Institute of Standards and Technology. "Artificial Intelligence Risk Management Framework (AI RMF 1.0)." NIST AI 100-1. U.S. Department of Commerce, Washington, DC. January 2023. DOI: 10.6028/NIST.AI.100-1.

National Institute of Standards and Technology. "AI RMF Generative AI Profile." NIST AI 600-1. U.S. Department of Commerce, Washington, DC. July 2024. DOI: 10.6028/NIST.AI.600-1.

International Organization for Standardization and International Electrotechnical Commission. "Information technology – Artificial intelligence – Management system." ISO/IEC 42001:2023(E). Geneva, Switzerland. December 2023.

Council of Europe. "Framework Convention on Artificial Intelligence and Human Rights, Democracy and the Rule of Law." Council of Europe Treaty Series (CETS) No. 225. Vilnius, Lithuania. September 2024. https://rm.coe.int/1680afae3c

European Parliament. "Parliament backs EU signature of Framework Convention on Artificial Intelligence." Press Release 20260306IPR37524. March 2026. https://www.europarl.europa.eu/news/en/press-room/20260306IPR37524/parliament-backs-eu-signature-of-framework-convention-on-artificial-intelligence

Rose, S., Borchert, O., Mitchell, S., and Connelly, S. "Zero Trust Architecture." NIST Special Publication 800-207. National Institute of Standards and Technology, Gaithersburg, MD. August 2020. DOI: 10.6028/NIST.SP.800-207.

Campbell, B., Bradley, J., Sakimura, N., and Lodderstedt, T. "OAuth 2.0 Mutual-TLS Client Authentication and Certificate-Bound Access Tokens." RFC 8705. Internet Engineering Task Force. February 2020. DOI: 10.17487/RFC8705.

OWASP Foundation. "OWASP Top 10 for Large Language Model Applications." November 2025. https://owasp.org/www-project-top-10-for-large-language-model-applications/

OWASP Foundation. "OWASP Top 10 for Agentic AI Applications." 2025. https://owasp.org/www-project-agentic-ai-threats-and-mitigations/

OWASP Foundation. "AIVSS Scoring System for OWASP Agentic AI Core Security Risks." Version 0.8. 2025.

Sporny, M., Guy, A., Sabadello, M., and Reed, D. "Decentralized Identifiers (DIDs) v1.0: Core architecture, data model, and representations." W3C Recommendation. July 2022. https://www.w3.org/TR/2022/REC-did-core-20220719/

Infocomm Media Development Authority. "Model AI Governance Framework for Agentic AI." Version 1.0. IMDA, Government of Singapore. January 2026. https://www.imda.gov.sg

Open Policy Agent Project. "Open Policy Agent." The Linux Foundation. 2016. https://www.openpolicyagent.org

5. Agentic AI Governance and Security

Syros, G. et al. "SAGA: A Security Architecture for Governing AI Agentic Systems." Proceedings of the Network and Distributed System Security Symposium (NDSS), San Diego, CA, USA. February 2026. https://www.ndss-symposium.org/wp-content/uploads/2026-s869-paper.pdf

Wang, X. et al. "MI9: An Integrated Runtime Governance Framework for Agentic AI." arXiv:2508.03858v4. 2025. https://arxiv.org/pdf/2508.03858

Arunachalam, K., Kayyidavazhiyil, A., and Santikellur, P. "POLYNIX: A Hybrid Policy Enforcement Framework for Zero-Trust Security in Virtualized Systems." 2026 IEEE 23rd Consumer Communications & Networking Conference (CCNC), Las Vegas, NV, USA. 2026. DOI: 10.1109/CCNC65079.2026.11366307.

Gaurav, S., Heikkonen, J., and Chaudhary, R. "Governance-as-a-Service: A Multi-Agent Framework for AI System Compliance and Policy Enforcement." arXiv:2508.18765v2. 2025. https://arxiv.org/pdf/2508.18765

Shapira, N. et al. "Agents of Chaos." arXiv:2602.20021. February 2026. https://arxiv.org/abs/2602.20021

Various authors. "A Survey of Agentic AI and Cybersecurity: Challenges, Opportunities and Use-case Prototypes." arXiv:2601.05293v1. 2026. https://arxiv.org/abs/2601.05293

Chan, R. et al. "The 2025 AI Agent Index." arXiv:2602.17753v1. 2025. https://arxiv.org/abs/2602.17753

Engin, Z. and Hand, N. "Toward Adaptive Categories: Dimensional Governance for Agentic AI." arXiv:2505.11579v2. 2025. https://arxiv.org/pdf/2505.11579

6. Identity and Trust

Rodriguez Garzon, S. et al. "AI Agents with Decentralized Identifiers and Verifiable Credentials." arXiv:2511.02841v2. 2025. https://arxiv.org/abs/2511.02841

Shuhan, H. et al. "Decentralised Identity Federations Using Blockchain." International Journal of Information Security. 2024. DOI: 10.1007/s10207-024-00864-6.

Josang, A., Ismail, R., and Boyd, C. "A Survey of Trust and Reputation Systems for Online Service Provision." Decision Support Systems, vol. 43, no. 2, pp. 618-644. March 2007. DOI: 10.1016/j.dss.2005.05.019.

7. Industry Reports and Web Sources

Gartner. "Market Guide for AI Governance." 2025. https://www.gartner.com

Gartner. "Predicts 2026: AI Governance Will Be a Board-Level Priority for 60% of Enterprises." 2025. https://www.gartner.com

Forrester. "The Forrester Wave: AI Governance Platforms, Q1 2026." 2026. https://www.forrester.com

IAPP. "AI Governance in Practice: 2025 Global Survey." 2025. https://iapp.org

IAPP-EY. "Annual Privacy Governance Report." 2025. https://iapp.org

Coalition for Secure AI (CoSAI). "AI Security Best Practices." OASIS Open Project. 2025. https://www.coalitionforsecureai.org

Cloud Security Alliance. "AI Safety Initiative: Security Guidance for AI Systems." 2025. https://cloudsecurityalliance.org

Munich Re. "AI Insurance Market Review." 2025. Key data point: cyber insurance policies increasingly include AI-specific exclusion clauses, with 67% of new policies in Q4 2025 containing explicit AI liability language.

Marsh McLennan. "AI Risk and Insurance Report." 2025. Documents the emergence of standalone AI liability coverage and the insurance industry's evolving approach to AI risk quantification.

AI Incident Database (AIID). Maintained by the Responsible AI Collaborative. https://incidentdatabase.ai

AIAAIC Repository. Maintained by Charlie Pownall. https://aiaaic.org

AVID (AI Vulnerability Database). https://avidml.org

MIT AI Risk Repository. https://airisk.mit.edu

MITRE. "ATLAS: Adversarial Threat Landscape for Artificial Intelligence Systems." https://atlas.mitre.org

OpenID Foundation. "OpenID for Verifiable Presentations." 2024. https://openid.net/specs/openid-4-verifiable-presentations-1_0.html. Relevant to AI agent identity verification in federated governance architectures.

Anthropic. "Model Context Protocol (MCP) Specification." 2024. https://modelcontextprotocol.io. Open protocol for standardizing AI agent connections to external tools and data sources.

Google. "Agent-to-Agent (A2A) Protocol." 2025. https://github.com/google/A2A. Open protocol for agent interoperability, complementary to MCP.

United Nations System Chief Executives Board for Coordination. "White Paper on AI Governance." CEB/2024/1/Add.1. 2024. Establishes the UN system's approach to AI governance, including principles for responsible AI use across UN agencies.

National Institute of Standards and Technology. "AI Agent Standards Initiative." Announced February 2026. Three pillars: standards development, open-source protocols, and security research for agentic AI systems. https://airc.nist.gov

SMB Group. "2025 SMB AI Adoption Survey." Key finding: 73% of SMBs using AI have no formal governance program; 41% report at least one AI-related incident in the past 12 months.

Deloitte. "State of AI in the Enterprise, 7th Edition." 2025. Documents enterprise AI adoption patterns, governance maturity levels, and the correlation between governance investment and successful AI deployment outcomes.

McKinsey Global Institute. "The State of AI in Early 2026." March 2026. https://www.mckinsey.com. Quantifies the acceleration of agentic AI deployment in enterprise environments and the widening gap between deployment velocity and governance maturity.

European Commission. "EU AI Act Implementation Guidelines: High-Risk AI Systems." Draft, February 2026. Practical guidance for providers and deployers of high-risk AI systems, including conformity assessment procedures and documentation templates.

ISO/IEC. "ISO/IEC 23894:2023 – Information technology – Artificial intelligence – Guidance on risk management." Geneva, Switzerland. 2023. Companion to ISO 42001, providing detailed risk management guidance for AI systems.

ISO/IEC. "ISO/IEC 42005:2025 – Information technology – Artificial intelligence – AI system impact assessment." Geneva, Switzerland. 2025. Framework for assessing the societal and individual impacts of AI systems.

www.ingramcontent.com/pod-product-compliance
Ingram Content Group UK Ltd.
Pitfield, Milton Keynes, MK11 3LW, UK
UKHW051117290926
15471UKWH00010B/1722

9 798950 533198